ECHOES

50 Years
of iMaestri

ECHOES ECHOES ECHOES ECHOES

Cassina 50 Years of iMaestri

New York Paris London Milan

An Echo from
the Past that
Celebrates
the Future
LUCA FUSO
6

The Genesis
of the Echo
IVAN MIETTON
8

The Alchemy
of History
EMANUELE COCCIA
10

Timeline
323

ECHOES
Exhibition,
Milano Design Week 2023
PATRICIA URQUIOLA
340

PHOTOS BY AGOSTINO OSIO
FOR ALTO PIANO

Bibliography
348

1
The Intuition
of iMaestri

Chronicle
of a Collection
BARBARA LEHMANN
16

iMAESTRI
Le Corbusier
Pierre Jeanneret
Charlotte Perriand
24

Charles & Ray
Eames
46

PHOTOS BY MATTIA BALSAMINI

2
Continuous
Research

The Research
Continues:
Origin, Evolution,
and Return
DOMITILLA DARDI
72

iMAESTRI
Gio Ponti
78

Vico Magistretti
92

Ico Parisi
110

Franco Albini
124

PHOTOS BY SCHELTENS & ABBENES

3
Building
Culture

4
Yesterday Today
and Tomorrow

5
Anticipating
Change

Unsettling
Chairs
BEATRIZ COLOMINA
MARK ANTONY WIGLEY
152

On the Avant-Garde,
as a Value of
Contemporary Life
and a Condition
of a Future
CÉLINE SARAÏVA
216

Past
into Future
JANE WITHERS
278

iMAESTRI
Carlo Scarpa
160

iMAESTRI
Charles Rennie
Mackintosh
222

iMAESTRI
Charlotte Perriand
284

PHOTOS BY TOMMASO SARTORI

Gerrit Thomas
Rietveld
172

Le Corbusier
236

Marco Zanuso
192

Erik Gunnar Asplund
250

PHOTOS BY DELFINO SISTO
LEGNANI, DSL STUDIO

Giacomo Balla
260

PHOTOS BY SARAH VAN RIJ &
DAVID VAN DER LEEUW

An Echo from the Past that Celebrates the Future

LUCA FUSO
Cassina CEO

My first memory of Cassina is the sudden appearance of a large white building set between a stream and the railway, a context that in no way revealed how this place could bring to life so many of the ideas that have written the history of design. I discovered, almost ten years later, that this white building preserved a company that has always been cutting-edge and has known how to intertwine its values of innovation, quality, and manufacturing excellence with the development and promotion of culture, supporting projects and initiatives that have contributed to affirming the heritage of Italian design throughout the world.

The Cassina family's intuition to collaborate with great architects and designers beginning in the 1950s gave rise to a pioneering journey that inaugurated industrial design in Italy and, over the following decades, has never allowed the company to lose sight of the importance of experimentation and the challenge of serial production.

Fifty years of the Cassina iMaestri Collection represents a milestone in the company's almost one-century-old history. With this important anniversary we are not only celebrating the most significant icons from the Modern Movement but, above all, a unique method devised over the years to reissue in the most authentic way, or even edit for the first time, the works of some of the authors who have most influenced twentieth-century architecture and design. An emblematic ability that involves the constant and painstaking philological study, which is carried out in close contact with the foundations and heirs of the Masters. In this process, Cassina's advanced research and development work is decisive to industrially produce these pieces, in some cases still unknown, and the aim is to make them available to a wider public, always with the utmost respect for the project and the author's original idea.

Since my arrival at Cassina five years ago, I have strongly believed that these icons, often considered standalone objects, could be further enhanced and placed at the center of a wider perspective. This vision is represented by "The Cassina Perspective," which has today become our company's philosophy: thanks to such a broad and eclectic collection that spans twelve decades, we can combine these timeless designs with the fruit of the most recent collaborations to give life to unique, welcoming atmospheres.

They are therefore not museum artifacts but works in continuous evolution, to be used daily. They are icons that look toward the future, also thanks to Cassina's commitment to adopting innovative production processes and circular materials, which is at the heart of the company's more conscious approach to determine a new perspective for greater sustainability. This anniversary is not only a celebration but an opportunity to look ahead and define the direction in which the echo of the past not only reverberates in the present but is amplified into the future.

The Genesis of the Echo

IVAN MIETTON
Curator

The starting point of this editorial adventure is the small town of Meda, north of Milan, the location of the company founded by Cesare and Umberto Cassina. It is here that the creations of the twentieth century's most talented architects and designers, made by craftsmen with recognized know-how, have been produced since 1927. It is here that this periodic and repetitive creative signal is sent to the world. It is from this place that the excellence of design "made in Cassina" resonates as an echo around the world.

Luca Fuso, the company's CEO, and Patricia Urquiola, its Art Director, decided to celebrate the fiftieth anniversary of the Cassina iMaestri Collection, devoted to the production of twentieth-century masterpieces, with a book. The idea is appealing, the task important. In browsing Cassina Historical Archives, meticulously ordered by its curator Barbara Lehmann, we can make a first observation: what these documents reveal, in addition to what they contain, is the values of the company whose memory they preserve.

From the abundance of these archives—photographs, sketches, diagrams, technical drawings and letters—various questions arise. How can we transcribe the richness of this material without the shortcomings of a work that would be too academic, while ensuring scientific rigor? It is essential to highlight the remarkable heritage preserved in the Cassina archives. It is also important to reflect the original character of this collection. The structure of the book as well as its original graphic identity were defined on the advice of Patricia Urquiola and with various proposals by the graphic designer Nicola Aguzzi. By acquiring a piece from the Cassina iMaestri Collection, we give ourselves a piece of history. The purpose of this book is to retrace that history through many sources, largely unpublished. Thus, there is an independent focus devoted to each of the Masters, organized around the same framework that recounts their biographies and analyzes the emblematic pieces they have created, supported by archival documents, such as preparatory sketches, technical drawings, letters and photographs. This investigative work in the Cassina archives is accompanied by additional research undertaken in the archives of the designers and with various museums that have made their knowledge available. The help and responsiveness of the Fondation Le Corbusier, the Archives Charlotte Perriand, the Fondazione Vico Magistretti, the Fondazione Franco Albini, and the Archivio del Design di Ico Parisi have been of great help in illustrating the work of these creators. On the institutional side, the Archivio del Moderno, the Museo di Castelvecchio, and the Glasgow School of Art have also been very helpful.

The book brings together contributions by a number of authors who shed light on the creative and production process initiated by Cassina with iMaestri Collection. The book is divided into five thematic chapters that analyze, from the viewpoints of different authors, the uniqueness of this collection. It not only provides a complete international panorama of twentieth-century artistic creativity, but it is also revelatory of the original character of the company. Barbara Lehmann retraces the history of the collection from its inception, from the work of Modernists such as Le Corbusier, Pierre Jeanneret, and Charlotte Perriand and the company's first reissues, all the way to the development of a veritable collection of masterpieces of design. Despite this, however, Cassina has not neglected the production of the most contemporary designers. Alongside furniture designed by Charles Rennie Mackintosh, Gerrit Thomas Rietveld, and Frank Lloyd Wright, the catalogue includes works by Gio Ponti, Ico Parisi, and Vico Magistretti. For her part, Domitilla Dardi highlights Cassina's avant-garde character; she shows how, thanks to the skills of its Research and Development Center, the creations of the masters of the future (Gio Ponti, Vico Magistretti) echo those of the masters of the past (Le Corbusier, Pierre Jeanneret, Charlotte Perriand, Gerrit Thomas Rietveld, and Charles Rennie Mackintosh). A large number of documents related to exhibitions organized or supported by Cassina are kept in the company's archives. Among the most emblematic events that have been documented is the exhibition *Italy: The New Domestic Landscape*, held at MoMA in 1972, for which Cassina produced Kar-a-sutra by Mario Bellini. In 1984, the researches of the company and the reconstruction of Mackintosh's furniture were exhibited at the Glasgow School of Art. Then, in 2012, it was the turn of Charlotte Perriand and Pierre Jeanneret's Refuge Tonneau (1938) to be produced thanks to Cassina. The list of the company's reconstruction program reveals not only its important cultural role but also a sincere and constant involvement in supporting art history.

In the third chapter of the book, Beatriz Colomina and Mark Wigley together study the dissemination of the Italian company's cultural values and analyze how it conceived the exhibitions and advertising campaigns from the past. Through the transversal view of the documents contained in the archives, one can hardly help but observe Cassina's aesthetic originality. With the help of documented historical examples, such as the Salon d'Automne (1929) and *La casa abitata* (1965), Céline Saraïva explains that elegance is both an aesthetic and a theoretical concept. She also notes the timelessness of its production and the perfect compatibility of the pieces of furniture with one another. Some speak of the "Cassina style," as if to stress the singularity of the brand.

Finally, Jane Withers describes how Cassina adapts to social changes and contemporary issues. In the 1970s, the company unhesitatingly supported radical designers such as Mario Bellini or Archizoom, while producing pieces by Gerrit Thomas Rietveld. Today, Cassina is facing new challenges that are largely environmental. The stakes are high, the theoretical and technical issues numerous, but the stress here should be on the company's research work.

The singularity of this editorial project also owes much to the various photographic commissions that cover the different themes of the book and shed a singular light on the creation of the Masters. The Italian photographer Mattia Balsamini engaged with the factory in Meda, playing with chiaroscuro to capture, in a mysterious atmosphere, the very special character of the pieces by Vico Magistretti, Le Corbusier, Pierre Jeanneret, and Charlotte Perriand. The Dutch photographer couple Scheltens & Abbenes are interested, for their part, in the structural components of furniture by the Masters. Using a graphic process consisting of colored lines, they bring out the singularity of these creations. Delfino Sisto Legnani of DSL Studio captures the masterpieces of iMaestri in museums. Like a futurist painting, Giacomo Balla's screen is presented at the Procuratie Vecchie, in Venice. The Doge table is photographed at Ca' Scarpa in Treviso, echoing the famous Italian architect's interior design. Gerrit Thomas Rietveld's creations are presented at the Kröller-Müller Museum in Otterlo, built by the architect in 1954. To illustrate the theme linked to the elegance of the iMaestri Collection, Sarah van Rij & David van der Leeuw compose veritable dream paintings and invite the viewer to wander through them. In a bygone yet timeless atmosphere, the Master's piece blends into the colorful composition that surrounds it, so perfectly bringing out the concept of elegance.

In the last chapter of this book, Tommaso Sartori captures Charlotte Perriand's furniture on the slopes of Mount Etna, as an echo of the place accorded by their creator to the harmony between humanity and nature. In this way, the Ventaglio table is photographed on a stony carpet of gray-black lava, soon to be covered with vegetation. Also in Sicily, the Italian photographer depicts the pieces of furniture by Le Corbusier, Pierre Jeanneret, and Charlotte Perriand inside the world's most beautiful piece of Land Art: the *Grande Cretto* by Alberto Burri. In the form of an irregular quadrilateral of several hectares, the artwork spreads over the sides of the mountain, encasing the town of Gibellina in a shroud of white cement. The visitor strolls through the alleys of this small town in Sicily utterly destroyed by an earthquake in 1968.

The book then presents a visual timeline retracing all the major creations and events that have marked the history of Cassina. The photographs from the *Echoes* exhibition, celebrating the fiftieth anniversary of the iMaestri Collection at the Salone del Mobile 2023, close the volume. This event, curated by Patricia Urquiola and Federica Sala, presents many rare pieces and prototypes from Cassina's archives in a site-specific exhibition design. A transposition of this book, the exhibition that took place at Palazzo Broggi transmitted to the public the creative echo of the Masters that has been resounding for fifty years.

The Alchemy of History

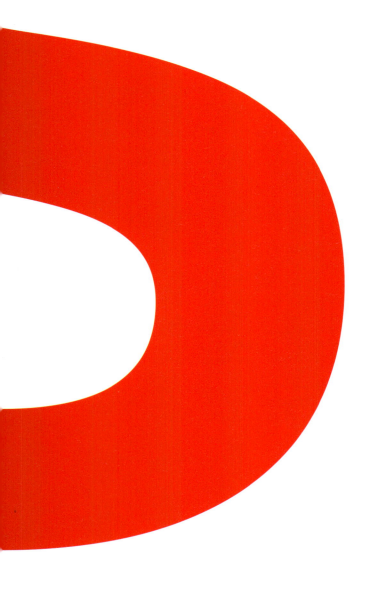

EMANUELE COCCIA
Associate professor,
École des Hautes Études
en Sciences Sociales
Centre d'Histoire et Théorie des Arts
(CEHTA)

The program of modernity has been based for at least two centuries on the rejection of history. The modern is and always has been whatever opposed the past. So Le Corbusier could observe with terse contempt that, "The practice of using styles of the past on aesthetic pretexts for new structures erected in historic areas has harmful consequences."[1] It is not just aesthetic naivety but a form of epistemological falsehood. To build as in the past means to lie to one's own time: "To imitate the past slavishly is to condemn ourselves to delusion, to institute the 'false' as a principle."[2] Likewise Gropius, in an introductory essay to one of the first Bauhaus publications, described adherence to the past as a form of inertia that makes it impossible to adequately answer the question "How do we want to live?" by formulating a general plan that is "the result of a universally valid thought." Because of this adherence we have never been able to build adequate housing: "Humans have the undoubted ability to build their dwellings in a sufficient and correct way, but their inner inertia and sentimental attachment to the past have so far prevented them from doing so."[3] What is really at stake is therefore the very condition of the possibility of design, which is at once modernity's critical avant-garde, means of construction, and divinatory map of anticipation. Moreover, returning to the past is not just a technical error or an aesthetic lapse. In the eyes of the moderns it was the locus of an anthropological paradox. "A step backward has never occurred; humanity has never retraced its footsteps." History is against nature. On this point cultural and geographical unanimity seemed universal. Even in Italy, where the movement to modernize architecture and design was partial, diminished, impeded, and less rigorous than what was happening in France or Germany, Gio Ponti himself could write that "the contemporary movement exists only as a movement of selection, of education, of real spiritual and technical content. Just as the false antique has nothing to do with antiquity, so the mercantile modern has nothing to do with modernity."[4] History only exists so that we can free ourselves from it, and design is the principle means of this liberation.

Of this urgent and necessary escape from the past, the home was both the universal theater and the undisputed protagonist, perhaps even more than the city. The new domestic landscape that design, especially Italian design, attempted to develop after the war was, as Germano Celant rightly pointed out in an exhibition a few years ago, the staging of a strange "invasion of the body snatchers." If the mineral shell of modern dwellings seemed more or less identical to that in the past—moreover we continue to live in buildings constructed centuries ago—the objects contained in homes began to be veritable futuristic relics, completely out of sync with other technologies. The home, for centuries unchanged, became the place to experience and experiment with this acceleration toward the future.

It was this context, both historical and speculative, that led to the program of iMaestri, begun by Cassina in the 1960s by reproducing designs by Le Corbusier, Pierre Jeanneret, and Charlotte Perriand, and, to follow, works by Gerrit Thomas Rietveld, Charles Rennie Mackintosh, Erik Gunnar Asplund, and Franco Albini.[5] It is in fact only by probing more deeply into this intellectual climate that we can measure the disruptive character and strength of this proposal, which seems to go not only against the original dogma of modernity and therefore of design, but above all against the aesthetic of the very individuals who have been elevated to exemplary models and masters. With a far from unconscious irony, iMaestri has forced, for example, the greatest prophet of the rejection of the past, Le Corbusier, to think of himself as a "past modern": he transformed the *very new* into historical forms, therefore open to reproduction, to transformation. In short, he inverted the avant-garde into tradition. But this was only a seeming paradox. Cassina's program was officially inaugurated in 1973, the year of the appearance of *Progetto e Utopia* (*Architecture*

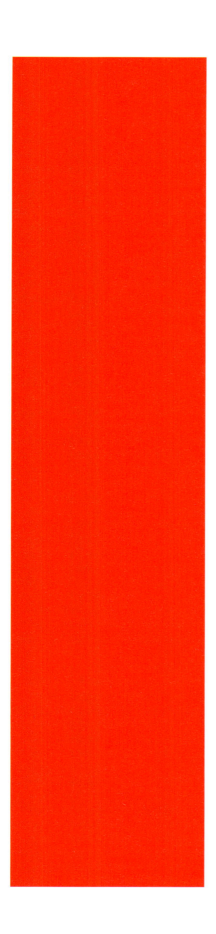

and Utopia), the manifesto book in which Manfredo Tafuri demolished any attempt to save form (and therefore felicity) in the city. It's hard not to see some sort of implicit response. It brought about an alchemical transformation—perhaps invisible but extremely powerful—of the modern project, on at least three planes.

In the first place, the very idea of modernity changed. The modern ceased to be a chronological limit that coincides with the present, to become a broader and potentially universal form of historical reflexivity. Modernity not only is and has a tradition, but it is tradition (and history) itself now being chosen in the form of the avant-garde. It would be hard to imagine a more radical upending. It is the history of design that becomes a form of research and renewal.

In short, there are masters in modernity, because there is nothing more modern—and creative—than a museum. This is the second element of transformation: the collection radically transforms the idea of the archive. For centuries the idea of the archive and the collection was directed at the past, at the patrimonial and archaeological management of something unavailable. Now the past is evoked to become contemporary with the avant-garde and assume the same forms as creativity. The archive is not a space for documentation, but one of the rooms of the laboratory; not the sleep of invention, but the garage where rather than thinking about tomorrow, the post-tomorrow is developed, a future that is no longer bound up with chronology. Thirdly, it is the very idea of the home that changes. Because this creative museum, which combines the times in the invention of the day after tomorrow, is now located in the most ordinary urban homes. Rather than the appendages or waiting rooms of the most important showcases of fairs or universal exhibitions, now homes themselves become the forges of history: the places where past and future mingle to invent a present that cannot be deduced from the first but is also free from the hostage-taking of the compulsion toward progress. With the project of iMaestri, Cassina brings the museum into the home and makes it the model of every new home.

There is something in this gesture that prolongs a trait typical of the design tradition, as Andrea Branzi[6] has formulated it. Geography is never a destiny. Places are always and only the surroundings of those who are capable of inhabiting and transforming them: more than objects of transformation, they are an echo, an aura of life, of which they constitute the extreme limit. Beyond the political determinations—so uncertain through the centuries and so unstable compared to other modern nations—the set of places that we associate with the idea of Italianness seem to share above all the particular resonance of what has happened over time in their midst. The name we give to these activities has now become banal: art. Italy, for those who live here, but above all for those who visit it or consider it from abroad, is a space at once geographic, cultural, social, and political, in which art seems to shape life in the most intense, pervasive, and radical way possible. It is not just a matter of material fact: it is not the number and antiquity of historical monuments that are uniformly distributed over its territory, and not only in the larger cities as is the case elsewhere, nor is it just the amount of artwork out of doors wherever you go. It is first of all the fact that art seems to be applied to every aspect of life, hence even to those considered most trivial, banal, close to physiological needs. This is the case with cuisine and fashion, for example, which transform two biological needs into the urge and need to transform a destiny into an act of choice. Even when eating, even when dressing, it is necessary to pass through art—to transform and transfigure in an arbitrary way the real, the given, what is before us regardless of the function it may have. The dish before our eyes and mouths containing not proteins and lipids, but unpredictable sensations. In Italy, due to the fact that one of the greatest patrons was the Church, the presence of art could never be conceived as something belonging to a privileged class (whether monarchs, aristocrats,

or burghers): the works of Titian or Canova, those of Caravaggio and Bernini, were in places open to anyone, from the poorest to the richest. Art is not a privilege or rare: it is omnipresent, accessible to everyone, at any time of day. The project of iMaestri prolongs this pervasiveness of art on a geographical, temporal, and social scale, making it the very hallmark of everyday life, the basso continuo of experience, whether dreaming or waking.

Bringing art everywhere to make it the form of experience is not an aesthetic project but a political one. It was in the fifteenth century, in fact, that in Europe the term "art," which originally meant "technology" or "technique" (*ars*), began to designate extremely heterogeneous activities of material and spiritual production, whose artifacts had nothing in common materially or formally, in terms of either use or function; at first mainly painting, sculpture, and architecture, but later also theater, dance, or the technique of making chairs, drinking glasses, tables, or chandeliers, also known as industrial design. The habit of isolating these specific techniques with such a generic name, which has lost its original meaning, began with a revolution that focused first of all on the way in which different human practices and activities were classified.

For centuries, in Europe, the whole of human activity was traversed by the distinction between activities worthy of free people, in the legal sense of the term, capable of exalting intellectual activity, and purely instrumental activities, which were literally typical of slaves. The former presupposed freedom and the capacity for discernment, and above all they exalted the freedom of those who practiced them and those who profited from their products. The latter did not produce any virtue, nor did they presuppose human knowledge or amplify it. The former were known as the *artes liberales*, the latter as the *artes mechanicae*. All the activities that today we call "arts" (painting, sculpture, theater, etc.) were classified as *artes mechanicae*: in the pages of Plutarch, Lucian or Seneca, a painter or sculptor is the equivalent of a plumber or a mechanic. It was from the generation of Leon Battista Alberti, and later of Vasari, that the idea developed that some techniques of manual manipulation of matter are worthy of free men, because they are capable of producing freedom and conveying spiritual contents. In the case of painting, for example, Alberti wanted to show that laying pigments on canvas was a means of understanding reality and spiritually developing a cognitive content equal to rhetoric or mathematics. Painting presupposes the exercise of one of the most complex parts of mathematics (perspective) and representing stories and a knowledge of humanity no less than literature or theology. Thanks to this intellectual revolution, a painter, the equivalent of a plumber, simultaneously became the equivalent of Philip Roth or Cicero and of a physicist specializing in string theory. To generalize the experience of art is to universalize the experience of one's own freedom.

One can ask what it means today to prolong and radicalize the gesture made by Cassina half a century ago. In a recent interview Patricia Urquiola spoke of a twofold objective: of "letting in as much vegetation as possible" and of dematerializing hardware. "The senescence curve of object technology is too tight," she continued. "It makes more sense to continually upgrade software through artificial intelligence than to change the box every year."[7]

These are two instances that seem to point in two decisive directions. On the one hand, design today has long since abandoned the blind obstinacy with which it sought to coincide with a geographical and chronological limit. Rather than thinking of itself as an attempt to take the forms typical of European and American culture to the extreme, it has learned to embody itself in forms of historicity and culture that are irrepressibly plural. Above all, it has crossed the threshold of our species. Far beyond European modernity, the new masters are all living, no species excluded: the home should aim to become a sort of extended museum of nonhuman as well as human civilizations, a space in which we meet and share our experience of freedom with all other species.

On the other hand, the digital revolution has enabled us to change the very idea of the home. It is no longer the mineral shell made of walls, roofs, and windows that constitutes the space through which we relate to whomever and whatever we love and form a relationship of intimacy with them. It is the digital space that designs the new domestic landscape: today smartphones are a kind of intangible living room by which we extend our home beyond the limits of urbanism and geography. It is as if the home has freed itself from metric space and therefore also from cities. Perhaps it is necessary to reproduce within this new space the same revolution that Cassina has brought about with iMaestri. To make this space the prolonged and daily experience of art: the stubborn search for our own freedom.

[1] Le Corbusier, *La Charte d'Athènes*, Paris, 1957, p. 91, n. 70.
[2] Ibid.
[3] Walter Gropius, "Wohnhaus-Industrie," Adolf Meyer (ed.), *Ein Versuchshaus des Bauhauses in Weimar* ("Bauhausbücher," 3, edited by Walter Gropius and László Moholy-Nagy), Munich, 1924, pp. 5–14, quote p. 5.
[4] Gio Ponti, "Modern House, Modern City," *Domus*, October 1933, XI, no. 70.
[5] Cf. Filippo Alison, "I Maestri: ideologia della ricostruzione," in Giampiero Bosoni (ed.), *Made in Cassina*, Milan, 2008, pp. 3–9.
[6] Andrea Branzi, *Introduzione al design italiano. Una modernità incompleta*, Milan, 2015.
[7] *Sguardi sul design contemporaneo. Interviste di Matteo Vercelloni*, Milan, 2021, pp. 78 and 80.

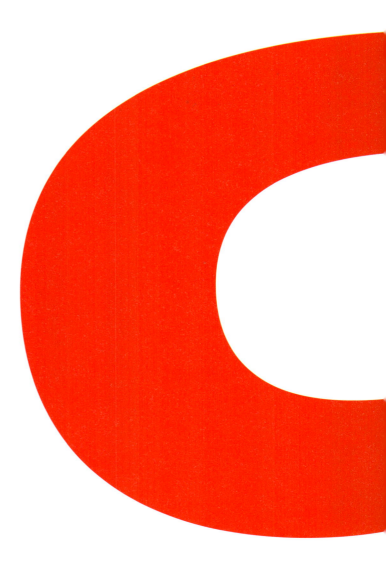

1

The Intuition

1

of

iMaestri

Cassina
Invents
iMaestri

The Intuition of iMaestri

Chronicle of a Collection

BARBARA LEHMANN
Curator of the Cassina Historical Archives,
Meda

Structuring Intuition

Intuition is the result of experience; it is direct knowledge of reality, conscious interpretation. It was clearly one of the qualities that led Cesare Cassina, the "tireless sensor of cultural, design, artistic, and productive trends,"[1] to make pioneering choices that proved successful and foundational for his company and the culture of design. The construction of the Cassina iMaestri Collection is one of the most significant examples of this. Its origin can be placed between the early 1960s and the mid-1970s.

While 1972 marked the birth of the name of the collection and 1974 its official presentation in a memorable exhibition at the company's Milan store, 1973 was the year when it acquired a coherent identity and actually became available to the general public. With the addition to the catalogue of reissues of the Zig Zag and Red and Blue chairs by Gerrit Thomas Rietveld and the presentation of Charles Rennie Mackintosh's furniture, both at the 15th Triennale di Milano and

1 Presentation of the Cassina iMaestri Collection, Cassina showroom, Milan, 1974

the Cassina Store in via Durini, the idea of a collection of works by the modern masters recognized by the scholarly community took concrete form. But the fertile soil in which the collection germinated was prepared at least a decade before this. Cesare Cassina's urge to direct production more decisively toward a modern vocabulary (which had already led him to introduce innovative industrial products in his long collaboration with Gio Ponti) induced him to add some furnishings considered supremely modern to the Cassina catalogue. These were four items of furniture by Le Corbusier, Pierre Jeanneret, and Charlotte Perriand, which entered the collection in 1965 following lengthy negotiations with Mme Heidi Weber, the Swiss gallerist responsible for disseminating Le Corbusier's works.[2] It was the enlightened entrepreneur, as well as friend, Dino Gavina and the publisher Bruno Alfieri who, already in 1963, urged Cesare to seize the opportunity of producing furniture that was a symbol of the Modern Movement. It was an opportunity taken after Gavina's refusal to include them in his company's production, contrasting with what he had done with the works by Marcel Breuer, in the conviction that he was bringing about an aesthetic renewal of the industrial product through designers with an undoubted modernist outlook. His refusal was motivated by the difficulty of industrially manufacturing such furnishings as they involved too much manual work.

The Intuition of iMaestri

2   Letter by Gio Ponti to Cassina, 1967

3   First poster of the iMaestri Collection, 1972

On signing the contract on October 23, 1964, Cassina thus acquired the reproduction and commercial rights of four models of furniture designed in 1928 in the Atelier at 35, Rue de Sèvres. Le Corbusier died in August 1965, shortly before the official presentation of the collection, at first identified by the acronym LC. Acquired as furnishings by Le Corbusier alone—since it was on these terms that they were offered by Mme Weber to Cassina—they were given their correct and more evident attribution also to Pierre Jeanneret and Charlotte Perriand only many years later,[3] when the philosophy underpinning the collection was increasingly concerned with the historical authenticity of the models. Le Corbusier was in fact the first international designer added to the Cassina collection with the purpose of explicitly sanctioning the work performed until then by the company in the wake of modernity. Alongside the criterion of exemplarity and authorship, the collection established another fundamental principle that would later characterize the Cassina iMaestri Collection, namely the principle of reissuing and producing models in a different period from the original one in which they were conceived. The principle aroused some controversy, especially when it was reiterated in 1972–73 with the inclusion of other early twentieth-century designers in the new Cassina iMaestri Collection. Regardless of the criticisms that saw it as a nostalgic or strategically artful move, it is undeniable that these decisions, conducted along the lines of a recovery of designs classifiable only in the first instance as belonging to the past, had an evident commercial success and provided a fundamental cultural frame of reference to define the relation between history and the planning of the new.[4] The words of Ernesto Nathan Rogers, written in the catalogue of the first brochure for the presentation of the LC Collection, clarified the reasons: "Objects become ancient when they have passed beyond being old; but this is a quality of a few selected objects. When they become ancient, they become today's heritage again and we can make practical and daily use of them for cultural consumption."[5] These words define the existence of a sacred precinct constituted by the paradigms of the history of furnishings; at the same time, they legitimize reconstruction since they clarify the relevance and therefore the classicism and timelessness of certain furniture by virtue of their cultural value. This is the profound significance of the reissues, which in the same brochure were described as a "dialectical pole" or as a necessary reference point for new designers.

Cassina, therefore, has every right to be seen as the company that first formulated and laid the foundations of a cultural development that was adopted by many other companies in the following years, sometimes sporadically or with impoverished formulas, in some cases leading to forms of counterfeiting that could be considered harmful to the market.

Cassina Historical Archives reveal a long series of studies conducted along these lines, some of which preceded the establishment of the collection in 1973. A little-known document from 1971 is highly significant and concerned with the structuring of the collection. This is a study commissioned to Virgilio Vercelloni titled *Numero 1 CENTRO CESARE CASSINA MEDA 1971* … The introduction explains the objective, which is to be not a catalogue of reproducible objects but "a set of stimuli for future research in the commitment to grasp a 'novelty' that contemporary culture imposes on us: the need to seek new relationships with figurative culture, the world of furniture design and practical objects."[6]

One after the other, photocopied drawings and black and white photos stir the imagination and the wish to continue experimenting in the present: from members of the Modern Movement such as Olbrich, Figini, Pollini, Breuer, Man Ray, El Lissitzky, the Naïfs, the Pop Art of Oldenburg and the (then almost contemporaneous) works by Christo, Bruce Nauman, Dan Flavin, and Yayoi Kusama. And among these Giacomo Balla, who would enter the collection many years later in 2020. A few lapidary words and questions: "Will the artistic avant-garde be able to help the consolidation and expansion of the Italian furniture industry?"

A thought-provoking document that paved the way for the iMaestri operation.

The document indisputably embodies the fundamental value assigned to cultural research as an integral part of the development of the project, and an expression of an increasingly mature urge to understand its roots.

The accounts by leading figures of the time, such as Adele Cassina,[7] Cesare's daughter, and especially the archival documents reveal a surprising tenacity in the search for modern designers (and others) to be included in the catalogue. The list of contacts is very surprising. It ranges from Salvador Dalí to Hoffmann and the Bauhaus, with whom Cassina signed a contract in 1968 for the production of Josef Hartwig's chess set and the fabrics created in the weaving laboratory at the Bauhaus (products that were never widely marketed).

Until that time, however, the numerous contacts established in previous years had led to a single effective product (in addition to the parenthesis of the agreement with the Bauhaus). Thanks to research by Daniele Baroni, a contract had been signed in 1971 for the industrial production of furniture by Rietveld, one of the founders of the revolutionary De Stijl theories. The start of production of Mackintosh's chairs in 1973—following the proposal made by Filippo Alison to Cesare Cassina in 1969, mainly intended to have an educational and formative purpose—began an activity of production and design that involved investigating the seminal sources of design culture characterized by a process structured on clearly defined principles. The program led to the marketing of reconstructions of exemplary works by the masters of Modernism developed not as pure and simple reproductions, fetishes of the distant past, but as products developed by a conscious creative process for real use. "Reconstructing is redesigning": this is how the program of the collection began, stressing the need for "concertation between the independent values identified in the original project and the production capacity of the time, with the consequent adaptation of the technologies and techniques used in the construction processes."[8]

This method, still valid today, involves scholarly reconstruction with possible minimum variations from the model identified, provided they are in keeping with the original design programs and respectful of the designer's hallmark.

The Echo of the Masters

In 1973 Filippo Alison became the curator of the Cassina iMaestri Collection. The collection's significance became increasingly clear, not only in terms of how to implement these

Barbara Lehmann

GIO PONTI ARCHITETTO

Milano, 25 Gennaio 1967
28/67 D - GP/EdF -

Signori Cassina
FIGLI DI AMEDEO CASSINA
Via Campo Sportivo, 1
<u>MILANO/MEDA</u>

Cari Cassina,

con le Galeries Lafayette voi vi siete
già accordati per le poltrone e sedie MAGISTRE<u>T</u>
TI etc.

Per le mie superleggere ve n'é una parte
che sarà esposta nello spazio detto Museo Domus,
dove ci sono dei prototipi importanti, che fanno ormai storia.

Io vi sarò grato di presentare qui le mie
superleggere in questi tipi:

  ...legno naturale e rafia naturale (1)
  ... e imbottitura bianca
  ... rafia nera
  ... e rafia naturale
  ...edi disegno 1)

  ...se esporrete una poltro-
  ... coperta in cavallino, e
  ...li (4) con copertura, una
  ...tica bianca, l'altra in

  ...luti, ringraziandovi,

  ...ranno in esportazione tempo-
  ...anno vendibili se non si op-
  ...rappresentante; le spese di
  ...a e ritorno saranno rimborsa-
  ...Lafayette. (segue)

(1) quelle color bruno chiaro delle quattro sedie
    in casa mia.

MILANO VIA DEZZA 49 TELEFONI 432.500 487.035 INDIRIZZO TELEGRAFICO: POFORO-MILANO

come ve le ho fatte fare Pongio,

BIANCO
BIANCO
NERO
(2)
BIANCO
BIANCO
NERO

(3)

The Intuition of iMaestri

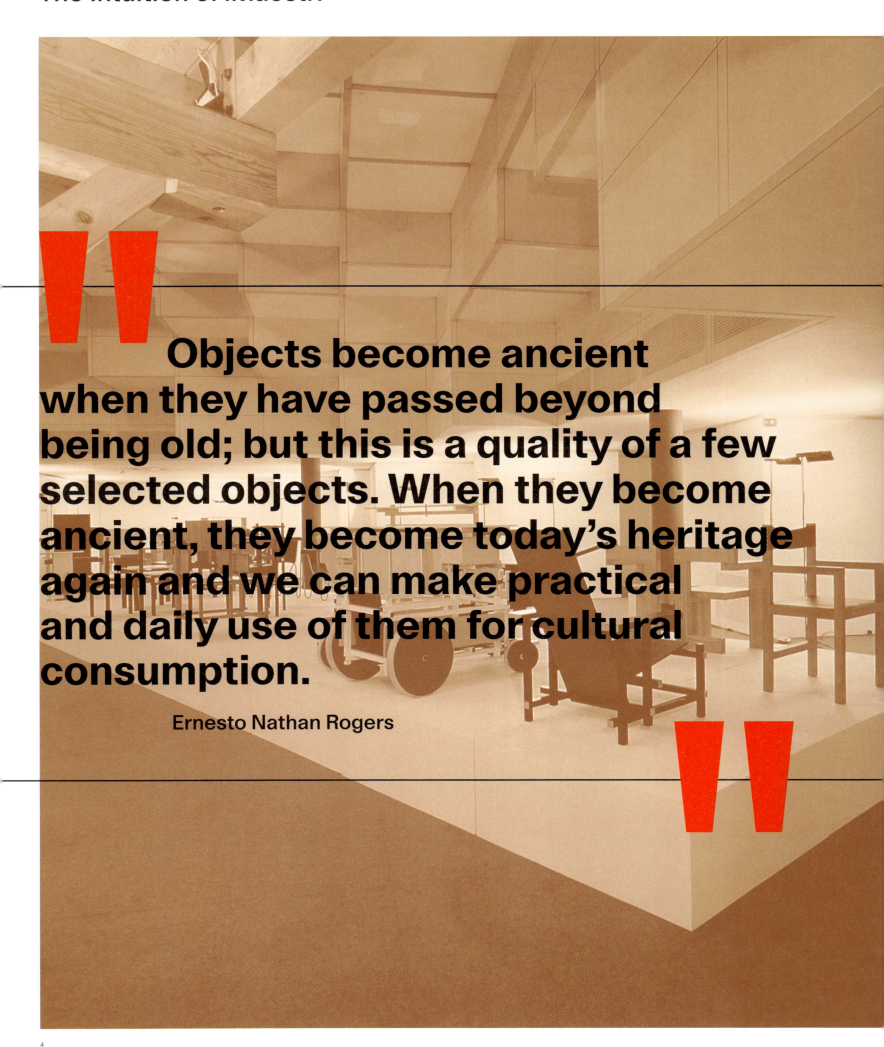

"Objects become ancient when they have passed beyond being old; but this is a quality of a few selected objects. When they become ancient, they become today's heritage again and we can make practical and daily use of them for cultural consumption."

Ernesto Nathan Rogers

Barbara Lehmann

4 Display for the presentation of the book by Daniele Baroni *I Mobili di Gerrit T. Rietveld*, showroom Cassina, Milan, 1977

reconstructions but also what to replicate. As already pointed out in the first reissues, what was superficially dismissed as an act of historical recovery was, in fact, an instrument aimed at the present and the future, to look ahead. The choice of what to place on the market arose from an assessment of its cultural significance in relation to the demands of the present, attuned to the increasingly emerging marketing strategies to offer products in keeping with rising needs.[9] The new research expanded a knowledge of the roots of the Modern Movement by exploring its genesis in different cultural fields, revealing varied interpretations and shared features in the international path toward modernity. The collection was expanded in 1983 with furniture by Erik Gunnar Asplund, the forerunner of modern Scandinavian classicism, and in 1986 with pieces by Frank Lloyd Wright, the American master whose projects, in complete osmosis with nature and their context, were a reference point in architecture and design.

The work of dissemination was intensified thanks to the collaboration with Alison. There were exhibitions in museums and at retailers, books and publications issued with the company's support to extend the knowledge of each object put into production and its designer. The basis of this cultural promotion was the idea of raising awareness among the general public of beauty, quality, and authenticity. The research was aimed not only at the models already put into production but extended to other designers (including Gaudí, Behrens, Gropius, and many others) to fully recount the roots of furniture design. Hence this was research not aimed at immediate production but at understanding the intrinsic laws of objects to intuit their permanent and topical values and the potential for resignifying them through the fundamental activity of redesign and physical reconstruction. These study models are today an important corporate heritage in historical and collective terms and, during production, they also provided the workers with a unique opportunity to learn new techniques and recover the skill of fine craftsmanship.

Close collaboration with the masters' heirs and official foundations who protect their copyright, together with the greatest experts, have always guaranteed a faithful approach to the reissues. A faithful but critical approach, aware of the need to use the chosen object in the present. The meeting between the Cassina Research and Development Center and Gerard van de Groenekan, Rietveld's most direct collaborator, was invaluable. His presence rendered possible a comparison between the original construction technique and Cassina's technological know-how. The synergy with Charlotte Perriand was likewise fundamental. From the mid-1970s until the late 1990s she contributed to the interpretation of the models of the collection designed with Le Corbusier and Pierre Jeanneret. She reintroduced, among other things, color for the structures of the tubular metal of the iconic Fauteuils Grand Confort, recovering some original values that had been initially omitted. As Franco Cassina playfully promised her, in reply to her request that he would issue her furniture after her death (this was, and still is, a requirement to move to the iMaestri category!), the Charlotte Perriand Collection was produced from 2004, making known the incredible activity of this woman, a pioneer of furniture design.[10]

A concern for the body, gestures, and the *art d'habiter* led to the creation of Charlotte Perriand's furniture that stands as resolved mediation between people and space. Works in which the resonances of early Rationalism, the Japanese world, and encounters—with figures such as Le Corbusier, Léger, Prouvé, Costa—are fused in an original expressiveness. The discovery of Charlotte Perriand's archive gave the company a new impulse to reinvigorate the work of dissemination introduced with the Cassina iMaestri Collection. On the occasion for major exhibitions organized internationally on the figure of Perriand, Cassina not only created some prototypes but also designed interiors, as in the case of the Refuge Tonneau and the Équipement intérieur d'une habitation: a cultural contribution that shifts the focus from the single icon to the interior, defining the relationship between the parts and the user, as well as reflecting changes in society.[11]

Italian Resonances

Since the beginning of the collection, the company has made an intense, pioneering journey, always at the forefront of innovation. Over the following decades it has built up a general catalogue with both continual new offerings and visions that have made their mark on the evolution of design, and new re-editions through the search for significant historical models identified in the archives of the heirs and foundations of the masters. Many of these innovative proposals have become successful projects and therefore benchmarks in the world of design, and the young designers of that time have now become important new references for subsequent generations.

The Italian companies' approach to design has increasingly become firmly established and successful worldwide. In the reinterpretation of an ever more recent past, the history of design has enshrined postwar Italian design and many of its masterpieces as exemplary. In the search for new archetypes for inclusion in the iMaestri Collection, Cassina began to reinterpret Italian history and inevitably rediscover its own past. The design excellences, now historicized along the timeline, also coincided with the company's history.

The breakthrough in the search for exemplary Italian designers and objects began in 2008, when Franco Albini, for his work in the culture of Rationalism, entered the iMaestri Collection as the first Italian architect. From a certain point of view we can speak of a return to the Cassina catalogue, since the late 1940s the architect had already collaborated with the company, establishing the foundations of his design method then matured in collaboration with the company Poggi. In 2015 the company's study of the origins of the history of Italian postwar design was further structured with the acquisition of the rights to some iconic models by Marco Zanuso. With the most significant works by these two masters, the collection thus incorporated the most important expressions of what has been termed "the analytical or aniconic line of Italian design" by its logical methodological approach to the project.[12] An analysis of the highest expressions of the postwar panorama, however, also includes an assessment of the *iconic line* of Italian design, characterized by the search for an aesthetic of the product in ideal continuity with decorative art. Ico Parisi and Gio Ponti were two important representatives of this line of thought and conduct that tended to be characterized by symbolic approximations.

The Intuition of iMaestri

5–6 Cassina press campaign, "Interni d'autore," B Communications, 1985
"La chaise longue" by Emilio Tadini
"Omaggio a Rietveld" by Gianfranco Pardi
Artwork inspired by the Red and Blue armchair
Cassina Historical Archives

Ico Parisi was reissued by Cassina in 2020. An author of original furniture for Cassina in the 1950s, his emblematic and quality designs helped spread Italian know-how overseas. Gio Ponti, on the other hand, has never left the catalogue. Since 1957, the Superleggera chair, an icon of both the company and Italian design, has been produced uninterruptedly, continuing to be contemporary to this day. A 1969 advertising campaign in the Italian magazine *Panorama* already used the slogan: "Logical structures, already classical, just devised" for this model. A concept that also accompanied another of the company's products, which paradoxically has not been produced for so long (since 1965) but dated 1928, namely the 2 Fauteuil Grand Confort, petit modèle by Le Corbusier, Pierre Jeanneret, and Charlotte Perriand, with the desire to globally position the company for its conceptual and productive excellence.[13] For this reason, there was no reissue of its most significant model, the 699, although through the years the production process has inevitably changed to some degree. While the assembly and the woven rush seat have maintained the expert craftsmanship that has always been a feature of the chair, the production of the wooden components is no longer made with the "carousel" and the "spindle molder," but by using five-axis CNC machines. Although Gio Ponti only became part of the Cassina iMaestri Collection in 2023, he was already universally considered a master. The fiftieth anniversary of the collection was marked by this transition and his positioning beside the other masters, some of whom were his contemporaries or who he had mentored and guided.[14] The partnership between Ponti and Cassina, moreover, was also exemplary, giving rise to over fifty models and countless interior design projects and memorable commissions. Today the Cassina Historical Archives preserve these models, as well as sketches, technical drawings, and personal correspondence, testifying to that unique relationship between a visionary industrialist and a designer equally rich in imagination who determined the character of Italian design.

The anniversary was also an opportunity to add other designers to the names of the great architects of the twentieth century. The new masters are now the pupils of the leading figures of the avant-garde from the first decades of the twentieth century. On the evolutionary line of Wright's organic principles are Charles & Ray Eames. The company acquired the rights to reissue their lighting designs, in 2023 presenting the prototype of the Galaxy lamp. Another is Carlo Scarpa, who merged the influence of the American masters with reflections on the lesson of Le Corbusier and De Stijl. Unlike the Eames model, the Scarpa's were already part of Cassina's catalogue since 2013, thanks to the acquisition of Simon International, the company founded in 1968 by Dino Gavina and Maria Simoncini.[15] Its most representative furniture collection, the Ultrarazionale, was in fact masterfully represented by the projects of the Venetian architect, who best expressed the urge to go beyond some limits of the Modern Movement, through his extreme sensibility in the use of materials. The presence of Carlo Scarpa's furniture in the Cassina collection is therefore to be considered a combination of two essential stories in the narrative of Italian design. Just as we can't say Italian design without naming Vico Magistretti, the youngest of the new masters. Also in this case we can talk about a special relationship between the architect and the entrepreneur and an output of about forty models, some of which have never left the collection since they appeared on the market, considered among the company's best sellers and icons of international design. Magistretti, a master of class and irony, argued that good design is a conceptual process and for this reason it cannot be ephemeral, as he stated, "It must never have an end, but it tends to repeat itself over a very long period and will remain valid even in a hundred years' time."

This is essentially the quality of the design classics, of those furnishings that, quoting Calvino, have never exhausted what they have to say.[16]

---

[1] Giampiero Bosoni, *Prefazione*, in Adele Cassina, *Cronache minori dalla periferia del design*, Mantua, 2021, p. 11.

[2] The production by Heidi Weber was the second authorized after the initial one entrusted to Thonet in the 1930s; since 1959, this furniture was made by small local Swiss artisans and was not widely distributed. The search for a producer with extensive distribution capacities and undoubted production abilities thus led the holder of the rights to the outstanding centers of furniture production in Italy.

[3] The joint design was acknowledged by the company a few years later as shown in some brochures (1974). Starting from her active collaboration in the 1970s, the role of Charlotte Perriand began to be stressed for the development of the collection, at the time called LC, though it was always kept in the background. It was increasingly shown that her role had been crucial thanks to the extended knowledge of the works and also in relation to the greater understanding and dissemination of the works of the codesigners.
Since 2023 the collection has been called Le Corbusier®, Pierre Jeanneret®, Charlotte Perriand®. The individual models repeat the original historical denomination in French preceded only by the numbering of the piece. This information is further enriched with details relating to adaptations and additions to the collection paying careful homage to the work of the three architects.

[4] Renato De Fusco, *Le Corbusier, Designer: Furniture, 1929*, New York, 1977, p. 55: "Reproducing the work of the masters, with the accompanying critical and scholarly inquiry, is one of the most tangible aspects of architectural research into the renewed history-design relationship. In the phenomenology of this relationship, the first term (history) lost all fanciful pretense of modifying reality and programming the new beyond any precedent and any code."

[5] Brochure LC 1965. Cassina Historical Archives.

[6] Pier Carlo Santini, *Gli anni del design italiano: Ritratto di Cesare Cassina*, Milan, 1981, p. 38.

[7] Cassina, op. cit., pp. 131–33.

[8] Filippo Alison, *La collezione Cassina iMaestri*, June 1989, press release. Cassina Historical Archives.

[9] Domenico De Masi, "Dieci frammenti di un discorso amoroso," in Maura Santoro (ed.), *Filippo Alison. Un viaggio tra le forme*, Milan, 2013, p. 14.

[10] Jacques Barsac, *Charlotte Perriand Complete Works. Vol. 3: 1956–1968*, Paris, 2017, p. 130.

[11] Added to this was the reconstruction of the interior of Le Corbusier's Cabanon in 2006.

[12] "Ponti/Zanuso," in Manolo De Giorgi (ed.), *45, 63: Un Museo del disegno industriale in Italia*, exhibition catalogue, Milan, 1995, p. 78.

[13] *Panorama*, 1969.

[14] Franco Albini began his professional practice in the office of Gio Ponti and Emilio Lancia, with whom he collaborated for three years.

[15] Barbara Lehmann, *Cassina e Simon: le ragioni dell'incontro di due eccellenze del design del mobile italiano*, Catalogo Cassina, Simon Collection, 2013.

[16] Italo Calvino, *Perché leggere i classici?*, Milan, 1991.

The Intuition of iMaestri

Le Corbusier
Pierre Jeanneret
Charlotte Perriand

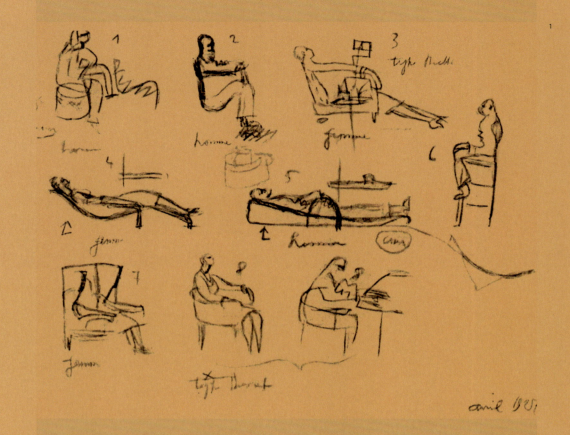

1 "The different ways of sitting, which seats need to be adapted to" Sketch by Le Corbusier, April 1927

2 Patent drawing of the Chaise longue basculante no. 673.824 by Mrs Scholefield, born Perriand, Gentlemen Jeanneret (C.E.) a.k.a. Le Corbusier and Jeanneret (A.P.), April 8, 1929

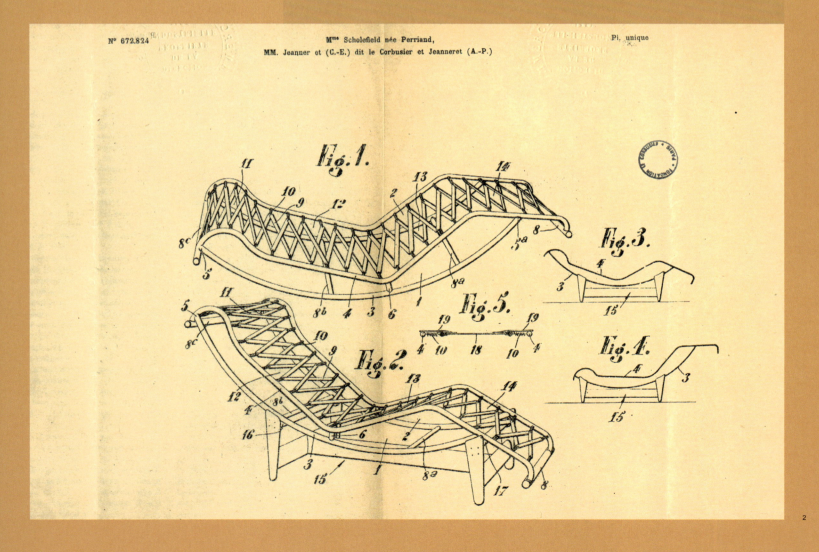

Le Corbusier / Pierre Jeanneret / Charlotte Perriand

Manifestos of the Modern Movement, Le Corbusier's theoretical writings *Vers une architecture* (1923) and *L'Art décoratif d'aujourd'hui* (1925) had a major influence on many contemporary architects and planners when they were published. "Reading these two books was dazzling. They took me past the wall that obstructed the future," Charlotte Perriand wrote in her autobiography. Carrying her portfolio of drawings, she knocked at the door of the architect's workshop to present her work. Despite a cold reception, she invited him to see her *Bar sous le toit*, which was exhibited at the Salon d'Automne. Satisfied by what he saw there, Le Corbusier hired Charlotte Perriand as partner to develop the furniture program, designing cabinets, chairs, and tables.

"My steps took me regularly to Rue de Sèvres until 1937. My role—unexpectedly—was to work as a partner of Le Corbusier and Pierre Jeanneret in developing their furniture program 'Cabinets, chairs and tables,' which they had announced in 1925 at the Pavillon de l'Esprit Nouveau, to continue their studies of them and ensure the production of prototypes by my craftworkers" (Charlotte Perriand, *Une vie de création*, Paris, 1998, p. 26).

Forming a close-knit team with Le Corbusier and Pierre Jeanneret, Perriand first worked on the renovation of the gallery of paintings at Maison La Roche (1923–25) and then Villa Church (1927–29).

Le Corbusier had devised a program for different ways of sitting. He had selected the chaise longue of William Morris, Maple & Co's Franklin armchairs, and the Surrepos Chaise longue by Dr. Pascaud providing a frame of reference for the research to be conducted by Le Corbusier, Pierre Jeanneret, and Charlotte Perriand. In 1928, they developed the prototypes of Chaise longue, of Fauteuil à dossier basculant, and Fauteuil Grand Confort (petit and grand modèle) to equip Villa Church. A first handcrafted series was produced, but it was extremely expensive compared to other contemporary models available on the market.

The Intuition of iMaestri

3

1887	Le Corbusier born at La Chaux-de-Fonds (Switzerland)	**1896**	Pierre Jeanneret born in Geneva (Switzerland)
1903	Charlotte Perriand born in Paris (France)	**1917**	Le Corbusier settles permanently in Paris
1921	Pierre Jeanneret moves to Paris and starts working with Auguste and Gustave Perret	**1921 - 1925**	Charlotte Perriand studies at the Union Centrale des Arts Décoratifs
1922	Pierre Jeanneret joins Le Corbusier's office	**1923 - 1925**	Le Corbusier and Pierre Jeanneret found Maisons La Roche-Jeanneret in Paris
1925	Le Corbusier and Pierre Jeanneret build the Pavillon de l'Esprit Nouveau		**20 Casiers standard P.E.N.**
1926	Charlotte Perriand takes part in the Salon des Artistes Décorateurs (SAD) with her Coin salon	**1927**	**Charlotte Perriand sets up her workshop in Place Saint-Sulpice and creates Le Bar sous le toit**
Charlotte Perriand joins Le Corbusier and Pierre Jeanneret's office	Le Corbusier and Pierre Jeanneret theorize the five points of modern architecture	In April 1927 Le Corbusier conceives the "new ways of sitting"	

3   Charlotte Perriand, Le Corbusier, and Pierre Jeanneret, Athens, 1933

4   Photo for the first advertising campaign by Unimark, circa 1968

Le Corbusier / Pierre Jeanneret / Charlotte Perriand

1928 — Charlotte Perriand exhibits the dining room suite with an extendable table, Fauteuil, and Tabouret pivotant at the Salon des Artistes Décorateurs (SAD) — **Development and prototyping of metal furniture by Le Corbusier, Pierre Jeanneret, Charlotte Perriand** — Foundation of the CIAM

1929 — Salon d'Automne, Paris — Charlotte Perriand resigns from SAD and founds the Union des Artistes Modernes (UAM)

1930 — First exhibition of the Union des Artistes Modernes (UAM) at the Pavillon de Marsan, Musée des Arts Décoratifs in Paris — Thonet France issues metal furniture under the name Le Corbusier, Pierre Jeanneret, Charlotte Perriand — **1930 - 1933**

Le Corbusier and Pierre Jeanneret build the Pavillon Suisse of the Cité Internationale Universitaire de Paris — Charlotte Perriand works with them on the furnishings of the student rooms and the hostel-library — **1931** — Le Corbusier and Pierre Jeanneret build Villa Savoye

1932 — Le Corbusier and Pierre Jeanneret build the Cité de refuge pour l'Armée du salut in Paris — Charlotte Perriand works with them on the furnishings of dormitories, refectories, kitchens, and nurseries

1934 — **Table pieds corolle, Appartement Le Corbusier** — **1935** — Study in La Maison du jeune homme, at the Universal Exhibition in Brussels with René Herbst and Louis Sognot

1937 — Charlotte Perriand ends her collaboration with Le Corbusier — **1938** — Pierre Jeanneret ends his collaboration with Le Corbusier

4

The Intuition of iMaestri

Pavillon de l'Esprit No

5–6 Pavillon de l'Esprit Nouveau
Le Corbusier, Pierre Jeanneret, Paris, 1925

7 Interior of the Pavillon de l'Esprit Nouveau, Bologna, 1977
Glauco and Giuliano Gresleri and José Oubrerie, architects

8 Interior of the Pavillon de l'Esprit Nouveau
Le Corbusier, Pierre Jeanneret, Paris, 1925

Le Corbusier / Pierre Jeanneret

veau 1925

From April 28 to November 30, 1925, the International Exhibition of Decorative Arts was held in Paris. Between the Place de la Concorde, the Grand Palais, and the Esplanade des Invalides, each country expressed its originality with the construction of ephemeral pavilions in which the most emblematic achievements in modern decorative art were presented. Two architectural currents were opposed: the Art Deco style and the modernist current, also known as the International avant-garde. Le Corbusier, in collaboration with his cousin Pierre Jeanneret, built a pavilion close to the Grand Palais. For the interiors, they developed a program of furniture that included the Casiers standard (standard cabinets) in wood, and a chrome-plated tubular steel table with a wooden top (LC12), as well as a second smaller table with a top in matte varnished sheet metal (LC19). The Pavillon de l'Esprit Nouveau was destroyed in 1926. A replica was rebuilt in 1977 at the International Building Fair in Bologna thanks to José Oubrerie, a former collaborator of Le Corbusier, and Glauco and Giuliano Gresleri. On this occasion, Cassina reissued, for the first time, the Casiers standard thanks to the work of Filippo Alison.

"The program: To reject decorative art. To affirm that the sphere of architecture embraces every least item of home furnishing, the street, the house, and even beyond. To illustrate how, by virtue of selection (the series and standardization), industry creates pure forms. To affirm the intrinsic value of the pure artwork. To show the radical transformations and structural liberties introduced by reinforced concrete and steel in urban housing. To show that an apartment can be standardized to meet the needs of many people. The practical living cell, comfortable and attractive, a veritable machine for living in, can be combined into great colonies in height and extent." (From Le Corbusier, *Oeuvre complète*, Vol. 1, Basel, 1910–29).

6

8

20 Casiers standard P.E.N.
1978

These cabinets are highly adaptable and express Le Corbusier's innovative idea of interior space organization. They can be installed as dividers or sideboards, as required. They are part of the Le Corbusier®, Pierre Jeanneret®, Charlotte Perriand® Collection.

The Intuition of iMaestri

Le Bar sous le toit

9   The dining room
Charlotte Perriand, 1928

10 Perspective sketch
of the dining room
Charlotte Perriand, 1928

11 Exhibition view of the
dining room at the Salon des
Artistes Décorateurs
Charlotte Perriand, 1928

In Paris, Charlotte Perriand lived in a former photographer's studio under the roof of a building on Rue Bonaparte. It had a huge glass roof overlooking the church of Saint-Sulpice. She laid out this small room ingeniously and, to gain the maximum space, replaced the classic front door of the apartment with a sliding door. She also created furnishings suited to the volumes of the apartment as well as the use she wanted to make of it. In the bar area, set in an attic room, she positioned the curved nickel-plated copper bar cabinet and a low sofa to optimal effect. A gaming table and low stools, made of chrome-plated copper upholstered in leather, completed the suite. Charlotte Perriand presented this interior design at the Salon d'Automne in 1927. This avant-garde furniture, made from industrial and modern materials, caused a sensation and brought her immediate fame. Le Corbusier took note and took on Charlotte Perriand as a partner "in charge of the program of furnishings: cabinets, chairs, and tables, as well as interior fittings." Together with her new activities in Le Corbusier's workshop, she continued to design the interior of her apartment, creating furnishings especially for her dining room, which was then exhibited at the Salon des Artistes Décorateurs in 1928. She devised a modular table consisting of a rectangular top embedded in a chrome aluminum frame and covered with black linoleum. It could be extended by a crank handle attached to a cream lacquered sheet metal case and comfortably accommodate a variable number of guests in the small space. Swivel chairs made of steel and leather were arranged around this extendable table. These chairs were issued by Thonet as B302 from 1930 for the version with a backrest and B304 for the version without a backrest. They were then produced by Cassina as part of the Collection Le Corbusier, Pierre Jeanneret, Charlotte Perriand. The latter created a stool with a chrome-plated tubular steel frame and rattan seat. Named the Siège salle de bains, it entered the Thonet catalogue as B305 and was then added to the Collection Le Corbusier, Pierre Jeanneret and Charlotte Perriand. At Cassina, this tabouret is available in a range of upholstery and color finishes.

Charlotte Perriand

1927

7 Fauteuil tournant
1978

8 Tabouret tournant
1978

9 Tabouret
1978

The Intuition of iMaestri

Salon d'Automne

34

Le Corbusier / Pierre Jeanneret / Charlotte Perriand

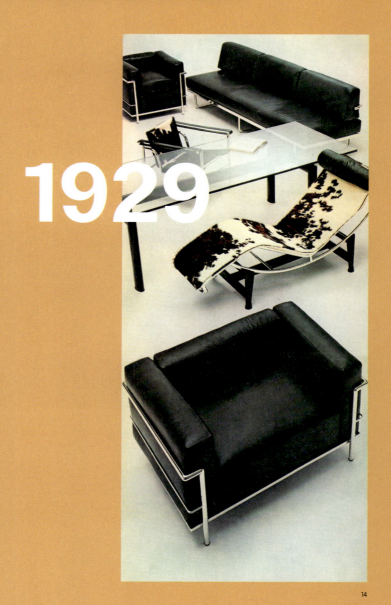

1929

It was at the 1929 Salon d'Automne that the range of tubular metal furniture was exhibited for the first time to the public. In a double-height space of nearly 90 sq m, Le Corbusier, Pierre Jeanneret, and Charlotte Perriand presented their works for the Équipement intérieur d'une habitation.

To divide and compartmentalize the living spaces fluidly, the idea of standard cabinets was taken on from Le Corbusier and Pierre Jeanneret's Pavillon de l'Esprit Nouveau of 1925, but in a metal and glass version. Now stackable and combinable, they met all storage needs and could be used in the living room, kitchen, or bathroom. The principal room, lit by powerful lamps, contained a table with a thick glass slab for the top and a base with an airplane wing profile around which were arranged Charlotte Perriand's swivel chairs (Fauteuil tournant), integrated on this occasion into the collection by Le Corbusier®, Pierre Jeanneret®, and Charlotte Perriand®. The Fauteuil à dossier basculant, the Chaise longue, and the Fauteuil Grand Confort completed the set.

12 Charlotte Perriand sitting on the Chaise longue à réglage continu by Le Corbusier, Pierre Jeanneret, Charlotte Perriand, 1928–29

13 Exhibition view of *Le Monde Nouveau de Charlotte Perriand* Reconstruction of the Salon d'Automne by Le Corbusier, Pierre Jeanneret, Charlotte Perriand, 2019 Fondation Louis Vuitton, Paris

14 Cassina poster of the Le Corbusier, Pierre Jeanneret, Charlotte Perriand Collection circa 1978

The Intuition of iMaestri

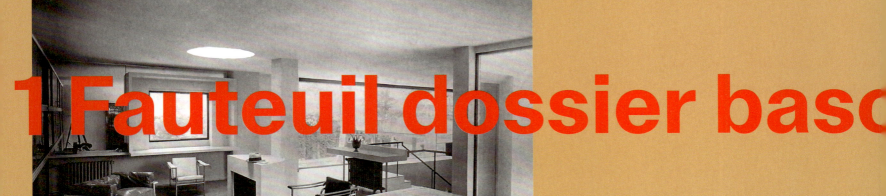

1 Fauteuil dossier basc

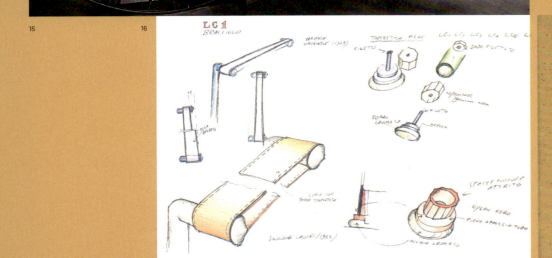

This slingback chair is a tubular chrome metal version of a traditional wooden colonial chair. The first prototypes were made for Villa Church and, to satisfy the client's requirements, had a padded seat and back. A few models were then made for the 1929 Salon d'Automne with a leather seat and backrest. Finally, a canvas version, with a natural leather trim, was presented at the Salon de l'Union des Artistes Modernes in 1930. It should be noted that versions of the slingback chair at the time all had armrests that were wider at the front than at the back of the chair.

Le Corbusier / Pierre Jeanneret / Charlotte Perriand

ulant 1928
1965

15 Interior design of the library
Le Corbusier, Pierre Jeanneret, Charlotte Perriand
Villa Church, Ville-d'Avray
Architecture by Le Corbusier, Pierre Jeanneret, 1929

16 Study sketches for the assembly of the Fauteuil à dossier basculant
Filippo Alison, late 1970s

17 Fauteuil à dossier basculant B301
Thonet Edition, 1930

18 Pierre Legrain
UAM exhibition poster, 1929

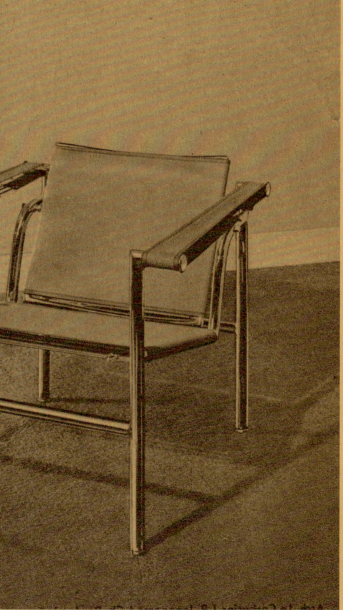

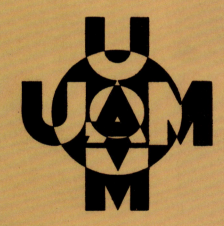

The range of furniture was then edited by Thonet in 1930, under the name "Le Corbusier, Pierre Jeanneret, Charlotte Perriand." They received the following reference numbers: B306 for the Chaise Longue, B301 for the Fauteuil dossier basculant, B302 for the swivel chair with a backrest, and B304 for the backless version, B305 for the bathroom stool, and, finally, B307 for the metal and glass table. Unfortunately, this avant-garde furniture was not successful because the production costs were too high and it failed to appeal to the public's taste. Thonet sold only 172 pieces of the Chaise Longue across Europe between 1930 and 1935.

In 1959, Heidi Weber, a gallerist in Zurich with an interest in Le Corbusier's work, contacted him for the reissue of the Chaise longue, the Fauteuil Grand Confort (petit and grand modèle), as well as the Fauteil dossier basculant. In 1964, she entrusted the manufacture of these models to Cassina, who eventually acquired the exclusive production and marketing rights in 1965.

The UAM

This association of artists, which included Charlotte Perriand, Pierre Jeanneret, Le Corbusier, Louis Sognot, Pierre Chareau, Sonia Delaunay, and Pierre Legrain, covered all fields of the visual arts. It exhibited collectively, for the first time in 1930, at the Pavillon de Marsan in Paris. On this occasion, the metal furniture designed by Le Corbusier, Pierre Jeanneret, and Charlotte Perriand was presented.

The Intuition of iMaestri

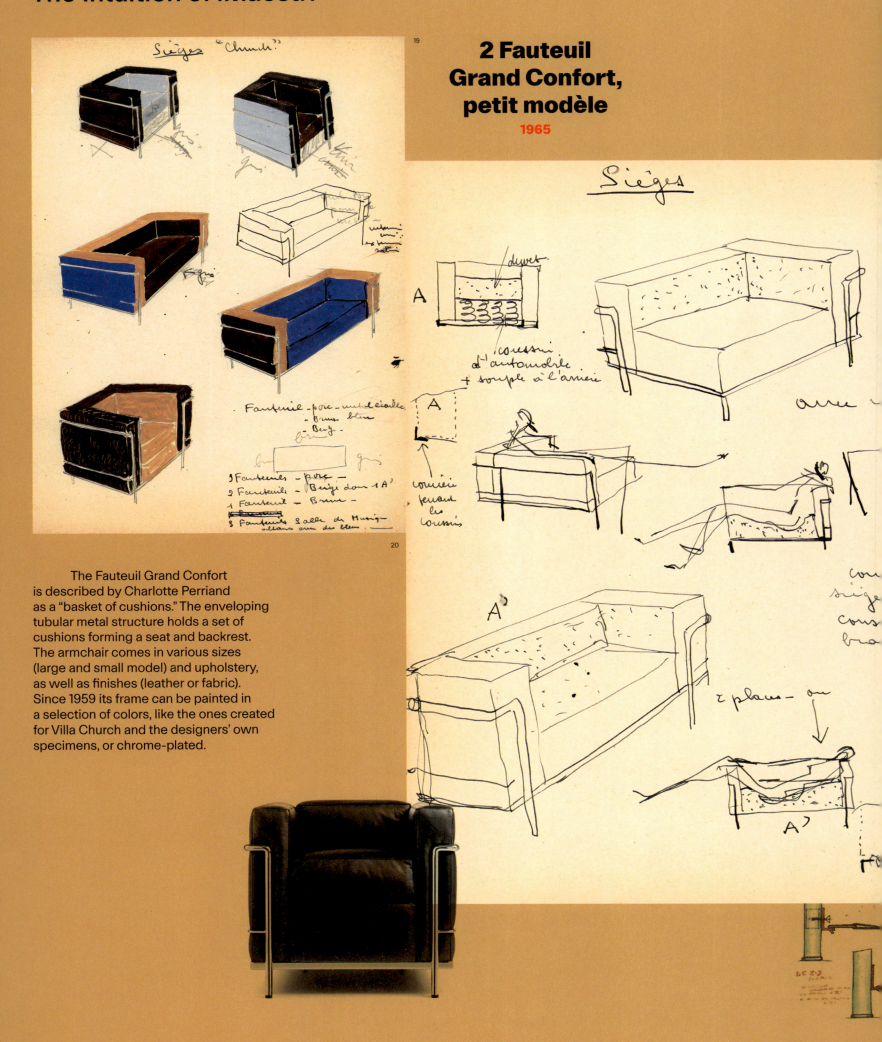

2 Fauteuil Grand Confort, petit modèle
1965

The Fauteuil Grand Confort is described by Charlotte Perriand as a "basket of cushions." The enveloping tubular metal structure holds a set of cushions forming a seat and backrest. The armchair comes in various sizes (large and small model) and upholstery, as well as finishes (leather or fabric). Since 1959 its frame can be painted in a selection of colors, like the ones created for Villa Church and the designers' own specimens, or chrome-plated.

Le Corbusier / Pierre Jeanneret / Charlotte Perriand

1928

19 Sketches of Fauteuil and Sofa Grand Confort, "Church" version
Charlotte Perriand, carnet de bord, 1928

20 Sketches of Fauteuil Grand Confort and Méridienne
Charlotte Perriand, carnet de bord, 1928

21 Study sketches of tubular metal bending and assembly of Fauteuil Grand Confort, models
Filippo Alison, late 1970s

3 Fauteuil Grand Confort, grand modèle
1965

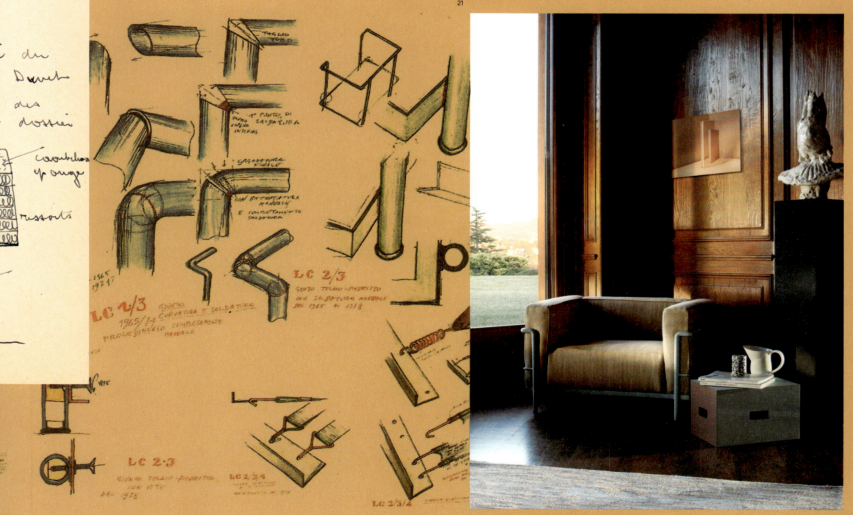

Le Corbusier / Pierre Jeanneret / Charlotte Perriand

1928
1965

This tilting chaise longue can be set in all positions, always balancing by itself, without any mechanical operation. Dubbed by its designers as a veritable "resting machine," it can be used as an armchair, a resting chair, a chaise longue, or a rocking chair.

It is an example of the iconic furnishings of the Modern Movement, where functionalism and decorative minimalism prevail.

22–23 Folding brochure on the history of the Chaise longue à réglage continu, 1974

24 Sketch of Chaise longue basculante, 1928

The Intuition of iMaestri

1928

6 Table tube d'avion
1974

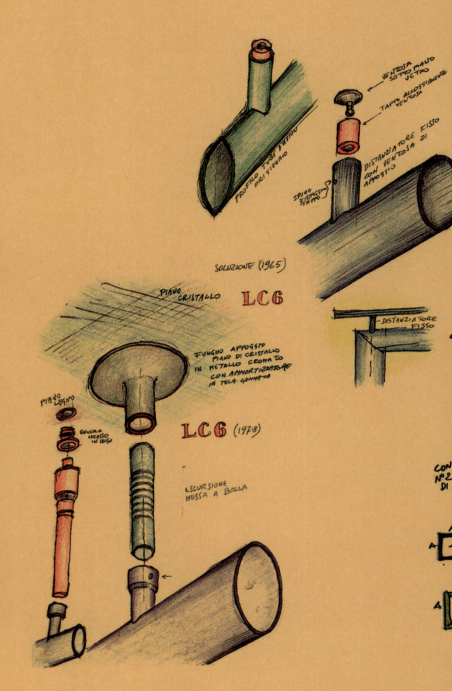

The structure of the table installed at Villa Church consisted of an ovoid strut, like those used in aviation to brace the wings of biplanes, which supported a thick sheet of glass resting on five points of support, allowing the height of the top to be modified. The version presented at the 1929 Salon d'Automne was green but other colors were presented later by Cassina.

Le Corbusier / Pierre Jeanneret / Charlotte Perriand

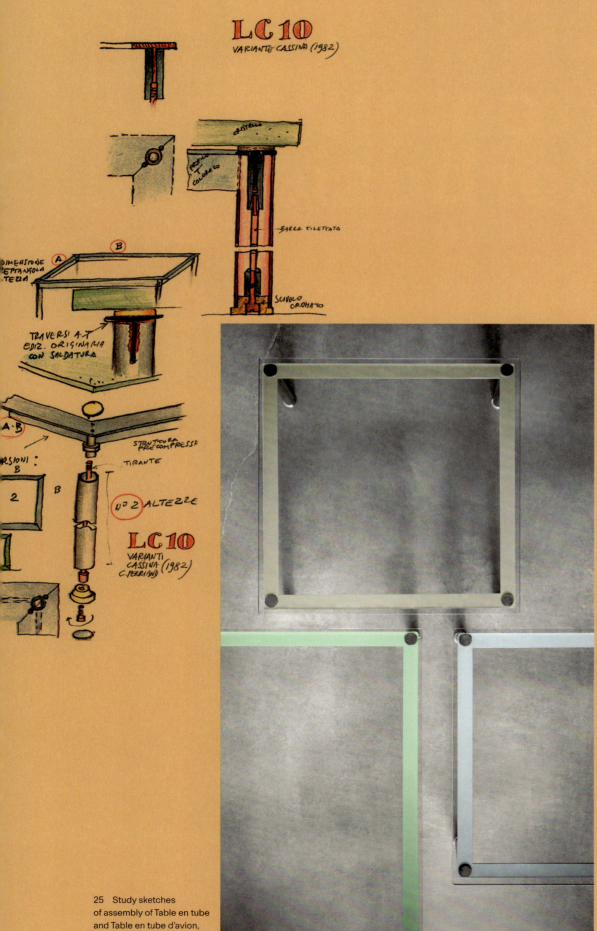

25 Study sketches of assembly of Table en tube and Table en tube d'avion, Filippo Alison, circa 1985

1928

10 Table en tube
1985

At the Salon d'Automne, this model was presented as a desk with a chrome finished frame and colored lacquer crosspieces. It was reinterpreted by Charlotte Perriand in 1984 and reissued the following year by Cassina in new variants better adapted to contemporary needs.

The Intuition of iMaestri

L'appartement de Le Corbusier

1934

In the early 1930s, Le Corbusier and Pierre Jeanneret undertook the construction of a residential building at 24 Rue Nungesser-et-Coli, in the 16th arrondissement of Paris. Le Corbusier reserved the last two floors as his personal apartment.

For the dining room, the three designers devised a large table with a thick marble top, derived from the one created for the Swiss Pavilion but with a slightly different base in cast iron with Corolle feet. For the living room, Le Corbusier designed a Canapé (sofa) with a tubular steel frame that held leather cushions padded with feathers. In 1974, Cassina reinterpreted the original and produced a version with a chrome structure. Variations then emerged, with a new chromatic range and two- or three-seater versions, available in leather or fabric. The sofa is part of the Collection Le Corbusier, Pierre Jeanneret, Charlotte Perriand.

5 Canapé, Appartement Le Corbusier
1974

26   Le Corbusier's apartment
Interior view, Paris, 1934

27   Le Corbusier's apartment
View of the dining room, Paris, 1934

Le Corbusier / Pierre Jeanneret / Charlotte Perriand

1935

La Maison du jeune homme

In 1935, Maurice Dufrène invited Charlotte Perriand, Louis Sognot, and René Herbst to design a 60-sq-m space in the French section of the Universal Exhibition in Brussels. They presented La Maison du jeune homme, a bold interior for a modern young man, both cultivated and sporting. René Herbst designed the space devoted to sports, Louis Sognot the sleeping quarters and bathroom, and Charlotte Perriand, with Le Corbusier and Pierre Jeanneret, furnished the study.

In front of a slate wall on which Charlotte Perriand designed the plan of the apartment and listed the various artists involved in the project, there was a large worktable with corolle feet. It was a variant of the one designed with Le Corbusier and Pierre Jeanneret for the dining room of Le Corbusier's apartment in Paris, in this case with a thick slate top.

The same type of structure was used to support the standard lacquered sheet metal cabinets separating the study from the gym. Le Corbusier placed the drawings of La Ville Radieuse on the central door and the map of Paris on the side. René Herbst furnished the exercise space with all the necessary equipment for gymnastics. The volume was enlivened by a large fresco by Fernand Léger and separated from the workspace by a net. At the desk, Charlotte Perriand placed her new model of a Fauteuil en bois et paille opposite her Fauteuil pivotant with a chrome metal structure, heralding her growing interest in the use of natural materials, such as wood, cane, and straw, in her furniture.

11 Table pieds corolle, plateau bois

1985

28 Exhibition view of La Maison du jeune homme
Charlotte Perriand, Le Corbusier, Pierre Jeanneret, Brussels, 1935

45

The Intuition of iMaestri

Charles & Ray Eames

The Intuition of iMaestri

CHARLES EAMES

1907 — Charles born in St Louis, Missouri

1925 — Designs lighting fixtures for Edwin F. Guth Fixture Company

1930 — Opens Gray & Eames Architects

1932-1933 — Doors, stained glass windows, and a chandelier for Pilgrim Congregational Church, St. Louis.

1934 — St Mary's Catholic Church, Helena, Arkansas; Helena Lighting Fixture

1936 — Meyer House, St Louis

1939 — Charles teaches at Cranbrook Academy of Art, Michigan - Architecture and furniture projects with Eero Saarinen

1941 — "Organic Design in Home Furnishings" competition at MoMA, with Eero Saarinen

RAY KAISER

1912 — Ray born in Sacramento, California

1933-1939 — Ray studies painting at the Hans Hofmann School, New York

1936 — Founding member of American Abstract Artists, New York - Exhibits her paintings at the Riverside Museum

1940 — Ray studies at Cranbrook Academy of Art

Charles & Ray Eames

Charles Ormand Eames Jr was born in St. Louis in 1907. After graduating from Yeatman High School and being dismissed from the architecture program at Washington University, for a kind of insubordination, Charles moved straight into his own architecture. Despite the Depression, he formed a series of practices from 1930 to 1936, building two churches in Arkansas and four homes in St Louis.

Esteemed architect Eliel Saarinen noted Charles's works and invited him to complete a fellowship at the Cranbrook Academy of Art near Detroit. This fellowship quickly transformed Charles into the school's first director of the industrial design program. After a short time at Cranbrook, Charles became friends with Eero Saarinen and other budding architects and designers.

Bernice Alexandra "Ray" Kaiser was born in Sacramento in 1912 and held an early interest in fashion design, theater, and the arts. She left her hometown for New York to attend the Bennett School for Girls, and in 1933, moved to Manhattan. Although she initially entertained the idea of studying engineering, she remained enamored by many artistic media and their respective social circles. Ray enrolled in Hans Hofmann's painting school from 1933 until 1939 and became a founding American Abstract Artists member. Following the advice of a dear friend, Ray applied to Cranbrook with hopes of expanding her artistic language.

1–2 Charles and Ray Eames at the Eames House in California in the 1950s

3 Charles and Ray Eames at the Eames Office in Venice, California, in the 1970s

The Intuition of iMaestri

Philip C. Johnson

September 14, 1949

Dear Charles:

Congratulations on your room at the Detroit show. It is by all odds the best of the lot, which I am sorry to say I am not saying as much as I had hoped.

However, we all admired particularly your little chandelier. Do you think it would be possible to make some more? Mrs. Edsel Ford was especially enthusiastic and I am asking for her as well as for myself.

When are you coming east to see my house now that it is done? I still have hopes of having some eames shots of it.

Yours,

Philip

Philip Johnson

Mr. Charles Eames
901 Washington Boulevard
West Los Angeles 24, California

PCJ/op

205 East 42 Street New York 17 N.Y.

Landis Gores, Associated

4   Letter from architect Philip Johnson to Charles about Edsel Ford's interest in the Galaxy light

5   Charles's and Ray's experiments with molded plywood began with a commission from the US Navy for 150,000 leg splints to help soldiers wounded in World War II

Charles & Ray Eames

It was at the Cranbrook Academy of Art that Charles's and Ray's lives and work began to intertwine. Their courtship lasted only a few months, sparked by Ray's assistance in Charles and Eero Saarinen's entry into MoMA's "Organic Design in Home Furnishings" competition. Immediately following their marriage in June 1941, Charles and Ray moved to Los Angeles with a great sense of optimism, bursting with exuberance for each other and their potential future in the arts and design.

The Eameses utilized the spare bedroom in their Neutra-designed apartment to experiment with molding plywood into complex furniture forms. When the US entered WWII, they pivoted this plywood manufacturing to, as Ray recalled, "aid in the war efforts without hurting anyone." With funding from the US Navy, the Eameses, alongside a small staff, manufactured leg splints, body litters, and aircraft parts. From these beginnings, they founded and operated the Eames Office, a design entity responsible for four decades of varied designs.

The Eames Office aimed, in part, to produce high-quality products for the masses from readily available industrial materials. Every object had to have what Charles called a "way-it-should-be-ness." Projects were modeled again and again in an iterative fashion until the final result was ready for the public.

And they constantly improved their designs after the first editions made it to the assembly line. There was an undeniable intuition for the rightness of particular forms, colors, and finishing details. Ray declared: "What works good is better than what looks good, because what works good lasts."

Open, curious eyes also led the Eameses into storytelling and educational pursuits. They gave impassioned lectures, designed international exhibitions, and created unique methods of communication with one of their most beloved tools: the camera. Charles's and Ray's visions were enmeshed—functioning as one; this vitality established the basis for the Eames Office's ongoing design work from that day onward.

After the deaths of Charles and Ray, the Eames Office, which is still run by the Eames family today, transformed into a cultural-commercial project dedicated to preserving, communicating, and extending one of the world's most influential design legacies. In 1988, the Library of Congress received close to one million documents, prints, and photographs from the Eames Office studio building, which was closed when the Eames Office moved to a new location.

Their works can be found in the permanent collections of numerous international museums, including the Centre Pompidou, Paris; Victoria & Albert Museum, London; Los Angeles County Museum of Art, CA; Metropolitan Museum of Art, New York, NY, and MoMA New York, NY.

The genesis of Cassina's Lighting Collection rose from the discovery of Charles and Ray's lighting designs, which were preserved and celebrated by the Eames Office. Interestingly, Charles Eames had a background in lighting fixture design. In 1925, he worked for the St.-Louis-based Edwin F. Guth Company, most renowned for the designs and patents of the Brascolite ceiling fixture and the first fluorescent lamp.

Later on, alongside architect Robert Walsh in Arkansas, Charles Eames built the St. Mary's Catholic Church in Helena and the St. Mary's Church in Paragould. Charles also designed the lighting fixtures and fittings for these two churches. Beginning in 2023, Charles and Ray Eames have joined the Cassina iMaestri Collection.

The Intuition of iMaestri

An Exhibition for Modern Living

After World War II, Charles & Ray Eames participated in *An Exhibition for Modern Living*, curated by Alexander Girard and held at the Detroit Institute of Arts, from September 11 to November 20, 1949.

Aside from the "hall of objects" where pieces of furniture actually in production were exhibited, a space gathered custom exhibition rooms designed by Alvar Aalto, Franco Albini, Hans Bellmann, Andres Dupres, Charles & Ray Eames, Pierre Jeanneret, Florence Knoll, Bruno Mathsson, George Nelson, Jens Risom, Eero Saarinen, Abel Sorensen, Richard Stein, and Van Keppel-Green.

Charles & Ray Eames worked closely to present a colorful space that was "not conceived of as a special room or section of a house, but rather suggests an attitude toward the space and objects with which one lives." Above their pieces of furniture, used as space dividers, suspended the sparkling-like ceiling fixture to be known as Galaxy.

Charles & Ray Eames

« This exhibition has its origin in the need of all of us to understand more about design. »

Alexander Girard

1949

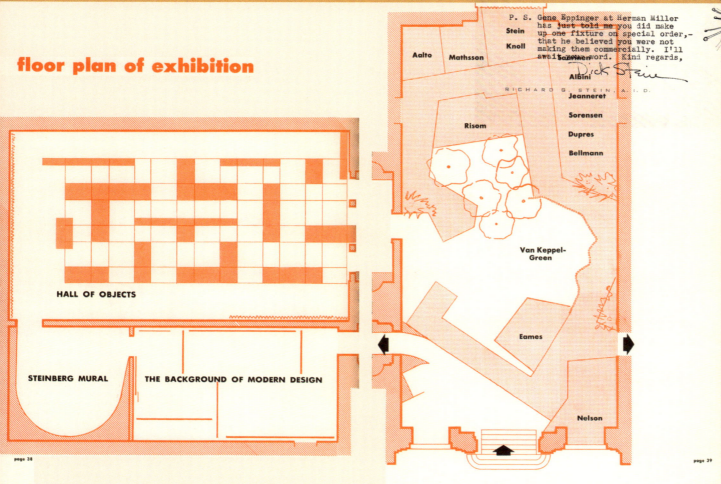

6   A collage created by Ray Eames of the Eames exhibition room at *An Exhibition for Modern Living* in Detroit

7   The Eames exhibition space at *An Exhibition for Modern Living*, featuring the Galaxy light

8   One of dozens of letters inquiring about the Galaxy light after it was shown in Detroit

9   Floor plan of *An Exhibition for Modern Living*

The Intuition of iMaestri

10 Charles and Ray during their early years of furniture and exhibition creation

CHARLES & RAY EAMES

1941 — Charles and Ray marry, move to Los Angeles, and start Eames Office

1942–1945 — Molded Plywood Leg Splint for US Navy

1944 — Graphic designs for *Arts & Architecture* magazine

1946 — *New Furniture Designed by Charles Eames* exhibition, MoMA, New York
- Eames Plywood Group

1947 — Textile designs for *The Competition for Printed Fabrics*, MoMA, New York

1948 — Eames Shell Chairs and La Chaise for "International Competition for Low-Cost Furniture Design" at MoMA, New York

1949 — *An Exhibition for Modern Living* at the Detroit Institute of Arts
- **Presentation of the Galaxy lamp**

1949 — Case Study House No. 8 (The Eames House) in Pacific Palisades

1950 — *Good Design* exhibition, Chicago Merchandise Mart and MoMA, NYC
Case Study House No. 9 (Entenza House) with Eero Saarinen
Eames Storage Units (ESU)

1951–1952 — The House of Cards, The Toy and The Little Toy

1953 — Film *A Communication Primer*
- Eames Hang-It-All

1956 — Lounge Chair and Ottoman

1957 — Film *Day of the Dead*
- Film *Toccata for Toy Trains*

1958 — *The India Report*
- Eames Aluminum Group

Charles & Ray Eames

1959
- Visit to the USSR; Film *Glimpses of the USA*
- Interior design, furniture, and a film for the Time-Life Building, New York

1961
- *Mathematica: A World of Numbers … and Beyond* exhibition
- Eames Contract Storage (ECS)

1963
- Eames Tandem Seating

1964-1965
- IBM Pavilion at New York World's Fair

1967
- Film *National Fisheries Center and Aquarium*

1968
- Eames Soft Pad Chaise for Billy Wilder
- Exhibitions *Photography & The City: The Evolution of an Art and a Science*, *Nehru: His Life and His India*

1969
- Exhibition and film *What is Design?*, Musée des Arts Décoratifs, Paris
- Film *Tops*
- Soft Pad Group chairs

1970-1971
- The Norton Lectures series at Harvard

1971
- *A Computer Perspective* exhibition

1972
- Film *SX-70* for Polaroid
- Film *Design Q&A*

1975
- *The World of Franklin and Jefferson* exhibition

1977
- Film *Powers of Ten. A Film Dealing with the Relative Size of Things in the Universe and the Effect of Adding Another Zero*

1978
- Charles Eames dies in St. Louis, Missouri

1988
- Ray Eames dies in Santa Monica, California. As per her and Charles's wishes, Eames Office continues to operate, still run today by the Eames Family

The Intuition of iMaestri

Galaxy

>> I got out of high school, then that summer—instead of going to the steel mill, and knowing I was going into architecture— I got a job at the Edwin F. Guth Fixture Company. (...) I got a job designing lighting fixtures, which is kind of an interesting transition from steel mill to architecture. >>

Charles Eames

Charles & Ray Eames

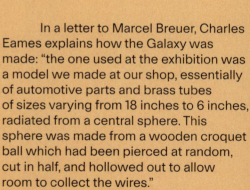

1949

2024

11 Charles, Ray, and Eames Office staff admiring the Galaxy in a packed crate, on its way to *An Exhibition for Modern Living*, in 1949

12 Cassina's Galaxy light prototype on display for the first time at the Salone del Mobile 2023

13 A response letter from Charles to Marcel Breuer's client regarding the availability of the Galaxy light

14 The Galaxy in its shipping crate, 1949

In a letter to Marcel Breuer, Charles Eames explains how the Galaxy was made: "the one used at the exhibition was a model we made at our shop, essentially of automotive parts and brass tubes of sizes varying from 18 inches to 6 inches, radiated from a central sphere. This sphere was made from a wooden croquet ball which had been pierced at random, cut in half, and hollowed out to allow room to collect the wires."

This experimental use of light, combined with technology and innovative materials, reflects the couple's design process, driven by curiosity and hands-on exploration. Despite the fact that the Eameses received many inquiries—from Philip C. Johnson to Marcel Breuer— the model has never been put into production until Cassina, following its fifty years of experience and research on historical pieces, decided to work with the Eames Office on their archive of lighting fixtures. After a few months of development, Galaxy made its grand debut in the Design World at the Milan Salone del Mobile where it was exhibited both at *Echoes* exhibition in Palazzo Broggi and in Cassina's historical showroom of Via Durini.

The Intuition of iMaestri

Photos by
MATTIA BALSAMINI

Mattia Balsamini unveils the space of the historical Cassina factory and plays with chiaroscuro to capture the essence of the pieces by Charles & Ray Eames, Vico Magistretti, Le Corbusier, Pierre Jeanneret, and Charlotte Perriand.

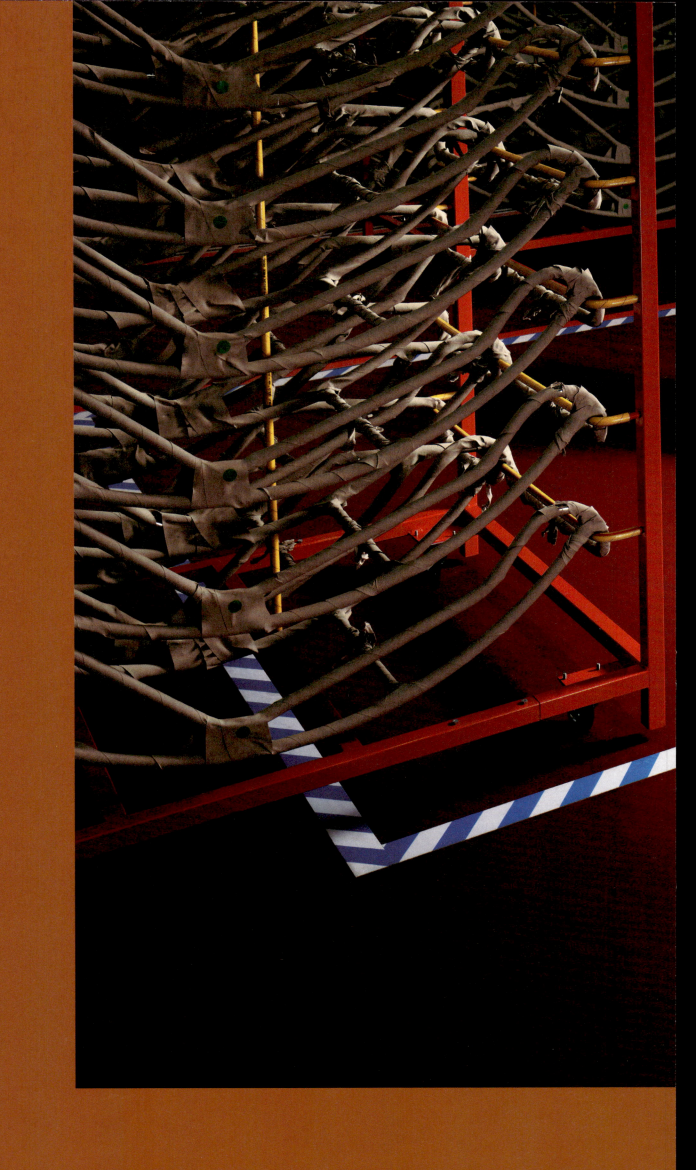

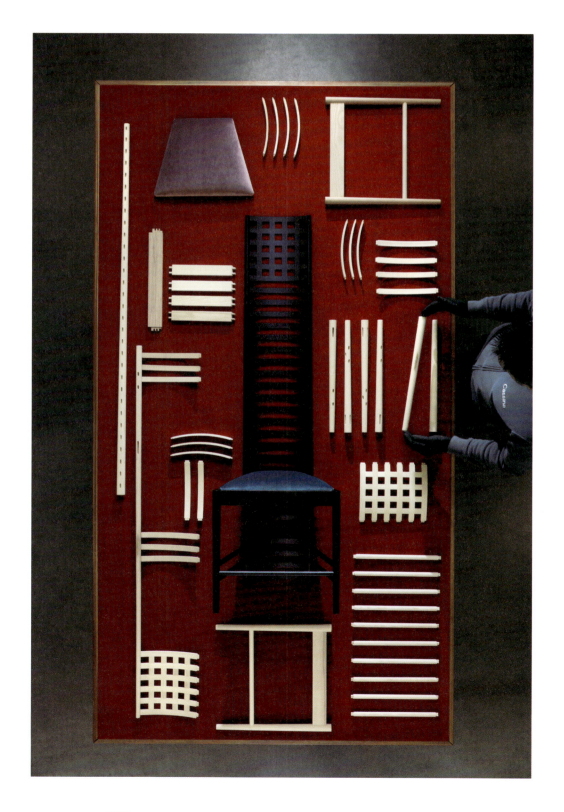

69

Continuous
Research

Cassina,
Continuity
Between Past and
Experimentation

The Research Continues: Origin, Evolution, and Return

DOMITILLA DARDI
Design historian

A home newly built and needing to be furnished. For the most fortunate Italians (and others) the 1960s and 1970s also meant this, a process of personal and collective identity that passed through the definition of their living space. But what did the market really offer in those years? The furniture industry was in turn finding its own identity and defining its target public. Not without complications, though. After the war, "the creation of simple and functional furniture encountered two fundamental difficulties. The first was that the general public, the mass public, was unwilling to accept the uniformity of serial products. It wanted to choose, and it chose with pleasure only striking furniture, of the sort that 'caught the eye.' The second was that Italian production was still in the hands of craftworkers and very small producers, and it was uneconomical for craftworkers to produce simple furniture in series, because they lacked the machinery to turn it out quickly, not to mention that it was unfulfilling, as there was no scope for expressing their manual skills."[1]

1 Cassina carpentry. Manual gluing of the Willow 1 chair by Charles R. Mackintosh

2 Cassina carpentry. Assembly of the Leggera chair by Gio Ponti

3 Assembly of 8 Sofa by Piero Lissoni

It was no small feat to make the transition from handcrafted production to industrial design, while providing a public in search of a new aesthetic identity with a valid alternative to furniture in antique styles. For this reason, the Cassina iMaestri Collection was the most farsighted project that a company could undertake in those years of change, at the height of post-modernity. It would be simplistic and erroneous to see it merely in terms of a scholarly concern with the past. It was a revolutionary achievement, the result of a strategic vision, but also of that capacity for instinctual insight that only great entrepreneurs or artists possess.

And today—with the extended perspective that history gives us—it has proved a pioneering achievement with a decisive effect on the future of contemporary design, and not just in Italy. It also offered the most effective synthesis to present a clear and recognizable corporate identity.

As we will see, the key to this was in research: technological research and historical-contextual research into designers. A continuous, passionate, tireless approach, constantly fanning the flames.

Continuous Research

Origin

As we know, behavior in humans arises from a complex balance that is partly determined by the genes in our DNA and partly by the influence of the environment in which we grow up. In a similar way, companies can also understand much of their identity by studying their origin, on the one hand, and, on the other, the changes that take place over time due to decisions, encounters, and the conditions that they evolve in.

In the case of Cassina, these factors can be exemplified in two foundational components: its origin in the handcrafted excellence of its carpentry and its development into an industrial manufacturer that underpinned the success of Italian design worldwide, capable of dealing with multiple production methods and different visions of design. Cementing the alpha and the omega of this story is research, embodied in equal measure in technique-technology (and here we find the DNA of know-how) and the dialogue with the designers (the environment), namely the "authors" of both past and present.

The Cassina iMaestri Collection was officially founded in 1973, when architectural theories demonstrated the validity of the palimpsest, the dialogue with history and superseding modernity, a year after Charles Jencks declared the death of architecture.[2] But it was developed, paradoxically, by introducing the masters of Modernism into the domestic landscape. It is a strategy that would act almost as an antidote to the twofold historicist eclecticism: that of furniture in period style (furniture that caught the eye, as mentioned above, a tendency that dies hard and is still rife today); but also that of the intellectualist architectural speculation of Post-Modern, which banished the masters of the Modern Movement.

It is symptomatic that, in the same years, Cassina was engaged in a dialogue with the young radical designers who would become the masters of the future. This is not a contradiction but the result of complexity. The Masters were in their own way the radicals of their time, designers who impregnated every expression of the scales of space, including furniture, with their vision of the world (not just architecture). Albini, Asplund, Le Corbusier-Jeanneret-Perriand, Mackintosh, and Wright were all dissidents in their day. Issuing their works, in that historical period, in a certain sense inventing the concept of the open-series edition by engineering the models, had nothing to do with a reassuring vintage fashion. On the contrary, it was a courageous vision, at least as much as giving space to experiments by young radicals. They could be considered as two sides of the same coin; and what united them was the approach to research, both productive and authorial. Just read the history.

As acknowledged by Cassina, Dino Gavina was the first to intuit the potential of reissuing furniture designed by the masters of the Modern Movement. The Bolognese entrepreneur jumped at the opportunity to reissue Marcel Breuer's furniture. He showed up at his studio in New York in 1962 armed with great determination and—it seems—a bouquet of white roses, which wrested a smile and permission from the former Bauhaus *enfant prodige*. "You have to give credit to Dino Gavina," said Rodrigo Rodriquez, "for understanding that there were furnishings designed in the past that deserved to be reissued today, or rather in the years we are talking about, the 1960s. Dino had already made contact with Marcel Breuer and began to manufacture the seats by this great exponent of the Bauhaus. To Cesare he suggested considering Le Corbusier's furniture, whose production rights were at that time held by Heidi Weber, shrewd and attentive in enhancing the value of the great master's nonarchitectural works."[3] For Cassina—in search of new ways of developing after its first successful phase of furnishing the ocean liners—looking at this potential of the historical edition also meant having a deep awareness of its target public: certainly not the masses, but an educated professional class in search of a new aesthetic and social identity.

This was the start of a major engineering operation, conducted in close contact with Charlotte Perriand. It continued even after Le Corbusier's death and would then lead to the editions of furniture designed exclusively by her. Later, attention would shift to other great masters: Rietveld, thanks to the intercession of Daniele Baroni, who arranged the contacts with his heirs in Utrecht; and then the complex operation on Mackintosh, handled by a key figure in the history of the collection, Filippo Alison, an architect and specialist professor of interior design at the University of Naples. It should be noted that the whole initiative of the editions of the iMaestri was conducted in tandem by intellectual-historical figures (primarily Gavina and Alison, and, for individual authors, names such as Baroni, Bosoni, and others), and the dialogue with production engineers. All this was done in conjunction with the heirs to the legacy, not only for the legal rights but as guarantors of fidelity to the original project. Alison represented both figures, being both an intellectual and overseeing the engineering of many of the earlier pieces in the collection. The discriminating factor for the choice of the latter, for the Neapolitan architect, was the possibility of enabling the archetype to live in the present, recognizing its use rather than it being a mere tribute to the relics of history. "If you want a designer product to fully communicate its cultural content, all the more one from a distant historical period, it has to be reproduced as an authentic object of use, so verifying the effects of its interaction with the homes and the sensibility of the present,"[4] explained Alison.

4   Sketch of different seatings designed for Cassina by Gio Ponti, circa 1960

5   Photomontage with the original Veliero bookshelf and its reissue

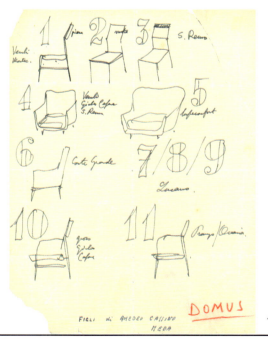

Domitilla Dardi

Continuous Research

"The Research Center was probably one of the first places where ideas were debated at all levels. I don't believe that many industries have pursued this possibility. It was very important, because innovation often arises in such contexts."

Gaetano Pesce

Domitilla Dardi

6   New methods of processing injection-molded polyurethane foam. Production phases: processing phases of Ciprea armchair by Afra and Tobia Scarpa, 1968

One aspect little known to the general public is the immense number of prototypes and tests leading to the choice of the models that would become, in all respects, icons of the design world. The success of Zig Zag and Red and Blue chairs, for example, is a merit that Rietveld will share forever with Cassina, who chose these two models from the many that were tested and prototyped. And these choices were the result of lengthy research, mediating between the possibility of serializing them and the contemporary sensibility of the home, as explained previously.

Obviously in the field of joinery, all the company's "genetic" skills were the true auxiliary of research. One inevitably thinks, for example, of ingenious solutions such as the "dry-mounted grooved" joint invented by the master foreman Fausto Redaelli, responding to Gio Ponti's request to pare down the sections of the 699 Superleggera chair. But an aptitude for research is part of the whole history of Cassina's output, even apart from its predisposition for the single material. This is its proud acceptance of the challenge of engineering that continues today. Recently, for example, two projects by Franco Albini tested the company's determination to adopt serial production. It is symptomatic that one of Cesare and Umberto's first meetings with designer-architects—even before they were called designers—was with Albini. It failed to develop into a regular collaboration, but today Albini has become one of the Masters whose projects have raised Cassina to very high levels of production, thanks to editions of the Veliero bookcase and the Radio in Cristallo. These are both works that were conceived as one-off pieces, designed by the architect for his own home in the late 1930s. Examples of bold engineering at the time, today they have succeeded in the challenge of serial reproducibility.

And research is always involved when dealing with the expansion of a historical series in its variants of finish and color. These are never dictated by a mere whim of the market, but always preceded by a careful scholarly reinterpretation of the historical sources in full respect of the original project. See for instance the research into color by Arthur Rüegg, a specialist in Le Corbusier's work, who was obviously consulted on the color variants.[5] And this leads back to the ties with historians and experts, who always respond to the call of the team working on the Masters.

Evolution

The picture of research would not be complete, unless, as already mentioned, the crucial question had been asked: Who will be the masters of the future? This seems to have been the impulse that led to the creation of the Cassina Research and Development Center in 1969, during the same period as the Cassina iMaestri Collection was developed. The Center is a unique laboratory, in which the most daring experiments are conducted on the most innovative materials. Above all, it is combined with research into new ways of living. "We had the technologies of expanded polyurethane," says Francesco Binfaré, who directed the center in those years, "and at one point I decided to carry out experiments on the body. I would put people in crates, inject polyurethane, and make casts of them. They were operations of collective creativity. It was the 1970s and experiments were being made. (...) Our work focused more on investigating aspects of functional complexity rather than technological complexity. And functional complexity is more an art than a science. Then, as we were mainly studying seating, what interested me most about these household products was their relationship with the body, their functioning as 'behavioral' objects."[6]

The radical groups, Archizoom at the forefront, were naturally at home in the Center, with Paolo Deganello developing the new idea of a chair with the AeO. And so was Mario Bellini, who would guide Cassina toward the interiors of means of transport, not ocean liners but cars, with the revolutionary and pioneering project Kar-a-sutra, presented in the exhibition *Italy: The New Domestic Landscape* at MoMA in 1972. But, most importantly, Gaetano Pesce, with whom Binfaré would found the first real Italian experimental brand. "We should not forget," stressed Pesce, "the role of the Research Center directed by Francesco Binfaré. It was a test bed for ideas and new materials and fostered a continuous exchange of ideas, reminiscent of a Renaissance *bottega*. The Research and Development Center was probably one of the first places where ideas were debated at all levels. I don't believe that many industries have pursued this opportunity. It was very important, because innovation often arises in such contexts. (...) Since the radical nature of the project made it difficult to produce these works officially under the Cassina brand, with Francesco Binfaré we came up with the idea of creating an alternative label and called it 'Bracciodiferro.' The experience also anticipated what Alessandro Mendini and Alessandro Guerriero later did with Alchimia, and then Ettore Sottsass with Memphis."[7]

Perhaps research now starts again from here. Who are the masters of the future today in a changed context, as we question ourselves about the coexistence between the material and the immaterial? The answer cannot lie in a single raw material or a single author, but in a choral and shared project. The processes will need to be metabolic and regenerative, otherwise we won't exist, as beings and even less as users. Waste is an invention of humanity, because in nature every residue returns to a cycle, and we can only study and learn from this, abandoning any presumption of superiority. Continuing to conduct research into what we are and what we would like to become, fusing historical and theoretical skills with technological and design skills, still seems the best possible formula. Studying and knowing remain the most revolutionary actions we can perform.

---

[1] Irene De Guttry and Maria Paola Maino, *Il mobile italiano degli anni '40 e '50* (1992), Rome-Bari, 2010, p. 12.
[2] Charles Jencks set the date of the death of modern architecture at exactly 3:32 p.m. on July 15, 1972, when a charge of dynamite destroyed the Pruitt-Igoe residential complex, built in 1951, in keeping with the most progressive ideals of Modernism.
[3] Giulio Castelli, Paola Antonelli, Francesca Picchi, *La Fabbrica del design*, Milan, 2007, p. 66.
[4] Filippo Alison, "I Maestri: ideologia della ricostruzione," in Giampiero Bosoni (ed.), *Made in Cassina*, Milan, 2008, pp. 3–9.
[5] See Arthur Rüegg, *Meubles et Intérieurs 1905-1965*, Zurich, 2012, pp. 135–37.
[6] Castelli, Antonelli, Picchi, op. cit., p. 76.
[7] Ibid., pp. 81 and 84.

Continuous Research

Gio

Ponti

1   Superleggera chair frames stacked in the factory, circa 1960

Chairs by Gio Ponti produced by Cassina

Gio Ponti

During the course of his prolific career, the Italian architect, designer, painter, author, and critic, Gio Ponti, made a deep impression on contemporary creativity in the twentieth century.

He designed office buildings, houses, furniture, and art objects, as well as industrial design objects. With this extremely rich and varied production, he was a major figure of Italian design.

To disseminate the finest of Italian production, with his protean talent he founded the magazines *Domus* in 1928 and then *STILE* in 1941, exerting an international influence as a formidable flag-bearer for the country's industry.

He also taught at the Politecnico di Milano from 1936 to 1941, training the next generation of Italian architects.

Finally, in 1954, he established the Compasso d'Oro, the award that singles out fine design produced in Italy and is still the most important award in the field of contemporary creativity. His most emblematic creations are the Pirelli Tower (Milan), the Co-cathedral (Taranto), the Superleggera chair, Villa Planchart and Villa Arreaza (Caracas), and the Hotel Parco dei Principi in Sorrento.

Postwar Italy saw the emergence of many individual and mainly family-run firms that interacted with one another and coalesced in a geographical network located mainly around Milan. They converged in the Brianza area and gave rise to an efficient, responsive, and flexible industrial fabric that was eager to prosper. It was a period of experimentation; there was great enthusiasm, and a whole new generation of architects was ready to embark on an adventure with these young companies. Kartell, Cassina, Zanotta, or Tecno, run by their enlightened owners, worked with young architects such as Vico Magistretti, Mario Bellini, Joe Colombo or Achille and Pier Giacomo Castiglioni. This association between representatives of the arts and industry gave rise to an applied art that was soon termed industrial design.

This was also the period of postwar reconstruction, revitalized by subsidies under the Marshall Plan, which proved crucial in reviving industry. Shipyards were gradually repaired and the construction of new ships planned. This met a growing demand for ocean liners to travel to the Americas. Gio Ponti was actively involved in refurbishing the interiors of these huge liners and turned to Cassina to meet its growing demand for furnishings, working on an impressive range of chairs and armchairs.

Between 1949 and 1953, he worked on the interior design of the transatlantic liner *Andrea Doria* (with the model 593 being chosen to furnish the first class spaces) and designed the model 504 chair to furnish the first classes of the *Conte Grande*. He also worked on the interior design of *Conte Biancamano* and *Giulio Cesare*. Finally, he took part in the refurbishment of *Africa* (1951) and *Oceania* (1952) for which he also designed the pieces of furnishings, all produced by Cassina.

Continuous Research

2 Communication campaign for the Superleggera chair

3 Gio Ponti and Cesare Cassina, circa 1960

1891 — Born in Milan

1921 — Graduates from the Politecnico di Milano

1923 — Artistic Director of Richard Ginori

1925 — Grand prix de céramique at the Exposition Internationale des Art Décoratifs de Paris
- Casa Ponti, Via Randaccio in Milan, homage to Palladio

1926 — Villa Bouilhet or "The Flying Angel," Garches (France)

1927 — Series of objects for Christofle

1928 — Founds the magazine *Domus*

1931–1939 — Cappella Borletti at Monumental Cemetery, Milan

1939 — Rai building, Milan
- Building in Piazza San Babila, Milan

1941 — Founds the magazine *STILE*

1949 — **Starts his collaboration with Cassina with the Scrolled chair**

1950 — **Interiors of the ocean liner *Conte Grande* (with Nino Zoncada)**
- **Mod. 477**

Prototype hotel room for the 9th Triennale di Milano

1951 — **Interiors of the ocean liners *Giulio Cesare*, *Andrea Doria*, and *Conte Biancamano***
- **Mod. 492**

Gio Ponti

1952 — Edison building, Milan | Interiors of the ocean liners *Oceania* and *Africa*, Trieste Model chair for first class made by Cassina | Mod. 646 Leggera

1953 — Mod. 504, Mod. 533, Mod. 586, Mod. 588, Mod. 589, Mod. 593, Mod. 663, Mod. 807 Distex

1954 — Villa Planchart, Caracas (Venezuela) — Mod. 719, Mod. 803, Mod. 851 Mariposa, Mod. 852 Round

1955 — Istituto Italiano di Cultura, Lerici Foundation, Stockholm — Stand at the 10th Triennale di Milano produced by Cassina | Villa La Diamantina or Villa Arreaza, Caracas (Venezuela) (1954–56) — Church of San Luca, Milan | Alitalia Office, New York — Mod. 676, Mod. 687, Mod. 688

1956 — Pirelli building, Milan — Mod. 811

1957 — FEAL House, 11th Triennale di Milano

1964 — Mod. 851, Mod. 699 Superleggera, Due Foglie sofa, Lotus armchair | Hotel Parco dei Principi, Rome — Mod. 113, Mod. 898, Mod. 899

1967 — Facade of the Bijenkorf department stores, Eindhoven

1970 — Co-cathedral, Taranto

1971 — Denver Art Museum, Colorado, with James Sudler and Joal Cronenwett

1979 — Dies in Milan

83

Continuous Research

Leggera

The inspiration for this model came from the traditional Chiavari chair, designed by Giuseppe Gaetano Descalzi in 1807 with a woven straw seat and ladder back. With the 646 chair, Ponti designed a more modern, lightweight, and airy chair with a bent back at the top. The frame was in ash and the chair came in several versions: with the seat in Indian cane, cellophane rush, or a padded cushion upholstered in fabric or skai, with a hollow back or again a padded cushion covered in fabric or skai. This design icon, the result of a perfect understanding between an industrialist and a designer, is now in the collections of MoMA. Today the Leggera is produced in ash or stained black walnut and available in a range of colors and upholsteries.

4   Chair 646/P. Version with armrests. Handwritten note by Gio Ponti

5   Brochure of the Mod. 646 with seat and back variants, circa 1960

Gio Ponti

1952
Mod. 646

Continuous Research

Gio Ponti

1953

Distex
Mod. 807

1954

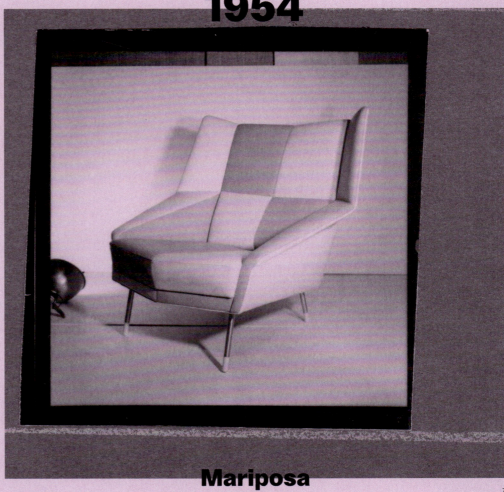

Mariposa
Mod. 851

Immediately recognizable by the obtuse angle of its straight back and its forward-sloping armrests, Distex was the culmination of Gio Ponti's research into well-being in the home. Combining comfort with aesthetics, this armchair used the vocabulary of forms inspired by the diamond, much loved by Ponti. It came in two versions: with open sides and a tubular brass frame or enclosed sides and wooden legs. The upholstery was in either wool or cotton fabric or Flexan faux leather, a new material whose primary qualities were stability and resistance to time and wear. The colors and finishes offered were many and varied. The patent filed by Figli di Amedeo Cassina is dated September 5, 1953.

The armchair was presented at the 10th Triennale di Milano (1954) on a stand designed by the Ponti, Fornaroli, and Rosselli offices. Production rights now belong to third parties. Cassina kept them until 1959.

Using Ponti's vocabulary of forms, the sofa and armchair set Mod. 851 was first made for the interior design of Villa Planchart in Caracas, Venezuela. Ponti, who wanted to emphasize the lightness of these furnishings, named it Mariposa, Spanish for butterfly. He played with color in the two-tone upholstery that enlivens and sets off the forms of the chair. The upholstery was in Vipla, an extremely tough technical fabric similar to vinyl, used mainly in the design of pleasure crafts, notably by Riva.

At the 11th Triennale di Milano in 1957, Studio Ponti, Fornaroli, and Rosselli, with the participation of Giovanni Varlonga, presented a pavilion designed as a lightweight, prefabricated aluminum structure with walls made of colored glass and concrete. It was erected in the Triennale garden. Its interior was fully furnished with items by Gio Ponti. Giordano Chiesa made a large backlit bookcase and a blue and purple laminated cabinet, like the one realized for Villa Planchart. Ponti also presented the set of armchairs and sofa Mod. 851 Mariposa, as well as the Round (1954), Due Foglie (1957), and Lotus (1957) armchairs produced by Cassina. Production rights now belong to third parties.

6   Mod. 807 catalogue photographic proofs, 1958

7   Mod. 851, photographic proofs

Continuous Research

Superleggera

"The little chair you see here is the protagonist of a singular adventure. I designed it simply, quickly, and without too much difficulty to add to the production of a company very famous among manufacturers of chairs in our Brianza. (The very kind 'sons of Amedeo Cassina' of Meda) (...). This chair is light, inexpensive, very sturdy, and if you visit the Cassina factory you will see a remarkable spectacle of chairs being tossed and falling after dizzying flights (in both height and length), and bouncing without ever breaking. At this price, no one makes chairs as strong as the sons of Amedeo Cassina, now famous worldwide for the passion with which they make their chairs and armchairs, and perform acrobatic games and feats of strength with them to demonstrate their unbeatable solidity." (Gio Ponti, "Senza aggettivi," *Domus*, 268, 1952).

Gio Ponti

1957

Mod. 699

"The 646 chair, the Leggera, saw the light of day around 1951. After its enormous success, when its manufacturing started to become more industrial, Ponti asked my father to slim it down a little, slice some wood off, because he wanted to make the seat and backrest like the Chiavari chairs. Father passed the request on to Fausto Redaelli, the head of the woodworking department, who was doubtful and reluctant to accept Cesare's order to cut away the amount of wood that was deemed excessive. But faced with Father's 'se te se bun no, lasa stà ch'el fo mi' (from the Brianza dialect meaning: 'if you can't do it then don't and I will'), Fausto prepared a perfect and very slim prototype. My father immediately sat down to try it, only to crash to the ground amidst the pieces. He and Ponti, however, did not give up and decided to repeat the experiment with more flexible wood, paying particular attention to the joints. From the choice of ash wood and the invention of a special dry-mounted and grooved joint ('a secco e zigrinato') the 699 Superleggera was born, to the great joy of its creator and its manufacturer." (Giulio Castelli, Paola Antonelli, and Francesca Picchi, *La Fabbrica del design. Conversazioni con i protagonisti del design italiano*, Milan, 2007).

Gio Ponti's research into strength and lightness culminated in the Superleggera chair. He wanted the lightest and strongest chair possible and pushed the craftworkers in the Cassina carpentry workshop to the limits of their abilities.

Faced with a considerable technical challenge, they made several prototypes that proved inconclusive. They completely redesigned the structure of the chair and adopted a triangular section of 18 mm for the legs. Its method of assembly was also redefined to improve its strength. In the end the chair, crafted in ash, weighed just 1.7 kg. It came in two versions (with an Indian cane seat or padded cushion) and was available in an extensive range of colors, as can be seen in the catalogue produced by the graphic designers Giulio Confalonieri and Ilio Negri in 1958. Gio Ponti played with its color combinations using different finishes for the ash wood frame (natural, bleached, stained black, and lacquered red and green) and the seating (in rayon, cane, cellophane rush, or with upholstery in fabric or colored skai) to offer customers a wider choice. He also produced a very elegant black and white version immortalized by Giorgio Casali and later Karl Lagerfeld. It is now available in natural ash or stained white, black, or red ash with a cane or padded seat.

8 Production phase of the back leg of the Superleggera chair, late 1950s

9 Detail of the joint between the seat frame and the front leg of the Superleggera chair, 1957

Continuous Research

1955

Mod. 835

1957

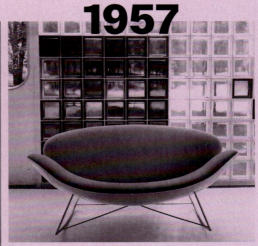

Due Foglie Dondolo

This set of model 835 and model 688 chairs were made by Cassina in a two-tone variant in white and blue specially for Villa Planchart in Caracas.

The Due Foglie sofa has a curved seat and elliptical padded backrest. It all rests on a tubular metal frame. Production rights now belong to third parties.

1954

Round
Mod. 852

Mod. 688

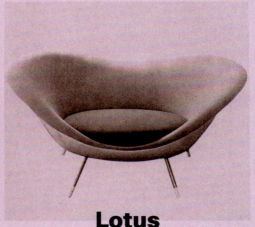

Lotus

The model's name reflects its rounded shape. It was also called an eight-piece armchair because it had only eight components. A seat and backrest, four tubular legs, and two curved pieces of wood ensured the rigidity of its assembly. This ingenious system was the subject of a patent application filed by Figli di Amedeo Cassina. The armchair was used to furnish the Villa Arreaza in Caracas, the Italian Cultural Institute in Stockholm, the Hotel Parco dei Principi in Sorrento, and the Alitalia agency in New York. Production rights now belong to third parties. Cassina kept them until 1959.

This armchair with a wraparound back was originally made for Villa Planchart in Caracas. The shape of its shell suggests a lotus flower as it opens. It rests on four tubular metal legs. It is interesting to note that Ponti used the same type of feet as the Mariposa. Production rights now belong to third parties.

Gio Ponti

1964

Principi
Mod. 113 — 2023

In 2023, to celebrate the introduction of Gio Ponti in the iMaestri Collection, Cassina reproduces the chair Mod. 113 under the name Principi. Originally made by Ponti in 1964 for the Hotel Parco dei Principi in Rome, Cassina now offers it with an upholstered fabric or leather seat.

This reissue stands out for its colors that pay homage to Ponti's philosophy regarding color.

Mod. 899

> « Everything in the world must be colorful. »
>
> Gio Ponti

After the Hotel Parco dei Principi in Sorrento (1960), the Studio Ponti worked on the interior design of the Hotel Parco dei Principi, located close to the gardens of Villa Borghese, in Rome.

Ponti furnished the hotel lobby in white and green tones. For the bar, he chose the 899 armchairs and sofa in cream skai and green velvet. He furnished the dining areas with chairs and armchairs designed by Carlo De Carli, also produced by Cassina. Production rights now belong to third parties.

Continuous Research

Vico

Magistretti

Continuous Research

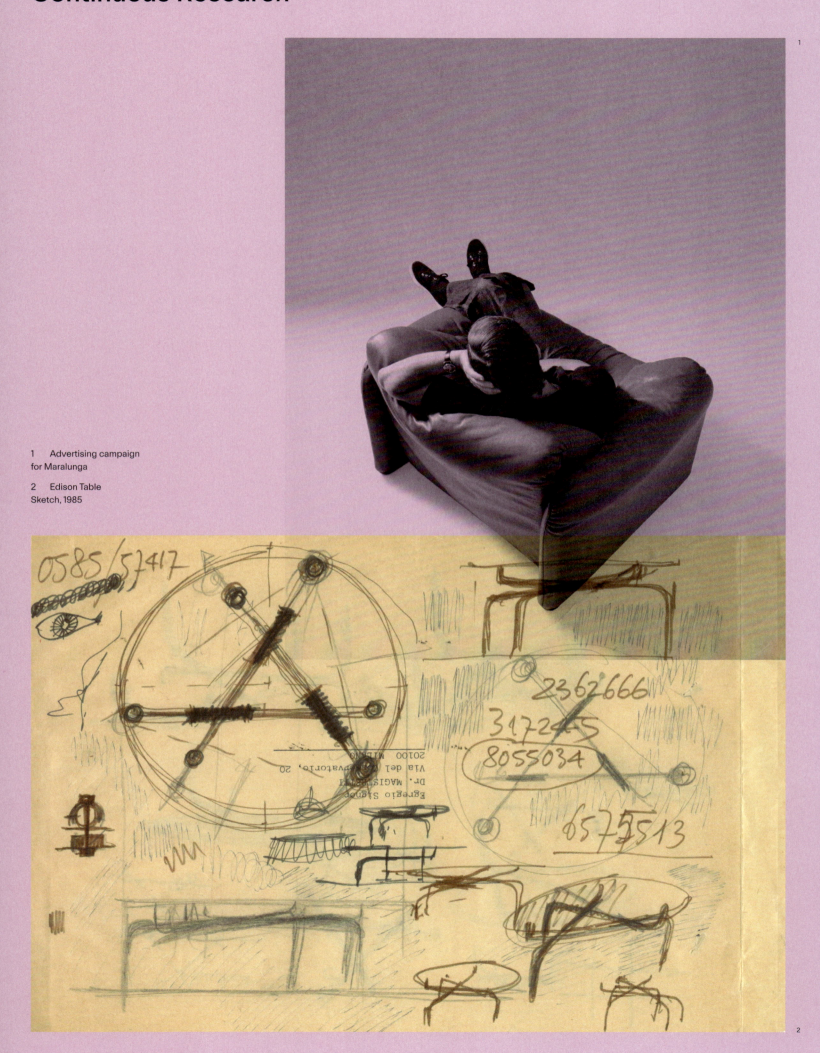

1 Advertising campaign for Maralunga

2 Edison Table
Sketch, 1985

Vico Magistretti

Ludovico "Vico" Magistretti was an Italian architect and designer born in Milan in 1920.

During the war, he studied at the Campo Universitario Italiano in Lausanne, Switzerland, and attended courses held by the architect Ernesto Nathan Rogers, a member of the BBPR practice. Returning to Milan, he graduated from the Politecnico di Milano in 1945 and worked in the firm previously inherited from his father architect Pier Giulio Magistretti. He designed many buildings in Milan, including the church of Santa Maria Nascente, the House of the Returned Soldiers, and a tower building near Parco Sempione.

In 1956, he joined the ADI (Associazione per il Disegno Industriale) and embarked on a very active career as an industrial designer working with the largest Italian furniture companies.

Cesare Cassina noticed Magistretti's work in 1960 at the 12th Triennale di Milano, where he presented a chair made of wood and straw for the furnishings of the restaurant of the Golf Club of Carimate. The Carimate chair produced by Cassina in 1963 was an immediate commercial success. The friendship between the architect Vico Magistretti and the entrepreneur Cesare Cassina led to a fruitful collaboration. Initially, many models of furnishings were made and referenced by their number in the commercial catalogue. Later they were given names, some of which became timeless classics immediately associated with the design. The best-known examples include the Selene chair (1969), the Gaudi chair (1970), the Maralunga sofa (1973), the Nuvola Rossa bookcase (1977), the Sindbad sofa (1981), and the Edison table (1985). This important output received three accolades at the Compasso d'Oro (1963, 1967, and 1979 for the Maralunga sofa).

His career as an architect continued to flourish. He built the Faculty of Biology at the University of Milan (1978–81), the Tanimoto House in Tokyo, Japan (1986), and the Cassa di Risparmio in Parma.

In 1995, he won his fourth and final Compasso d'Oro for lifetime achievement. A member of the Royal College of Arts (London) and the Accademia di San Luca (Rome), he saw his work added to the collections of major museums around the world, such as the Centre Pompidou in Paris, the MoMA in New York, and the ADI Design Museum in Milan.

"I remember Cesare Cassina passing through that window the models I had given him a week before." This saved time, useful for producing new ideas. Italian design was waiting to be invented: "There was an urgency, a kind of hectic atmosphere in which these people (…) took risks, loved to take risks, and we both took risks, because in the end—and this is the most wonderful thing about the work—if these objects didn't work, they wouldn't sell."

Continuous Research

1920	Born in Milan
1946	Exhibition RIMA, Palazzo dell'Arte
1947 - 1955	Church of Santa Maria Nascente, QT8, Milan
1953 - 1956	Torre al Parco, Milan (with Franco Longoni)
1958 - 1961	Golf Club Carimate (with Guido Veneziani)
1963	**Mod. 892 Carimate** **Mod. 896** **Mod. 897** - **Compasso d'Oro for the Mania lamp**
1965	**Mod. 765** **Mod. 772** **Mod. 781** **Mod. 921** **Mod. 922** **Mod. T8**
1945	Graduates from the Politecnico di Milano
1946 - 1948	Homes for returned soldiers, QT8, Milan
1948	Gran Premio at the 8th Triennale di Milano
1956 - 1959	Casa Arosio, Arenzano
1961	San Felice housing development, Milan
1964 - 1965	**Casa Cassina, Carimate** - **Mod. 905** **Mod. 912** **Mod. 913**
1967	**Mod. 122** **Mod. 781** **Mod. 928** **Mod. 937** - **Compasso d'Oro for the Eclisse lamp**

3   Vico Magistretti seated on his Sindbad sofa

4   Vico Magistretti working with Cassina's cabinetmaker, 1963

Vico Magistretti

1973 — Mod. 675 Maralunga

1975 — Mod. 707 Fiandra

1977 — Mod. 114 Nuvola Rossa

1979 — Cassina showroom Via Durini, Milan

1981 — Mod. 666 Paddock - Compasso d'Oro for Atollo and Maralunga / Mod. 118 Sindbad

1983 — Mod. 123 Veranda

1985 — Mod. 790 Edison / Mod. 963 Cardigan / Mod. 929 Villabianca

1989 — Mod. 678 Portovenere

1992 — Mod. 706 Donegal

1993 — Mod. 710 Calibur / Mod. 798 Genoa

1994 — Compasso d'Oro Lifetime Achievement Award

1995 — Mod. 709 Palmaria

2006 — Dies in Milan

Continuous Research

Carimate

The Mod. 892 chair was originally made for the restaurant of the Carimate Golf Club near Como. Originally a piece of industrial design by Vico Magistretti, it drew on the design of traditional rustic chairs. It was made of beech, natural or dyed with aniline. The seat was available in two versions: in woven straw or padded and upholstered with leather or faux leather.

"I remember also making a chair for an architectural work. It was my first industrial product. It was that red chair we made in 1959–60, which was discovered at the Triennale by Cesare Cassina. It's called Carimate. It was one of the chairs that sold widely. Various restaurants used it. It recalled the image of some children's games, which was innovative. All this was devised for the 1960 Triennale, when a series of other objects were exhibited that still strike me as extraordinary, even today." The model was produced by Cassina until 1985. Production rights now belong to third parties.

5   Carimate
Sketch, circa 1960

6   Carimate red version
aniline-dyed beech wood
frame

5

Vico Magistretti

1963
Mod. 892

Continuous Research

Mod. 905

Vico Magistretti

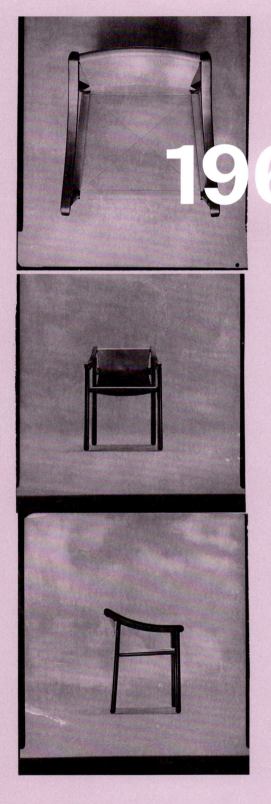

1964

The originality of the Mod. 905 chair lies in its solid beech frame supporting a saddle leather seat and back. The bentwood armrests slot into the top of the cylindrical legs. Note the attention to detail paid by Vico Magistretti with the elegant leather strap supporting the backrest. The chair was integrated into the interior design of Cassina House (1964–65).

1967

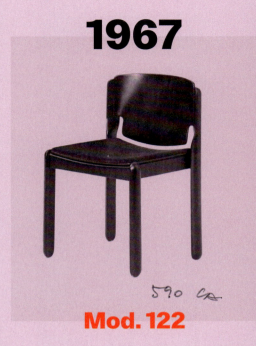

Mod. 122

The frame of the chair is in natural walnut or beech aniline-stained brown or ebony. The seat is made of curved and padded plywood. Its ingenious design makes the chair stackable. The model was produced by Cassina until 1982.

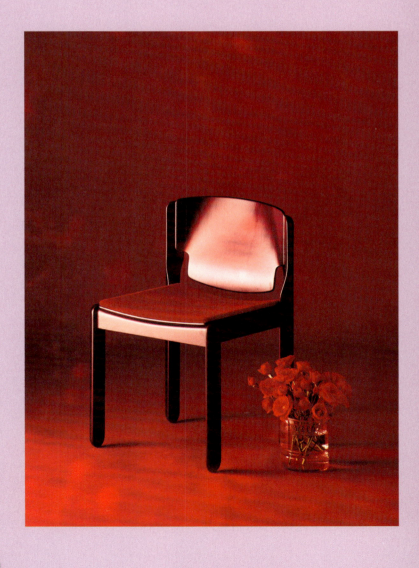

Continuous Research

Maralunga

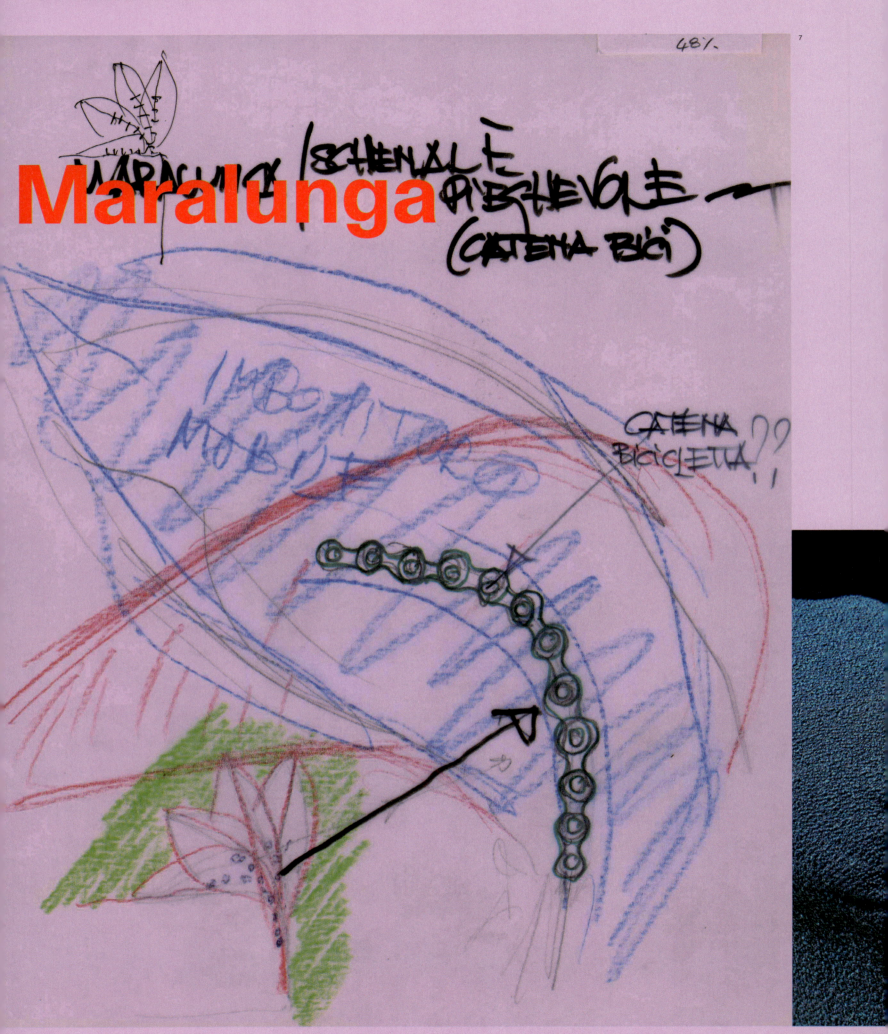

Vico Magistretti

With Maralunga, Vico Magistretti presented a dual-purpose sofa with a high or low backrest. The height-adjustable headrest is made possible by an ingenious system, patented by Cassina, which uses a simple bicycle chain. The frame is made of steel coated with polyurethane foam and the cushions are filled with polyester padding and Fiberfill dacron. Cassina upholstered it in either fabric or leather. Magistretti received the prestigious Compasso d'Oro for this model, which has been in continuous production for forty years.

"I was designing something for Cesare Cassina. It developed out of an armrest with a cushion attached. Looking at it and swinging it, I thought of making a cushioned adjustable headrest for a sofa and I exchanged a glance with Cesare Cassina. The result was the Maralunga sofa, one of the best-selling Italian designs." To celebrate Maralunga's fortieth anniversary, Cassina has developed the Maralunga 40-S, now with removable covers. It is distinguished from the others by visible stitching along its outlines. The Maralunga series comprises armchair, pouf, and the sofa in two- or three-seater versions. Finally, the Maralunga Maxi is a version with increased depth for even greater comfort.

1973

Mod. 675

7   Maralunga Sketch, 1973

>> **Looking at it and swinging it, I thought of making a cushioned adjustable headrest for a sofa and I exchanged a glance with Cesare Cassina. The result was the Maralunga sofa, one of the best-selling Italian designs.** >>

Vico Magistretti

Continuous Research

1975

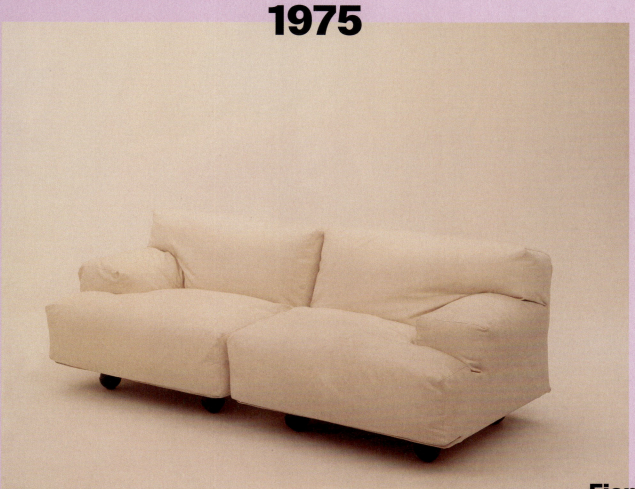

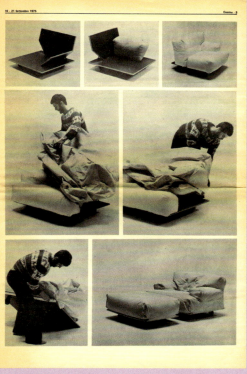

Fiandra
Mod. 707

This sofa with a beech plywood frame covered with polyurethane foam and polyester padding embodies Vico Magistretti's elegance and timeless style. It is also a strong, comfortable, and, above all, modular sofa. In fact, the basic element is available in different sizes, with or without armrests, which allows Cassina to offer a sofa adaptable to all configurations. The model was produced by Cassina until 2001.

8   Cassina
Trade document for Salone del Mobile, 1975

Vico Magistretti

1977

Nuvola Rossa
Mod. 114

(…) it is not just a game, but also an approach (…). And that's how Nuvola Rossa was born and where it got its name from: these diagonal wood pieces, the smoky Native American camps, the wigwams, Emilio Salgari, and John Wayne, fighting everyone. And in the end, the stories fit (above all that of the daughter of Nuvola Rossa by Salgari), the magazines, the objects. And it folds away, like a stepladder at home, and can be carried away in a box. That's it.

Vico Magistretti

With Nuvola Rossa, Vico Magistretti offered a folding bookcase, easy-to-transport, that could be placed against a wall or in the middle of a room to divide it. The frame consists of wooden uprights arranged diagonally and supporting the shelves. Originally produced in natural beech, and white or black chestnut, it has been in the Cassina catalogue continuously since 1977.

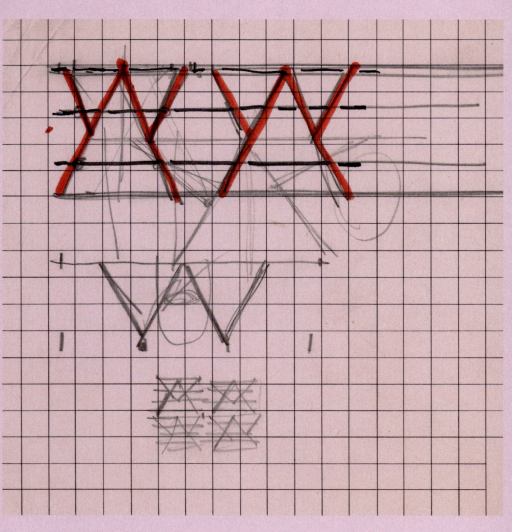

9   Nuvola Rossa
Sketch, circa 1977

Continuous Research

Paddock
Mod. 666

With Paddock, Vico Magistretti offered an original sofa inspired by industrial production. Its exposed tubular metal frame supports the seat and back of three independent places. Available in fabric or leather upholstery, it is suited to the living room of a private dwelling as well as a hotel lobby or airport lounge. "It is a new way of reducing the elements of a sofa to essentials." (Vico Magistretti).

1979

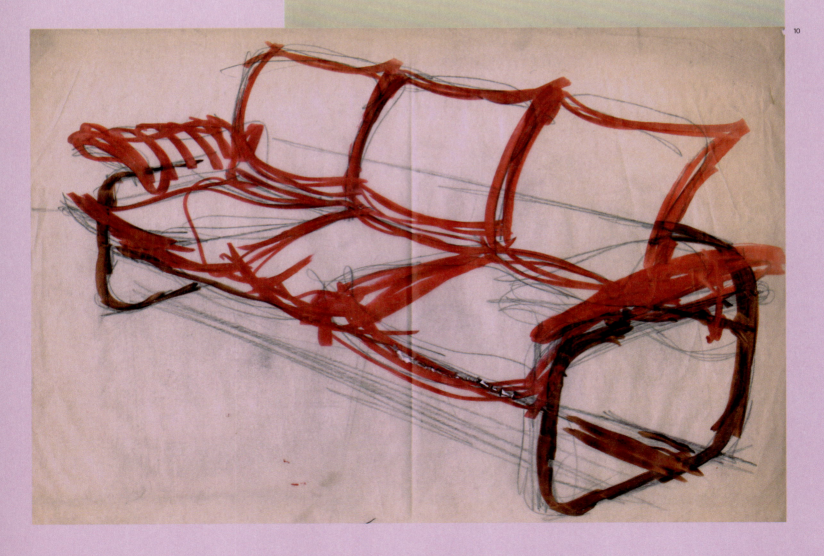

10   Paddock
Sketch, 1977

Vico Magistretti

1981

Sindbad
Mod. 118

With Sindbad, Vico Magistretti designed a sofa "without upholstery" with a seat cover that seems to have been simply thrown over its frame. "I thought of the blanket on an English horse (…)," he said, describing the initial idea of a blanket covering a sofa. Conceived as an interchangeable part of the sofa, the blanket is simply fixed to the upholstered structure with two clasps that can be opened on the inner sides of the seat. It comes in linen for summer and wool for winter but an elegant thick leather version trimmed with colorful fabrics was also available. The model was produced by Cassina until 1998.

11   Sindbad Sketch, 1981

» *Nothing is as beautiful as the gesture of someone who throws a large piece of fabric or leather over a sofa or armchair to see how it looks.* »

Vico Magistretti

Continuous Research

1983

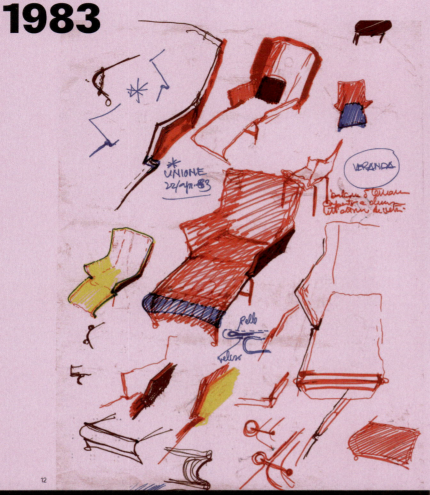

1985

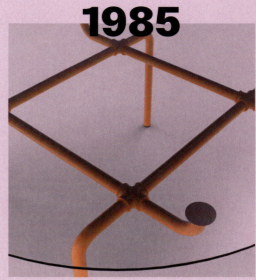

Edison
Mod. 790

Inspired by the poetry of the readymade, the Edison table was designed for Magistretti's dining room. The structure is made of metal pipes connected to one another by means of cross joints in the colors glossy black, gray, blue, duck-beak orange, which varies according to the shape of the top, whether it be rectangular, square, or round. With a wooden or crystal top when first issued, Edison was reissued in 2021 with a glass-only top to leave the tubular frame visible, available in matte black or duck-beak orange.

"One of the most elegant arrangements for connecting four steel tubes is used in gas lighting systems, with a simple cast-iron cross joint. I used it to connect the elements of the frame of a series of tables (with birch or crystal tops) that I called Edison, named after the old gas company in Milan."

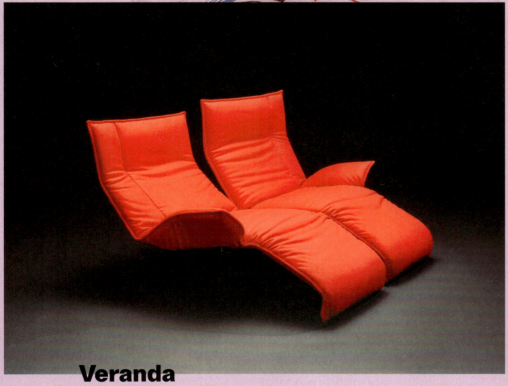

Veranda
Mod. 123

12   Veranda
Sketch, 1983

The model was produced by Cassina until 2008.

Vico Magistretti

1985

Villabianca
Mod. 929

This chair is characterized by the broken line of its back leg which, at the same time, serves as an armrest. Available in colored stained wood, the frame supports the back and seat in resin. It's covered with a cushion in polyester padding upholstered with fabric or leather. Again, Vico Magistretti succeeded in offering a stackable seat suitable for all uses. The model was produced by Cassina until 1997.

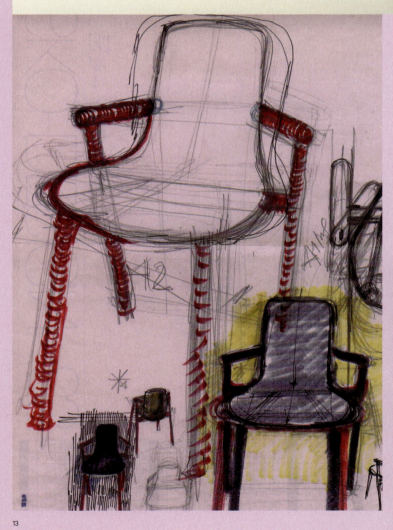

13 Villabianca
Sketch, 1985

1995

Palmaria
Mod. 709

The model was produced by Cassina until 2001.

Continuous Research

Ico

Parisi

1   Console with ramage, 1949

2   812 Sofa
Cassina catalogue, 1958

Ico Parisi

Ico Parisi was an Italian architect, designer, painter, sculptor, and ceramist; together with Carlo Mollino and Gio Ponti, he was a figure emblematic of Italian 1950s style. Born in Palermo in 1916, his family moved to Como, where he became a building inspector in 1936. He was apprenticed to Giuseppe Terragni's architectural office and moved in artistic circles in Como, where he met the painter Mario Radice and the Rationalist architects Cesare Cattaneo, Pietro Lingeri, and Alberto Sartoris. With a passion for cinema and photography, in 1936, at age twenty, he took photographs for the magazine *Quadrante* (no. 35, 1937) of a masterpiece of modernist architecture by Giuseppe Terragni: the Casa del Fascio in Como.

"Look closely at it. Do you see it as a cold building? It is pure emotion and poetry."

He founded Studio Alta Quota in 1937 with his architect friends Silvio Longhi, Fulvio Cappelletti, and Giovanni Galfetti, but World War II interrupted his artistic activities and he was sent to the Russian front but was discharged from the army in 1943. He resumed his work as a designer and was mainly engaged in interior design, exhibition design, and the production of furniture.

In 1947 he married Luisa Aiani, and the following year they opened Studio La Ruota, a space devoted to creativity and cultural exhibitions. He met Lucio Fontana, Bruno Munari, Osvaldo Licini, and Fausto Melotti, working with them on some interior design projects.

His architectural work became a comprehensive vision of the concepts of the integration of the arts and interdisciplinarity in creation, to which he was deeply attached.

In 1950, he built Carcano House and invited Mario Radice to paint a fresco in it. In 1952, he commissioned a sculpture by Francesco Somaini and a mosaic by Mario Radice for Bini House. For the 10th Triennale di Milano in 1954, with Silvio Longhi he designed the Living Room Pavilion and invited the sculptor Francesco Somaini and the painters Mauro Reggiani and Bruno Munari to produce works for it ("Padiglione per soggiorno alla Triennale," *Domus*, no. 301, December, 1954, pp. 7–9). Finally, in 1957, together with Francesco Somaini, Gian Paolo Allevi, and Manlio Rho, he presented the Casa delle Vacanze project at the exhibition *Colori e forme della casa d'oggi*.

At the same time, his work as a designer increased immensely. Promoter of a free style, his creations were initially produced by craftsmen from the Como region, engaged in making quality furniture mostly as one-off pieces. Ico Parisi then experimented with a more industrial production, with companies like Cassina, MIM, Bonacina, and Singer & Sons, turning out objects that have now become icons of Italian design.

Gio Ponti said that Ico Parisi's creations were enthusiastically turbulent, full of life, and highly imaginative. In fact, the late 1960s marked a radical turning point in his conceptual research. With his Contenitori Umani (Human Containers) produced in collaboration with the sculptor Francesco Somaini and presented for the first time at the Milan Salone del Mobile in 1968, he began a new strand of utopian and existential research into different ways of living. The culmination of this work came between 1974 and 1976 with the Operazione Arcevia, a community architectural project to repopulate the Italian countryside, which was suffering from rural exodus. This work was presented as part of the 76th Venice Biennale and then exhibited at the National Gallery of Modern Art in Rome (1979).

Continuous Research

3 Ico Parisi next to his console

4 865 Sofa

1916	Born in Palermo, Sicily	**1936**	Building inspector
	1937 Founds Studio Alta Quota with Silvio Longhi, Fulvio Cappelletti, and Giovanni Galfetti		
	1947 Marries Luisa Aiani		**Mod. 816 PA' 1947**
1948 Founds Studio La Ruota		**1949**	Carcano House, Maslianico, with works by Mario Radice and Fausto Melotti
1950	Casa Notari, Fino Mornasco, with a work by Mario Radice	**1952**	Casa Bini, Como, with artworks by Francesco Somaini and Mario Radice
1953	**Mod. 813**	**1954**	Gold Medal at the 10th Triennale di Milano, with Silvio Longhi and Luigi Antonietti and works by Francesco Somaini and artists Mauro Reggiani and Bruno Munari
Mod. 812	**1955**	**Mod. 691**	**Mod. 815 Olimpino**

Ico Parisi

1957 — Casa per le Vacanze at the exhibition *Colori e forme della casa d'oggi* with Francesco Somaini and Gian Paolo Allevi

Mod. 856 / Mod. 839

1958 — Casa Parisi, Como, with works by Francesco Somaini, Lucio Fontana, and Bruno Munari

Mod. 865

1960 — Mod. 875 / Mod. 860

1964 — Ferrara Chamber of Commerce

1966 — Casa Orlandi, Erba

1967 — Casa Fontana, Lenno with Grazia Varisco, Mario Ceroli, Gabriele de Vecchi, and Enzo Degni

1968 — Contenitori Umani project with Somaini

1972 — Casa Esistenziale project

1973 — Publishes *Ipotesi per una casa esistenziale*

1974 — Operazione Arcevia project with Italo Bartoletti, Enrico Crispolti, Antonio Miotto, and Pierre Restany

1996 — Dies in Como

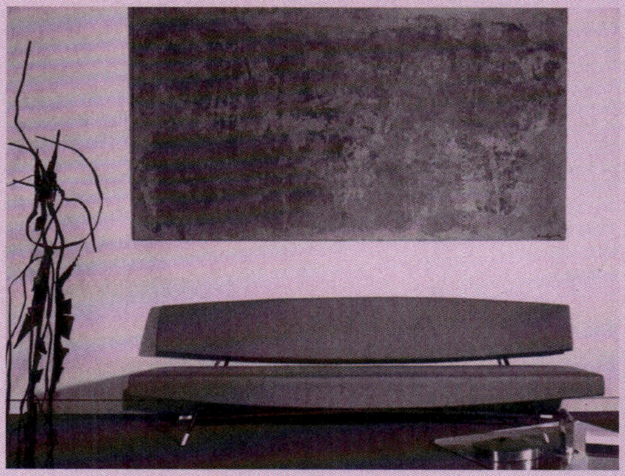

Continuous Research

PA'1947

5   Sketch of the console, 1947
6   Perspective drawing of the console, 1947

In 2020, Cassina decided to reissue this console table designed in 1947 by Ico Parisi as a private commission. The concept was created as a few lines drawn on a sheet of paper: a straight, horizontal line and two oblique lines defining a tensile structure of perfect proportions.

In the vein of the consoles in walnut wood made by artisans in Brianza, such as Fratelli Rizzi for Singer & Sons of New York, or Mobilificio Bega, it embodies an organic design with elegant and refined lines that suggest a foal with tapering legs ready to run. The rectangular top has four square notches into which the upper sockets for the legs are screwed, like real leg joints, forming a Y shape, characteristic of Ico Parisi's work. The legs taper along their whole length and terminate in gilded brass tips.

Ico Parisi

1947

Mod. 816 — 2020

Continuous Research

1954
Mod. 813

Prototyped by Ariberto Colombo in 1951, the armchair 813, called A Uovo, was put into production by Cassina two years later, in 1953. It comprises a molded plywood wraparound structure supported by a base in black painted metal or gilded brass. Ico Parisi, who wanted an ergonomic and comfortable chair, decided with the specialists at Cassina to opt for a foam rubber seat upholstered with a colorful elastic Flexa fabric.

The 813 armchair was presented at the 10th Triennale di Milano, in the Padiglione per soggiorno, a striking structure built by Ico Parisi, Silvio Longhi, and Luigi Antonietti that reflects the architects' research into the properties of reinforced concrete. The model was produced by Cassina until 1958.

7

Ico Parisi

1955

Mod. 691

This refined chair has an ash-wood frame to which are attached the seat and back in molded plywood, upholstered in fabric or skai; it was the more popular piece of Parisi, used for private as well as public interiors including the Lorena Hotel in Grosseto (1960). The chair was awarded a special mention at the Compasso d'Oro in 1955.

7 813 armchair
Snapshot for the 1958 catalogue

8 Padiglione per soggiorno
10th Triennale di Milano
Exhibition view, 1954

Continuous Research

Olimpino

9 Dining room with Olimpino table and 691 chairs, 1955

Ico Parisi

1955

Mod. 815 — 2020

In 1955, Ico Parisi designed this table as part of the furnishings of a house on Monte Olimpino by Lake Como. Initially produced to order by Brugnoli Mobili in Cantù, it features a painted metal structure supporting an impressive glass top. Slender and airy with its Y-shaped metal legs, joined to each other by a bar running down its center, the table is also extremely refined in its finishes. The tips of its arrow-shaped feet are made of solid ash and fastened to the metal frame with elegant brass screws. This model has been produced by Cassina since 2020.

Continuous Research

1957

Mod. 856

Ico Parisi ingeniously managed to lighten this lounge chair, while securing the optimal rigidity of the whole, by using teak crosspieces inserted into the metal structure. This ensures it is lighter than if the frame had been made of solid metal, while remaining sturdy and durable. It was available at the time with skai, leather, or velvet upholstery. The model was produced by Cassina until 1966.

1958

Mod. 839

Mod. 865

The originality of the 839 armchair lies in its airy lines made possible by the use of a molded plywood shell for the seat and a plywood ring for armrests, supported by a lightweight lacquered metal frame. Available in skai or colored fabrics, the chair won the gold medal at the *Colori e forme della casa d'oggi* exhibition in Como, in 1957. The model was produced by Cassina until 1961.

For Cassina, Ico Parisi designed this lounge chair and sofa, with a supporting frame consisting of lightweight blackened iron tubing with its extremities painted white, making the whole light and timeless. The model was produced by Cassina until 1962.

Ico Parisi

Mod. 875   1960
2020

Cassina's privileged relationship with Ico Parisi resulted in the introduction of the 875 armchair in its commercial catalogue in 1960. It is a comfortable armchair with perfect proportions endowed with a generous, airy appearance thanks to its delicate chrome metal base. The metal frame, originally padded with foam rubber upholstered with fabric, is now made of expanded polyurethane, enabling Cassina to keep as close as possible to the Master's initial design.

Between 1954 and 1964, Cassina added to its catalogue some models by Ico Parisi that became emblematic of Italian design (Mod. 865 armchair and sofa). Their style and construction reveal a designer deeply attached to cabinetry (Mod. 691 chair available in beech, ash, or birch), while also conducting research into new forms (Mod. 813 armchair called A Uovo) and materials, notably molded plywood (Mod. 839 armchair). Ico Parisi's production for Cassina was characterized by light and airy lines, in some cases organic, endowing his furnishings with a quality that is both modern and poetic. He embodied this in his many interior designs together with models by Gio Ponti and Gianfranco Frattini, all produced by Cassina. In early 1959, the Figli di Amedeo Cassina firm opened its showroom at Meda with an exhibition of furniture by Gio Ponti, Gianfranco Frattini, and Ico Parisi. Parisi also designed the layout and exhibition installation. For the occasion, Cassina produced a catalogue in collaboration with the graphic designers Ilio Negri and Giulio Confalonieri.

Continuous Research

Franco

Albini

Continuous Research

1 INA office building
View of the staircase, 1950–54

2 Olivetti showroom
Paris, 1958

Franco Albini

Italian designer, architect, and urban planner born in Robbiate (Como) in 1905. After graduating from the Politecnico di Milano, he worked briefly at Studio Ponti & Lancia, notably on the design of the Borletti Chapel (1929–30). In 1931, he opened his own architectural office with Renato Camus and Giancarlo Palanti and made a name for himself with the Casa Ferrarin development project in Milan. From an early date he was interested in the principles of the Rationalist movement (which advocated displaying only whatever had a real function and banishing any ornament that was not an integral part of the structure). A committed architect, he took an early interest in debates on modern architecture and soon joined the International Congress of Modern Architecture (CIAM) founded by, among others, Gerrit T. Rietveld, Pierre Chareau, and Charlotte Perriand. He worked on many social housing projects in Milan. They included the Francesco Baracca (1932), Fabio Filzi (1936–38), Gabriele d'Annunzio (1938), and Ettore Ponti (1939) housing estates. At the 6th Triennale di Milano, he presented the results of his research into social housing and the concept of "existenzminimum" with La stanza per un uomo. Designed for a modern man, sporting and intellectual, this double-height modular space displayed Franco Albini's poetic rationalism, embodied in a creative vocabulary based on the concepts of lightness and suspension.

We find these features in the furniture he designed in the late 1930s: the Mitragliera floor lamp (1938), the Radio in Cristallo (1938), and the Veliero bookcase (1940) made from glass and metal cables. They all have in common this lightness that is characteristic of his work. These models also reveal his unfailing concern to achieve the utmost simplification of the load-bearing structures to facilitate their production, while preserving the lightness of the lines. By this time aesthetic values and technology were inseparable in his work.

In the 1950s, he worked on the restoration and renovation of various museums in Genoa: Palazzo Bianco (1949–51), Museo del Tesoro (1952–56), Palazzo Rosso (1952–62), and designed most of his furnishings, which became iconic. It was during this period that he made many of his emblematic models, such as the Cicognino side table (1953), the Luisa chair, winner of the Compasso d'Oro in 1955, the Infinito bookcase (1956), the Stadera desk (1957–58), and the Tre Pezzi armchair (1959) with Franca Helg.

He then carried out major projects, such as the design of La Rinascente department store in Rome, and a set of office buildings and housing for INA in Genoa (1957 to 1961). He received a second Compasso d'Oro in 1958 for lifetime achievement.

In Paris, in 1959, he designed the Olivetti showroom, in which the interior design reflected his constant research into the concepts of lightness and suspension. The typewriters were suspended on triangular displays attached to large vertical mahogany uprights and illuminated by delicate Murano glass pendant lamps.

During 1962–64, he began working on the design of the stations of the Milan Metro line M1, for which he was awarded the Compasso d'Oro together with Franca Helg. In 1968, his work was the subject of a solo exhibition at the 24th Venice Architecture Biennale.

In 1970, together with Franca Helg and Antonio Piva, he designed the interior of the Museo di Sant'Agostino. In 1976 he was awarded the Gold Medal of the Municipality of Milan.

Continuous Research

1905 — Born at Robbiate, near Como

1929 — Graduates from the Politecnico di Milano

1938 — Mod. 842 Radio in Cristallo Designs the Mitragliera lamp - Villa Pestarini, Milan

1940 — Mod. 837 Canapo Mod. 838 Veliero - Albini apartment

1949 - 1954 — Professor at the Istituto Universitario di Architettura in Venice

1950 — Mod. 833 Cavalletto - INA office building, Parma

1951 — Begins his partnership with Franca Helg – Studio di Architettura Franco Albini and Franca Helg

1952 - 1962 — Palazzo Rosso

1953 — Mod. 834 Cicognino Mod. 839 TL3

1954 — 10th Triennale di Milano, national competition for the renovation of the Salone d'Onore

Mod. 840 Stadera

1955 — Mod. 832 Luisa - Compasso d'Oro for the Luisa chair

1956 — Mod. 835 Infinito - Villa Zambelli, Forlì

128

Franco Albini

1957 — Exhibition *Colori e forme della casa d'oggi*, Villa Olmo, Como

1958 — Olivetti showroom, Paris
-
Compasso d'Oro, Gran Premio Nazionale

1962 — Orion television set for Brionvega
-
Begins collaboration with Antonio Piva

1964 — Professor at the Politecnico di Milano
-
Compasso d'Oro for the Milan Metro stations

1967
-
1969 — Milan Metro M2 Centrale Station
-
Series of lamps AM/AS
Table lamp 601

1975
-
1974

1957
-
1961 — Grands Magasins La Rinascente, Rome
-
INA Residential and Office Buildings, Genoa

1959 — **Mod. 836 Tre Pezzi with Franca Helg**

1962
-
1964 — Milan Metro M1 line (with Franca Helg, Antonio Piva, and graphism by Bob Noorda)
-
Lobby and shopping arcades of the Hotel Cavalieri Hilton, Rome

1965 — Begins collaboration with Marco Albini

1968 — Personal exhibition at the 24th Venice Biennale of Architecture
-
Stores and offices for Brionvega, Arzano

1969
-
1974 — Snam office building, San Donato Milanese

1977 — Dies in Milan
-
Studio di Architettura Franco Albini, Franca Helg, Antonio Piva, Marco Albini

3 Franco Albini, Walter Gropius & Palma Bucarelli Bauhaus exhibition at the Galleria Nazionale d'Arte Moderna, Rome, 1961

4 The Franco Albini Collection Cassina showroom, Milan, 2008

Continuous Research

Radio in Cristallo

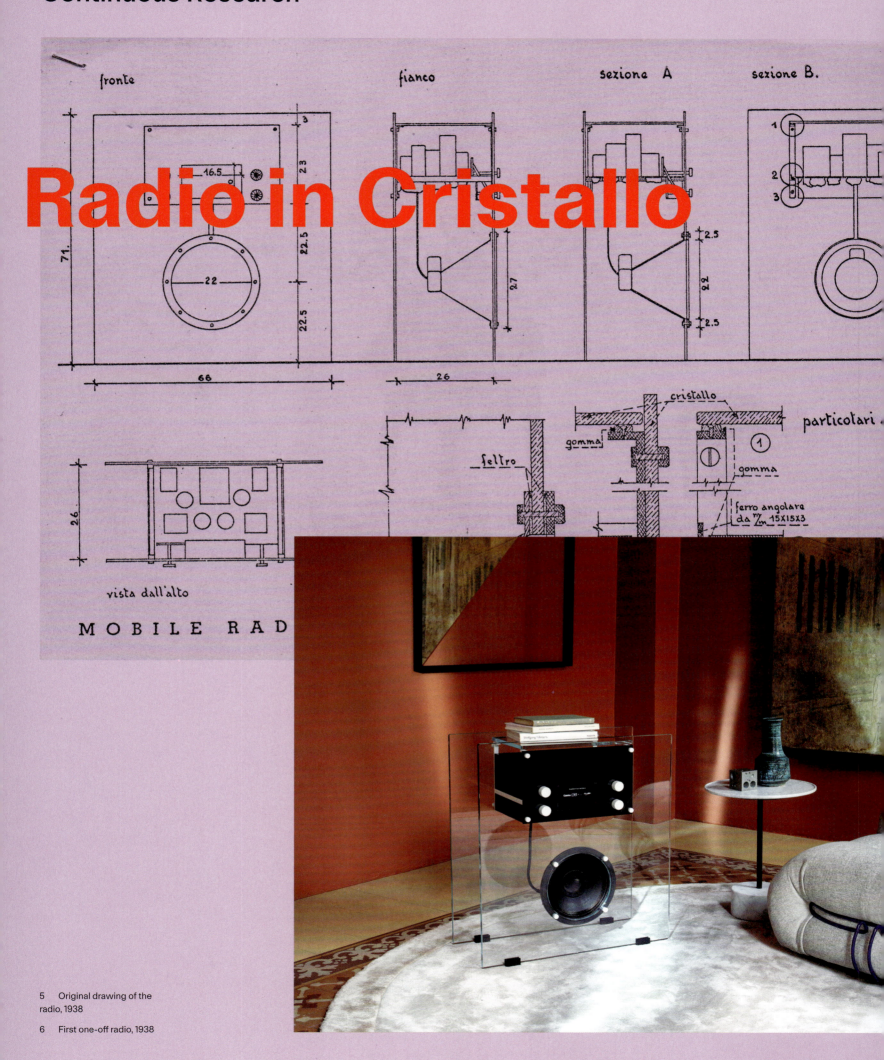

5   Original drawing of the radio, 1938
6   First one-off radio, 1938

Franco Albini

1938

Mod. 842 — 2021

After receiving as a wedding gift a wooden radio, Franco Albini completely dismantled it and designed a new one with the electric components placed between two glass panels that served as the casing of the whole. He decided to make visible what had previously been concealed. He adopted the fundamental principles of Rationalism in architecture ("to express the building's internal arrangements on the exterior" Carlo Lodoli, 1690–1761) and embodied them, for the first time, into a domestic appliance. He rejected the principle of ornament and showed only what was functional to ensure that it was completely legible.

This one-off model preserved by the Fondazione Franco Albini has been industrially produced by Cassina since 2021.

Continuous Research

Veliero

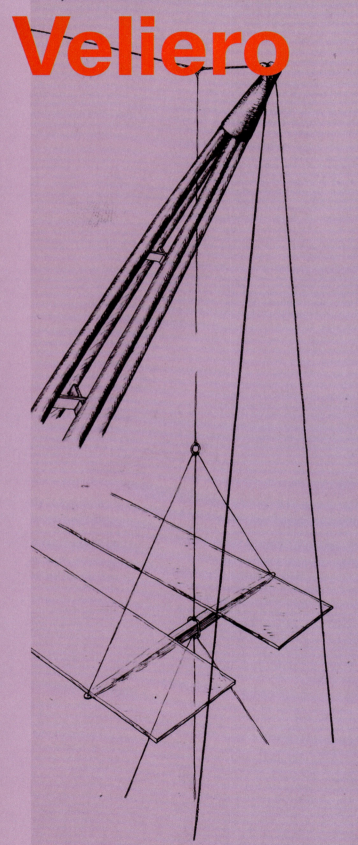
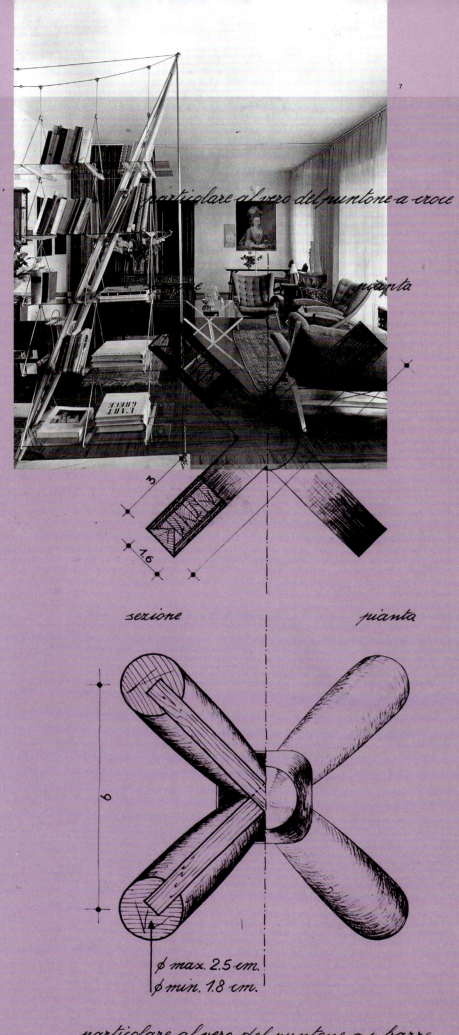

Franco Albini

1940
Mod. 838 — 2011

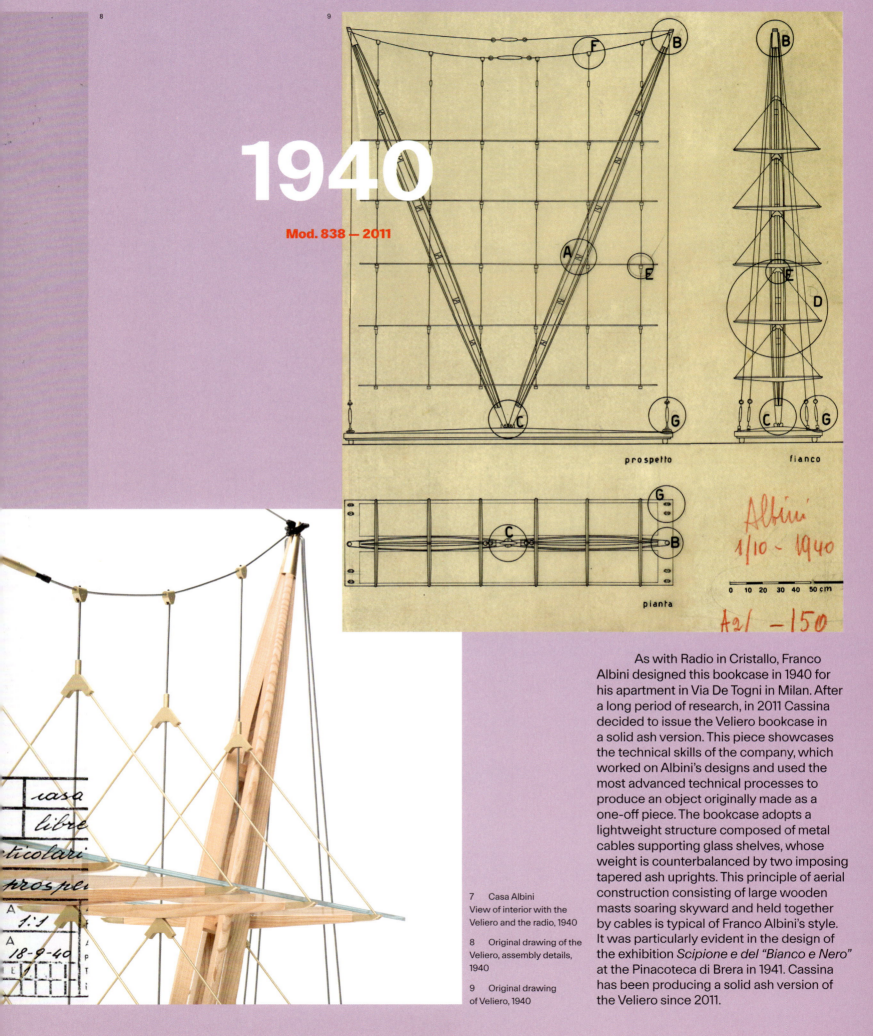

7 Casa Albini
View of interior with the Veliero and the radio, 1940

8 Original drawing of the Veliero, assembly details, 1940

9 Original drawing of Veliero, 1940

As with Radio in Cristallo, Franco Albini designed this bookcase in 1940 for his apartment in Via De Togni in Milan. After a long period of research, in 2011 Cassina decided to issue the Veliero bookcase in a solid ash version. This piece showcases the technical skills of the company, which worked on Albini's designs and used the most advanced technical processes to produce an object originally made as a one-off piece. The bookcase adopts a lightweight structure composed of metal cables supporting glass shelves, whose weight is counterbalanced by two imposing tapered ash uprights. This principle of aerial construction consisting of large wooden masts soaring skyward and held together by cables is typical of Franco Albini's style. It was particularly evident in the design of the exhibition *Scipione e del "Bianco e Nero"* at the Pinacoteca di Brera in 1941. Cassina has been producing a solid ash version of the Veliero since 2011.

Continuous Research

1940

Canapo
Mod. 837 — 2009

This rocking chaise longue was first made in 1938 in a tubular metal version for the Via Cimarosa apartment. Two years later, it was given a solid walnut frame, curved, to which a supporting canvas was attached. The model was exhibited at the 7th Triennale di Milano in 1940 at the presentation *Criteri per la casa d'oggi* and produced by the company AR.AR, which issued it in only a few copies. It was then produced by Poggi in maple walnut or oak in 1959, and by Cassina in 2009.

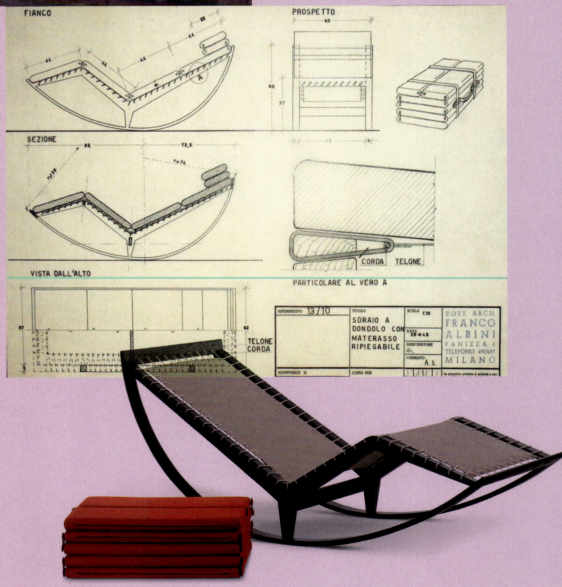

10 Rocking chair and Tre Pezzi armchair in Villa Zambelli, Forlì (with Franca Helg), 1956

11 Original drawing of the rocking chair

Franco Albini

1950

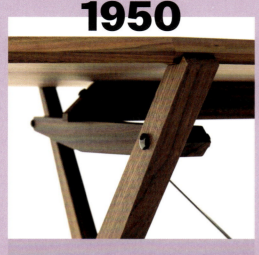

Cavalletto
Mod. 833 — 2008

The Cavalletto desk is a trestle table. Its lightweight frame and top were originally made from solid walnut. The frame is braced by two burnished brass struts placed under the top. Exhibited for the first time in Milan in 1948, during the exhibition *Lo stile dell'arredamento moderno*, it was then produced by Poggi in 1950 in versions in rosewood or ash and finally by Cassina in a version in ash or walnut.

1953

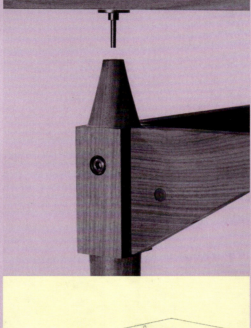

TL3
Mod. 839 — 2013

Designed in 1949, this table was presented for the first time in Milan at the exhibition *Mostra dell'Arredamento Fede Cheti*. It has a slender rectangular frame with a solid wooden top resting lightly on it. The table can be dismantled easily to facilitate packaging and transport. It was produced by Poggi in 1951 in a teak version and then by Cassina, since 2013, in ash or walnut with a glass top.

1954

Stadera
Mod. 840 — 2015

Franco Albini designed this as part of the furniture for Caterina Marcenaro's apartment in Genoa. It has a self-supporting structure in lacquered steel, on which rests an asymmetrical two-level wooden top. A version with a marble top and base was also made to furnish the INA offices in Genoa between 1957 and 1961. This asymmetrical desk was issued in 1957 by the Altamira firm and then by Poggi in 1958 and Cassina since 2015. Its unique foot structure creates the appearance of apparent instability that, through the play of balance generated by the different proportions of the sides, evokes the form of a steelyard, after which it was named.

Continuous Research

1953

Cicognino
Mod. 834 — 2008

This small three-legged side table was initially manufactured by Poggi in mahogany, walnut, or birch. Its distinctive feature is that the third foot extends into a handle, enabling it to be moved easily. Cicognino has been produced by Cassina since 2008 in a version in natural beech, stained black or amaranto, or in canaletto walnut.

Its elegant lines make it a classic of design, now in the collections of MoMA in New York and the Design Museum of the Triennale di Milano.

Franco Albini

1955

Luisa
Mod. 832 — 2008

With this project, Franco Albini explored the intrinsic capabilities of wood to design a chair that is elegant, light, and sturdy. It took several years of research to arrive at the final version produced by Poggi in 1955. The work was not in vain, since it immediately received the prestigious Compasso d'Oro award in the same year. Luisa is a timeless object. Despite its light and simple lines, it is the outcome of extremely technical research and a demonstration of the skills of the craftworkers in Meda. With this model, Franco Albini poetically emphasizes all the elements that make up the structure. Luisa is then produced by Cassina from 2008 in black-stained natural beech or canaletto walnut. Of great historical value, this icon is part of the collection of MoMA in New York and the Design Museum of the Triennale di Milano.

12 Original drawing of the Luisa chair, 1955

Continuous Research

1956

13 Exhibition view of the
*Mostra di Scipione e del
"Bianco e Nero"*
Pinacoteca di Brera, 1941

14 Details of the Milan
Metro handrail
Milan, 1959

Infinito
Mod. 835 — 2008

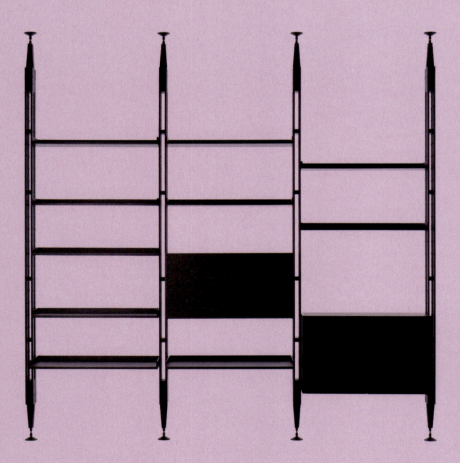

Designed between 1956 and 1957 by Franco Albini, this bookcase has a self-supporting wooden frame, fixed to the floor and ceiling by small blackened cast aluminum legs. It is fully modular and can be installed against a wall or in the center of a room to divide it in two. Franco Albini remained faithful to his vocabulary of forms, and this bookcase, with large vertical tapered uprights seeming to soar skyward, recalls the many temporary exhibition designs that he devised in the 1930s.

It is also interesting to note that Albini was a remarkable industrial designer, because his furnishings embody deep reflection on the union between aesthetics and the constraints of production. He invariably managed to realize a wide range of design objects that facilitate transport and assembly and dismantling. Infinito has been produced by Cassina since 2008 in black-stained natural beech or canaletto walnut.

Franco Albini

1959

Tre Pezzi
Mod. 836 — 2009

Like other prestigious CIAM members (Charlotte Perriand, Mart Stam, etc.), Franco Albini began to explore the properties of tubular steel in the 1930s. He made a few prototypes of his rocking chaise longue as well as a model of a chair with a self-supporting tubular structure, exhibited at the 6th Triennale di Milano in 1936 (La stanza per un uomo). Twenty years later, he designed with Franca Helg this wingback armchair consisting of three pieces fixed to a tubular frame. Comfort seems to be the key word of this project. The seat is deep and padded, as is the back, which develops into the armrests. Finally, a broad headrest in the shape of a half moon offers comfortable support for the head. The design of the lateral tubular structure recalls the handrails of the Milan Metro, which Albini designed with Franca Helg, Antonio Piva, and Bob Noorda.

Continuous Research

Photos by
SCHELTENS & ABBENES

For this photoshoot dedicated to Cassina's constant research, the Dutch photographer couple Maurice Scheltens & Liesbeth Abbenes focused on the structural components of the Maestri pieces of furniture. Using a graphic process composed of colored lines and stripes that create a two- and three-dimensional space, they aim to underline the singularity of these creations.

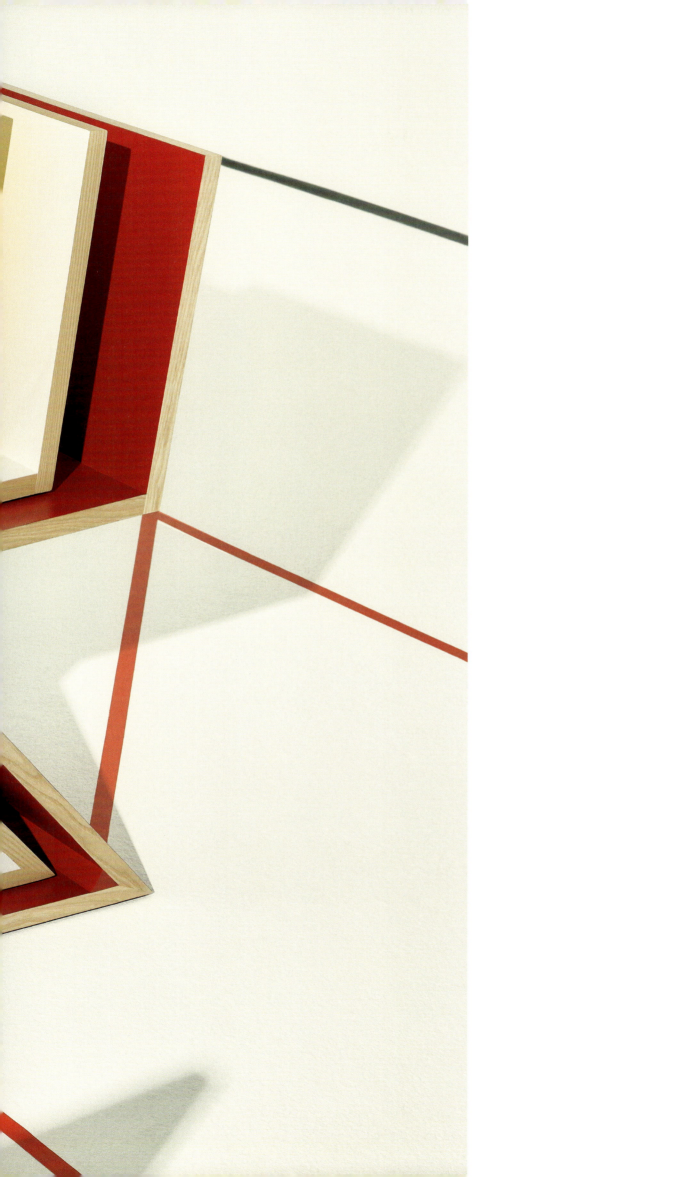

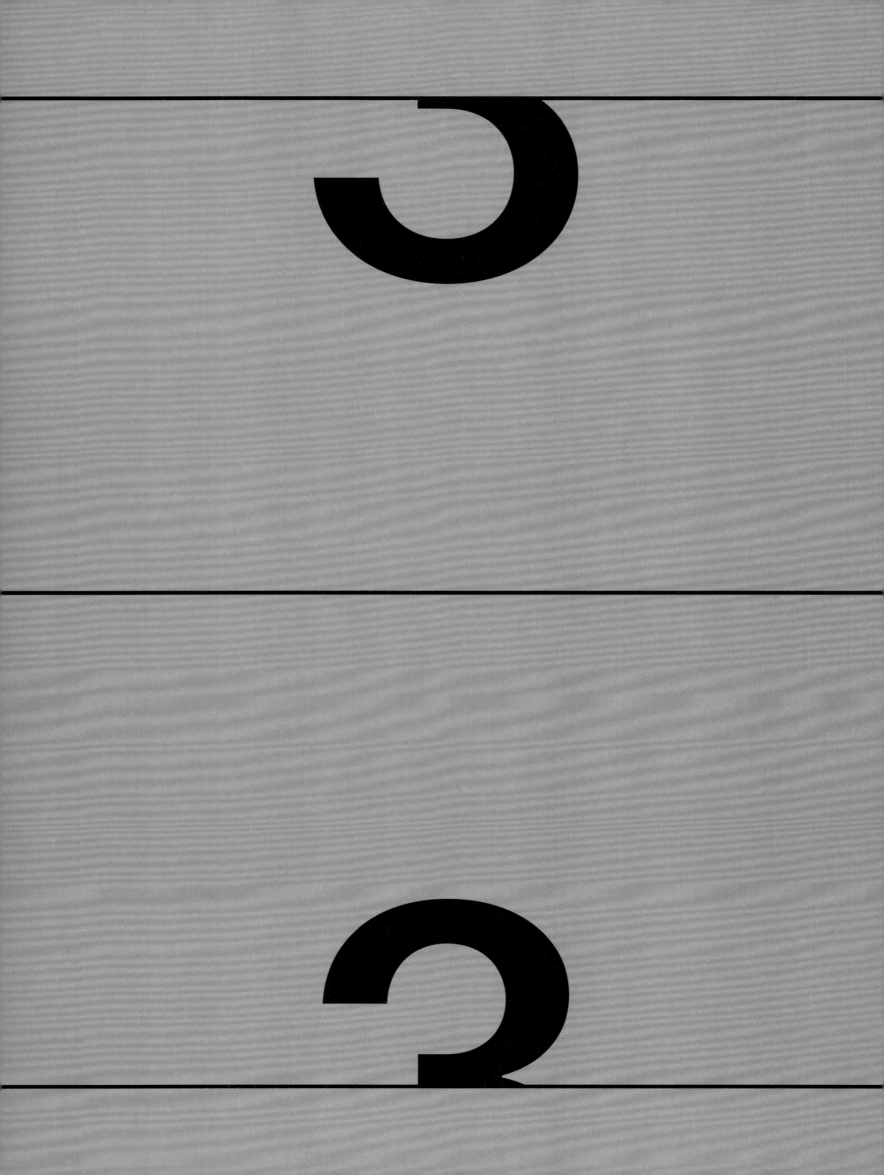

Building

Culture

Cassina,
a Company
That Spreads
Cultural Values

Building Culture

Unsettling Chairs

BEATRIZ COLOMINA
-
MARK ANTONY WIGLEY

Historians, theorists, and curators of architecture and design

    Chairs have the capacity to make us see the world differently. In that sense, they reinvent the world and therefore our species. There is nothing innocent about a chair. If Neolithic buildings already lifted humans off the ground, chairs reposition the eye, the body, and the brain. Yet, chairs are never stable, never fixed objects. They are unsettled and unsettling.

    Take the four chairs (Fauteuil à dossier basculant, Fauteuil Grand Confort grand and petit modèle, Chaise longue à réglage continu) first designed by Le Corbusier, Pierre Jeanneret, and Charlotte Perriand in 1928 that Cassina started to manufacture in 1965, and only then became so successful that they attained the status of cultural icons dispersed across the globe as avatars of modernity. They were the product of a close mutually interactive three-way collaboration when Perriand was in charge of the Équipement intérieur d'une habitation in the studio, continuing her earlier independent interior design work. The chairs were first published in the April 1929 issue of *The Studio*, to accompany the two-page manifesto of Charlotte

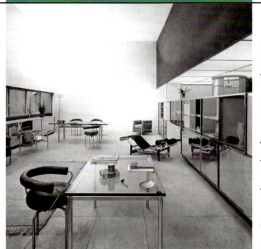

1 Exhibition view of Équipement intérieur d'une habitation, at the Salon d'Automne 1929 in Paris, with furniture by Le Corbusier, Pierre Jeanneret, and Charlotte Perriand

Perriand in favor of metal ("METAL plays the same part in furniture as cement has in Architecture. IT IS A REVOLUTION. AESTHETICS OF METAL"). Thonet sponsored the presentation of the new tubular chairs that November in the Salon d'Automne where a whole set of sitting and storage types by the three designers was seen to constitute a domestic interior. It was effectively a kind of showroom in which visitors could imagine themselves occupying the empty furniture—understood as "équipement" for dwelling in the city, like the mobile camping equipment that domesticates the outdoors. The crisp white rectangular volume of the domestic space is defined only by the equipment, plain rugs on the floor, and a fur blanket on the bed. It is a house without walls. The distinctions between spaces for working, eating, resting, cooking, sleeping, bathing, and toilette are only defined by the equipment. The display was a manifesto for the idea of dwelling constructed solely by what used to be called furniture.

  Each piece suspended the body in a different way. They are more a way of moving the body than letting it rest. Each chair enables a certain kind of movement. The minimum architecture is no longer one chair, but an ensemble of different chairs that are orthopedically and visually different, each so tuned to a different way of collaborating with the body that it is not obvious that they are of the same family.

Building Culture

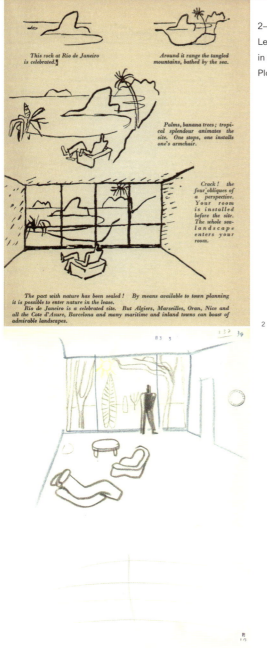

2–3 Drawings by Le Corbusier, published in *La Maison des hommes*, Plon, Paris, 1942

While Perriand and Jeanneret were putting the exhibition together in Paris, Le Corbusier was touring Latin America for several months and his lecture in Buenos Aires of October 19, "L'aventure du mobilier" argued that the "renewal" of the modern house demands the rethinking of furniture. Chairs become equipment—each standardized to offer a different form of "active" sitting. Only the chaise longue is a "machine of resting" and even it is active in being able to "take all positions."[1] The body is suspended as if floating and turning at different angles, not just in the room but in the landscape.

Le Corbusier explains the six-kilometer serpentine strip of housing, suspended under a highway, for Rio de Janeiro that he drew during the trip in terms of placing a single generic armchair in front of the magnificent landscape: "One stops. One installs an armchair. Crack! A frame all around. Crack! The four obliques of a perspective. Your room is installed in front of the site. The whole sea-landscape enters your room."[2] Architecture is made for and by a chair. And not just one. A chaise longue is added to the armchair in a drawing of how the sky and nature have "entered the dwelling" that Le Corbusier would repeatedly publish. It is his idealized image of the most minimal yet complete interior, and therefore the prototype of architecture itself.

Shortly after the 1929 exhibition, Perriand had drafted a contract for Thonet to manufacture the pieces that the company signed and the pieces were already produced as "Thonet Chairs," as if already available, even before the company started production in 1930, attaching a metal seal naming the three designers on each chair and promoting them globally alongside those of Mies van der Rohe, Mart Stam, and Marcel Breuer. Thonet's usual practice was to give licenses to manufacturers in other countries but was already disconcerted to see unauthorized versions displayed in a July 1930 decorative arts exhibition in Stockholm and even more disconcerted to learn that Le Corbusier was trying to set up an agreement with the Berlin firm Deutsche Stahlmöbel to make and sell the chaise longue everywhere in the world except France. Le Corbusier, in turn, was infuriated when the Swiss company Bigla started to produce an unauthorized version in 1931.

The set of chairs were produced widely and exhibited at MoMA in February 1933 in what was meant to be a permanent "Architecture Room" to convey "modern interior architecture."[3] But they were difficult to manufacture, expensive, and didn't sell well. Thonet didn't even bother to advertise them after 1933, when they distributed the rights to a range of different companies.[4] Le Corbusier never received any royalties and started to talk of setting up new licenses in 1949, being frustrated to hear of a few chairs by the manufacturers authorized by Thonet still for sale in department stores in the early 1950s. In 1958, during a visit to Le Corbusier in Paris, the interior designer and gallerist Heidi Weber offered to produce the four chairs in Zurich; in 1959 Le Corbusier granted Weber and the publisher Hans Girsberger the right to make the pieces. Charlotte Perriand had already been instructed to send all the drawings made at the studio at 35 Rue de Sèvres. But the four chairs, first exhibited in Weber's gallery in December 1958, were now identified as Le Corbusier's only and marked with the initials "LC." The joint collaborative signature had given way to a single one—even if Le Corbusier acknowledged that the royalties would be divided equally between the three of them.[5]

When Cassina took over the rights in October 1964 and started production in 1965, Le Corbusier's signature was literally cast into the tubular metal along with a number, as if to pin it down as a singular artwork, even if the chairs themselves continued to evolve in these new versions. Heidi Weber had reached out to Cassina when her small workshop could no longer handle the level of production, offering the opportunity to reach an entirely new market. Cassina was already working with a new generation of designers including Ponti, Albini, Magistretti, and Bellini, but launching the new edition of chairs from 1928 moved the company directly toward a new cultural space and global reach. It also dramatically transformed the status of the chairs, as if finally realizing the original dream of Le Corbusier, Pierre Jeanneret, Charlotte Perriand to develop standard yet relatively luxurious mobile equipment for modern life.

The first presentation of the edition was in the Sala Espressioni in Milan that had been set up by Gio Ponti. The critic and editor Bruno Alfieri displayed the four "classic" chairs in a kind of gleaming white sandwich of space formed by lifting up the central square section of the floor into a podium and lowering a matching section of the ceiling above it.[6] A full-size version of Le Corbusier's drawing of the "modular man" stood behind the chairs, reaching up to touch the ceiling, accompanied by some plants and four colored lithographs by the architect. On all four sides of the podium, Cassina's logo was inserted inside the "C" of "LC" in Le Corbusier's signature font, one signature nested inside the other to convey the symbiotic partnership of designer and manufacturer. Everything was visible to the public through the street window with the huge letters "LC" written across it.

wall opposite a dense multileveled photographic history of modern architecture and art. Three pages in the July issue of *Domus* used the same typography to advertise the concept: "Objects by masters of architecture and design that time has valorized with historical and critical recognition, understood today as anticipation of the most modern concepts of living. The collection that Cassina is selecting and realizing will consist of pieces catalogued and exhibited in the most important museums of the world. Objects of art, therefore, but to be offered to a wider public in order to restitute the function of that which was born by function."[9]

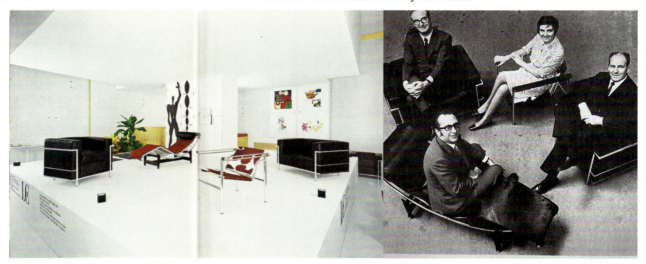

This launch of the edition that would permanently transform the status of the four designs was also highly visible in the press. The display was symptomatically preceded by a half-page advertisement in the September 30, 1965 issue of the Milanese paper *Corriere della Sera*. The promise made to the reader was that the four mass-produced chairs were "designed to give an unmistakable imprint to any truly qualified interior arrangement."[7] But the audience was also the design community. Cassina published a sophisticated thirty-two-page catalogue entitled simply "LC" in huge letters on the cover against a white background. It was edited by Alfieri to accompany the exhibition, acknowledging Le Corbusier's recent death at the end of August that deepened the meaning of remaking the 1920s designs. The texts were by a who's who list of designers and critics, including Sergio Bettini, Gio Ponti, Max Bill, Ernesto N. Rogers, and Vittorio Gregotti. It was a kind of call-to-arms to defend the very idea of modern design and the timeliness of "classic" works by "Masters," "for the world of today and tomorrow."[8]

The four Cassina family members photographed themselves sitting in the four chairs, looking up at the camera in an empty photography studio, as if Cassina itself was at home in the space made by the ensemble of chairs, just as their customers could remake their homes and cultural identities by purchasing one of them. Once again, to own a chair is not simply to seat oneself more comfortably within one's home. It is to be modern by being at home in the twentieth century. The chair is home.

After acquiring the license to make Gerrit Thomas Rietveld works in 1972, Cassina went even deeper into the cult of designers, launching the concept of "iMaestri" with a showroom display of a series of six identical open wooden cabinets labeled "Cassina IMAESTRI" in a colorful typeface, each holding two chairs. They formed a kind of

Images of the two Rietveld chairs from 1918 and 1934 were accompanied by short historical paragraphs on his philosophy and how the chairs were connected to architecture and art. To buy such a chair is to enter the history of design and become a participant. In 1973 the focus was Charles Rennie Mackintosh with parallel exhibitions in the showroom and the Triennale di Milano. Finally, the series was formally established in September 1974 with a show of Le Corbusier, Rietveld, and Mackintosh together—with a three-dimensional "M" looking like a folded piece of furniture as the logo. It was a huge campaign—

4 Presentation of the furniture by Le Corbusier, Pierre Jeanneret, and Charlotte Perriand exhibited at Sala Espressioni, Ideal Standard, Milan, 1965

5 The Cassina family sits on the models by Le Corbusier, Pierre Jeanneret, and Charlotte Perriand. From bottom left: Franco, Cesare, Adele, and Umberto, late 1960s

6 First poster of the Red and Blue chair by Gerrit Thomas Rietveld, Cassina iMaestri Collection, 1972

Building Culture

7 The Chaise longue à réglage continu, exhibited in the Cassina showroom designed by Mario Bellini in 1968

with posters, advertisements, brochures, and traveling exhibitions. The Mackintosh exhibition, for example, immediately traveled to the Museum of Modern Art (MoMA) in New York in 1974 and three other American Museums, with Cassina bringing the original drawings from the archive in Scotland and the chairs from Italy. Foldout sales leaflets in 1975 featured the Cassina iMaestri Collection on one side, as "the origin of contemporary interior design," with the design philosophy of the three "Masters" described in detail. The text insists that the idea of "reproposing" a selection of classic designs is neither "sterile," "snobbish," or "academic." On the contrary, it is about the ongoing validity of certain concepts launched in the past. The concepts are not just represented as historical images but proposed again, relaunched as modernizing agents. The other side of the leaflet featured the "contemporary" Italian designers Mario Bellini, Afra and Tobia Scarpa, Archizoom, and Vico Magistretti, as if the past and present energize each other.

The effect is a sense of design history, reinforced by a series of scholarly iMaestri books on the furniture of Mackintosh in 1973, Le Corbusier in 1976, and Rietveld in 1977. The company saw its own work to put modern chairs back into circulation as a form of scholarship. The idea was to do extensive material, documentary, and oral history investigation into the original formation of the furniture in order to use contemporary technologies and production methods to develop chairs that are different yet faithful to the concept, and therefore neither originals nor copies.[10] Historical preservation understood as an act of transformation. Even a seventy-nine-page sales catalogue devoted to the three Masters in 1980 reads like a lavishly illustrated design history book.[11] Images of the new versions of the chairs in empty studio spaces have the quality of historical images.

But the key technology was always the showroom. Cassina opened a showroom in New York in 1967 and a new one was inaugurated in Milan in December 1968 with a Mario Bellini design that symptomatically foregrounded the chaise longue in an elevated metal cage like a dangerous but stimulating animal. Such showrooms were soon installed around the world in a global network communicating directly to the public. If the modern house is a showroom, the showroom is a house, a place to visualize yourself living a different kind of life.

Cassina eventually treated a set of their contemporary Italian designers (including Ponti, Magistretti, Scarpa, Zanuso, and Albini) as "Masters" tied to the established legacy of Le Corbusier, Rietveld, and Mackintosh that had been expanded by the addition of Asplund in 1981 and Frank Lloyd Wright in 1986. Earlier designs by living architects were identified as classics and remade with the same attitude of historical preservation-transformation. The first Italian to be included was Albini, when a selection of his projects was added to the series in 2008.[12] The main concept of the campaign from the beginning was to give chairs and their designers the paradoxical status of being at once modern and timeless—fusing the stability of centuries with the excitement of the present. Renato De Fusco, in the book on Le Corbusier's chairs commissioned by Cassina, described the "revival" of "unexplored or incomplete developments" by canonic designers as a "cultural movement" to interrupt the endless cycles of consumer products.[13] But it was, of course, the launch of a longer cycle through the idea of the paradoxically new-yet-old, old-yet-new standard furniture that might be more expensive but would not need to be replaced.

Building Culture

8 Cassina advertising, *Sei riflessioni sul prossimo millennio* by Bozell, Testa, Pella, Rossetti, 1991–92

Mastery of design was mastery of time. Already in 1963 and 1964, Cassina was advertising chairs by Magistretti and Mangiarotti in *Domus* with the slogan "Cassina: The modern that lasts" —even posing the chairs in front of Greek temples.[14] The first advertisements for the new editions of 1928 chairs in 1965 likewise insisted that the objects "testify to the full vitality and functionality of objects of use created rationally outside of fashion."[15] A 1974 advertisement added Bauhaus, Antonio Gaudí, and Shakers designs to the series and showed them rising up from a stone quarry as if a kind of primeval formation.[16] Cassina advertisements in 1993 showed the pieces in empty landscapes with the questions: "What do we think in one thousand years?"; "Who would we invite in one thousand years?"; "What would we talk about in one thousand years?" The text below, next to the Cassina name, says "some things change, others remain." The same point was made in reverse with an advertisement from 2008 showing a gorilla looking at us while leaning casually but possessively on the Fauteuil Grand Confort that had been relaunched in 1965, as if channeling the timeless monolith surrounded by proto-human Simians in Stanley Kubrick's *2001: A Space Odyssey*.[17]

This idea of stitching the timely and the timeless was already written into the polemics of Le Corbusier, who famously treated the Parthenon as a perfected machine and, in reverse, treated machines as a form of architecture. Likewise, the associated idea of the master—seemingly at odds with the logic of industrialization, mass production, and the disposal of no longer useful objects in the relentless pursuit of efficiency—was written into the promotion of modern architecture. Take the catalogue of the influential 1932 exhibition of Modern Architecture at MoMA that not by chance toured department stores where consumers could purchase their own piece of modern architecture in the form of furniture. It insisted on the mythology of Le Corbusier, Gropius, Mies van der Rohe, and Oud as "the four masters" of the new style, repeatedly using the word "masterly" to describe the work being exhibited.[18] This cult of the modern master was very active in the years leading up to Cassina's self-transformation. Peter John's *The Masters of Modern Architecture* appeared in 1958, Peter Blake's *The Master Builders: Le Corbusier, Mies van der Rohe, Frank Lloyd Wright* in 1960, and the box sets monographing eleven *Masters of World Architecture* in same year.

Cassina didn't just leverage the canonized signature of famous designers. It redesigned the perception of designers, and became an active part of the ongoing theoretical promotion of modern architecture. The company never simply makes furniture. It changes the conversation about it, precisely reconstructing polemical designs (like the 1929 Salon d'Automne interior, Perriand's and Pierre Jeanneret's 1938 Refuge Tonneau, and Le Corbusier's 1952 Cabanon), sponsoring exhibitions (like the recent ones on Perriand and Magistretti), publishing comprehensive scholarship (like the four volumes of the complete works of Charlotte Perriand), and relaunching unique designs (like Albini's 1938 Radio in Cristallo). In this way, Cassina extends the endless fluidity of co-production, co-authorship, and co-interpretation of the ever-shifting pieces of furniture that circulate the world in vast galaxies hidden by the buildings they are placed in. This radical fluidity is usually disguised in design discourse that credits designs to only singular individuals and thinks of furniture as singular static forms. But more details, formal and technical variations, and the names of other designers, craftspeople, critics, clients, exhibitions, and publications are eventually recovered. Perriand's and Jeanneret's names, for example, started to be restored in 1978 when Perriand became an important ongoing collaborator with Cassina—redesigning all the pieces that year—with her and Jeanneret's signature now added alongside that of Le Corbusier. In 2004 they officially became members of "iMaestri" and recently the original title of each piece has been restored. After the deaths of all the so-called masters, the designs continue to be adjusted by deep, ongoing historical work in the archives of all the respective designers in collaboration with the rights holders. In other words, design continues. The chairs remain, as they were from the beginning, restless and unsettled.

The "iMaestri" project furthers our understanding of the deep complexity and unfinishedness of thinking, making, occupying, and reading chairs. After all, the stories we tell ourselves about the history of each chair are actually part of the very fabric of chairs, part of what we sit in.

[1] Le Corbusier, "L'aventure du mobilier," in *Précisions sur un état présent de l'architecture et l'urbanisme*, Paris, 1930.

[2] Le Corbusier and François de Pierrefeu, *Maison des Hommes*, Paris, 1942, p. 69. For a more extensive analysis, see Beatriz Colomina, *Privacy and Publicity: Modern Architecture as Mass Media*, Cambridge, MA, 1994, pp. 319–24.

[3] The furniture pieces were gifted to the museum by Thonet and too expensive for even Alfred Barr, the Director of the Museum, to buy for personal use. Patricio del Real, "Object Lessons: Early Modernist Interiors at the Museum of Modern Art," *West 86th: A Journal of Decorative Arts, Design History, and Material Culture*, vol. 25, no. 1, Spring–Summer 2018.

[4] Arthur Rüegg (ed.), *Charlotte Perriand. Livre de bord 1928–1933*, Basel, 2004, p. 273.

[5] The reduction of authorship from three down to one had already occurred in other contexts. MoMA, for example, acknowledged all three designers when first exhibiting the chairs in 1933 but only referred to Le Corbusier in the 1941 catalogue of *Organic Design in Home Furnishings*.

[6] The Sala Espressioni space was choreographed by Gio Ponti for the Ideal Standard company and images of the installation of the Cassina chairs were published to illustrate an article in memory of Le Corbusier by Bruno Zevi in *Ideal-Standard – Rassegna dei problemi del benessere*, July–November 1965.

[7] The phrase and Cassina Logo inside the LC of Le Corbusier was repeated in advertisements in *Domus*, and the double logo was even used as the opening of Gio Ponti's coverage of the new furniture in the September issue.

[8] Bruno Alfieri, in *LC Le Corbusier*, Milan, 1965.

[9] *Domus*, 512, July 1972.

[10] This relentless research and the Cassina iMaestri Collection were curated by the designer and design researcher Filippo Alison.

[11] *Le Corbusier/Rietveld/Mackintosh*, Meda, 1980.

[12] The idea of treating contemporary Italian designers like Albini as "maestri" was already established by books like Marina Montuori, *Dieci maestri dell'architettura italiana. Lezioni di progettazione*, Milan, 1988. Bruno Zevi's concept of "nuovi maestri" became the basis of Giovanni Durbiano, *I nuovi maestri: architetti tra politica e cultura nel dopoguerra*, Venice, 2000.

[13] Renato De Fusco, *Le Corbusier, Designer: Furniture, 1929*, New York, 1977, p. 55.

[14] *Domus*, 413, April 1964.

[15] *Domus*, 431, October 1965.

[16] *Domus*, 539, October 1974.

[17] *Domus*, 911, February 2008.

[18] Henry Russell Hitchcock and Philip Johnson, *Modern Architecture: International Exhibition*, New York, 1932, p. 16.

Beatriz Colomina / Mark Antony Wigley

Building Culture

Carlo

Scarpa

1   Sketch for the Sarpi table
Graphite and pastel on paper
Carlo Scarpa, Sandro Bagnoli, circa 1974

2   Sketch of the Cassina House, Carimate (unbuilt)
Scale 1:100
Carlo Scarpa, 1963

Carlo Scarpa

After graduating from the Accademia Reale delle Belle Arti in 1926, Carlo Scarpa designed several private houses in Padua, such as Villa Campagnolo, Villa Martinati, and Villa Velo, with Franco Pizzuto.

The following year, he opened his own architectural office and began a collaboration with the Cappellin foundry, becoming its artistic director after Vittorio Zecchin. At the same time, he produced interior design projects such as the Cappellin showroom in Florence (1928), Casa Donà in Murano (1929), Caffè Lavena in Venice (1931), and the Sfriso showroom in Campo San Tomà (1932).

When Cappellin failed, Scarpa turned to Venini and worked as artistic director from 1932 to 1946. During this period, together with the Murano craftworkers, he continued his research into forms and colors, combining tradition and modernity and helping to modernize the famous glassmaking company. In 1934, he was awarded the honorary diploma of the Triennale di Milano for his products with Venini. In the same year he married Onorina Lazzari, and their son Tobia was born in Venice a few months later.

Scarpa then devoted himself to the renovation of a number of public spaces. These included the interior design of the Casino at the Lido of Venice, the redevelopment of the Faculty of Economics at Ca' Foscari (1936), the Teatro Rossini (1937), and, just after the war, the renovation of the Gallerie dell'Accademia (1945). He began his collaboration with the Venice Biennale that lasted almost thirty years.

During the 1950s, he devoted himself to the restructuring and restoration of a number of museums, such as Palazzo Abatellis in Palermo (1953), the historical section of the Museo Correr in Venice (1953), the Uffizi Gallery in Florence (1954–56), the Gipsoteca Canoviana in Possagno (1955), the Museo Civico di Castelvecchio in Verona (1956), and, finally, the picture gallery of the Museo Correr (1957).

At the same time, he worked on the designs of numerous exhibitions, such as those devoted to Giovanni Bellini (1949), Giambattista Tiepolo (1951), Toulouse Lautrec (1953), Piet Mondrian (1956), and Frank Lloyd Wright at the Triennale di Milano (1960). Finally, he created shops and showrooms for Olivetti (1957), Salviati (1960), and Gavina (1961). As an architect, he built many varied projects such as Ca' Foscari (1954–56), Veritti House in Udine (1956), the ENI Village at Borca di Cadore (1959), the Zilio tomb in Udine (1960), and the gardens of the Fondazione Querini-Stampalia (1961–63). He received the commission from Cesare Cassina for a private house at Ronco di Carimate near Como (1963–64), then he built the Fondazione Masieri in Venice (1968) and, finally, the Brion tomb in Treviso (1969).

His career as a designer really began when he met Dino Gavina, the owner of Simon International. Until then Scarpa had designed furnishings only in the form of one-off pieces made for special clients, such as those for Ferruccio Asta in Venice or Villa Zentner in Zurich. With Gavina, he experimented with industrial production by revising some of his earlier designs, as in the case of the Doge table (1968). As in architecture, Scarpa excelled in using combinations of materials. Wood, metal, glass, or brass form the basis of a design that is both complex in detail and simple in its entirety.

Scarpa was capable of working on quite modest projects, such as the Zilio tomb in Udine (1960), at the same time as he was working on others that were much more complex, such as the Banca Popolare di Verona (1973–80).

Building Culture

3   Carlo Scarpa, Dino Gavina, Pier Giacomo, and Achille Castiglioni, circa 1960

1906 — Born in Venice

1920 — Studies at the Accademia Reale di Belle Arti

1926 — Qualification in architectural design

1927 — Opens his architecture office in Venice

1931 — Interior design of Caffè Lavena, Venice

1932 — Competition for the Accademia Bridge, Venice

1933 — Lecturer at the Istituto Superiore di Architettura in Venice

1935 - 1937 — Birth of his son Tobia - Renovation of Ca' Foscari, Venice

1937 — Renovation of the Rossini Theater, Venice

1940 - 1941 — Vettore Rizzo tomb, San Michele Cemetery, Venice

1941 — Design of Il Cavallino gallery of modern art, Venice

1942 — Refurbishment and interior design of Villa Pellizzari, Venice

1943 — Capovilla tomb, Venice

1947 - 1949 — Head Office of the Banca Cattolica del Veneto in Tarvisio, Udine

Carlo Scarpa

1951	Veritti tomb, Udine - Meets Frank Lloyd Wright in Venice
1953 - 1954	Renovation of the National Gallery of Sicily, Palazzo Abatellis, Palermo
1957 - 1958	Olivetti Showroom, St Mark's Square, Venice
1963 - 1964	Project for Cassina House, Carimate - Villa Zentner, Zurich
1969	Brion Tomb, Treviso
1972	Mod. W05 Orseolo
1974	Mod. W02 Sarpi Mod. W10 Rialto

1953	Development of the Museo Correr, historical section, Venice
1956	Restoration and development of the Museo Civico di Castelvecchio, Verona
1961 - 1963	Ground floor of the Fondazione Querini-Stampalia, Venice
1968	Mod. W01 Doge - Masieri Foundation, Venice
1970	Mod. W04 Delfi
1973	Banca Popolare di Verona, Verona
1978	Galli tomb, Genoa - Dies in Japan

The range of his work reflects the breadth of his knowledge. A protean artist, Scarpa is recognized worldwide for his achievement, which is both technical and sophisticated, a mingling of tradition and modernity. His knowledge of materials and manufacturing techniques enabled him to endlessly enrich his creative vocabulary while creating major pieces of Italian architecture and design.

Scarpa received numerous awards during his prolific career: Diploma of Honor for Glass Objects at the 21st Triennale di Milano (1938) and at the 22nd Venice Biennale (1940), Olivetti National Prize for Architecture (1956), IN-ARCH National Prize and Gold Medal (1962), President of the Republic's Prize for Architecture (1967), and an honorary degree in architecture (1978). The Ultrarazionale collection was the first project of the young Simon International company (1968). Created in collaboration by Dino Gavina and Carlo Scarpa, it sought to present new furniture that would preserve the great traditional values while moving beyond the limitations of Rationalism and taking account of the constraints imposed by industrial production.

In 2013, Cassina acquired Simon International and, through it, a catalogue of iconic products by Carlo Scarpa, Marcel Breuer, and Kazuhide Takahama. Sharing the same advanced values, Cassina and Simon were the first two companies to undertake reissues of furniture, with Marcel Breuer's pieces for Simon (1962), and those by Le Corbusier, Pierre Jeanneret, and Charlotte Perriand for Cassina (1964). Dino Gavina and Cesare Cassina also founded Flos (1962), a cutting-edge lighting company, with the industrial production of models by the Castiglioni brothers and Tobia Scarpa. These two shared stories are united in this new collection.

Building Culture

Doge

Carlo Scarpa

1968

Mod. W01 — 2013

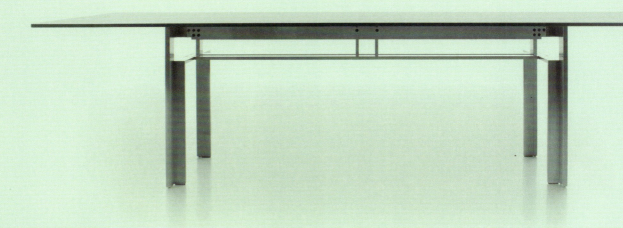

In 1968, Carlo Scarpa designed a large table in polished steel and glass adapted from the one he had designed for Villa Zentner in Zurich. In fact, after seeing that model with a marble top, Gavina suggested that Scarpa issue a version with a 20 mm glass top to reveal its structure. The table went into production and quickly became the symbol of the Ultrarazionale current of the time. Available in five sizes, Doge retains the iconic sculptural steel base that sets off the table's architectural character. It also retains its exposed burnished screws as well as the brass inset spacers.
To celebrate the addition of Carlo Scarpa to the iMaestri Collection, Cassina is offering a limited-edition version of Doge (Doge Laguna) in partnership with Tobia Scarpa. The glass top is sandblasted to opacify the material, then annealed, so creating this characteristic corrugated effect. Finally, the top is also fully beveled by machining to present a slender outline and shape, a transparent crystalline frame. This sophisticated detail creates a contrast with the center of the table.
Doge is found in the collections of major museums such as the Metropolitan Museum of Art. Cassina is reissuing it today, in steel or aluminum, with the top available in glass or marble.

Building Culture

Delfi

168

Carlo Scarpa

1969

Mod. W04 — 2013

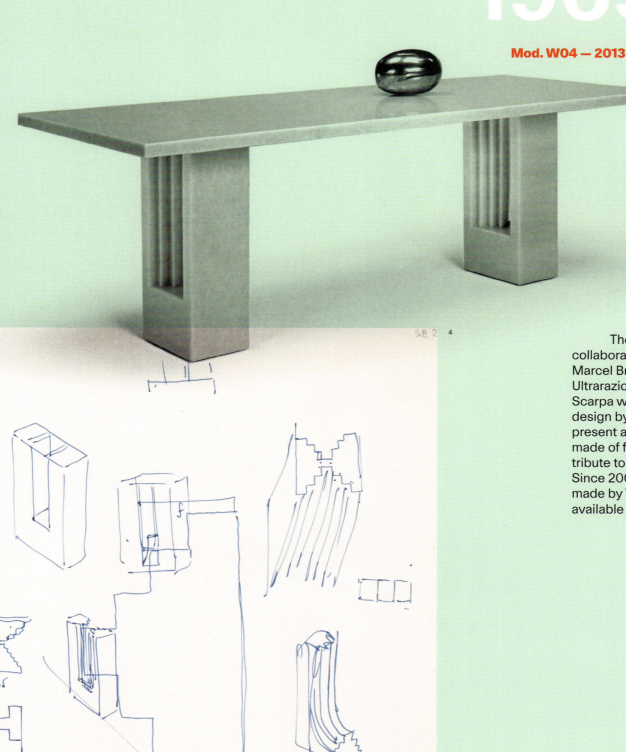

The Delfi table emerged from the collaboration between Carlo Scarpa and Marcel Breuer on Simon International's Ultrarazionale collection in 1969. Carlo Scarpa worked on a 1930s Rationalist design by Breuer, and reworked it to present a table with two monolithic feet made of fluted and hollow marble in tribute to the past and great architecture. Since 2009, another variant of the table, made by Tobia Scarpa, has also been available with a crystal top.

4   Sketch of the Delfi table, circa 1969
Details of the marble base

Building Culture

1972 – 73

Orseolo
Mod. W05 — 2013

Designed in 1972–73 for Simon International, the Orseolo table has been reissued by Cassina since 2013. The originality of this piece lies in its thick polyester lacquer finish—matte or gloss—hot-poured to completely cover its structure as well as its joints in satin-finish cast aluminum, endowing the whole with an extremely sophisticated character. Scarpa here combined form and function by designing elegant joints that at the same time, being points of maximum stress, ensure the full support of the table.

5   Sketch of the Orseolo table, circa 1972

Carlo Scarpa

1974

Rialto
Mod. W10 — 2013

This bookcase was originally designed by Carlo Scarpa for his home in Vicenza. Its originality lay in the extreme modularity of these elements thanks to a spacer. Dino Gavina redesigned it to adapt it to industrial production. It was edited by Simon International (1972) and later by Cassina.

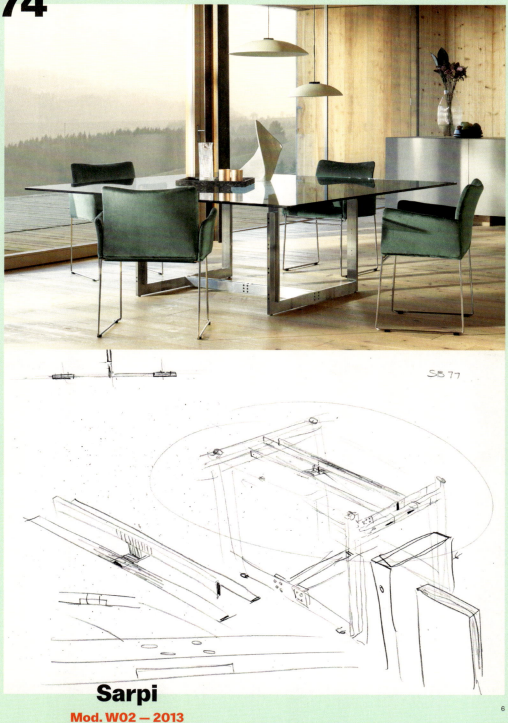

Sarpi
Mod. W02 — 2013

Produced by Simon International in 1974, this table features a transparent glass top (square, round, rectangular, or octagonal) resting on a four-legged frame in brushed satin-finish steel fixed to an H-shaped base by burnished metal screws. The careful detailing, especially the brass supports of the glass top, reflects the extreme refinement of Carlo Scarpa's design. In 2009, in collaboration with Tobia Scarpa, Cassina edited a version with an elliptical top.

6   Sketch of the Sarpi table
Detail of the metal frame
Graphite on paper, circa 1974

Building Culture

Gerrit Thomas Rietveld

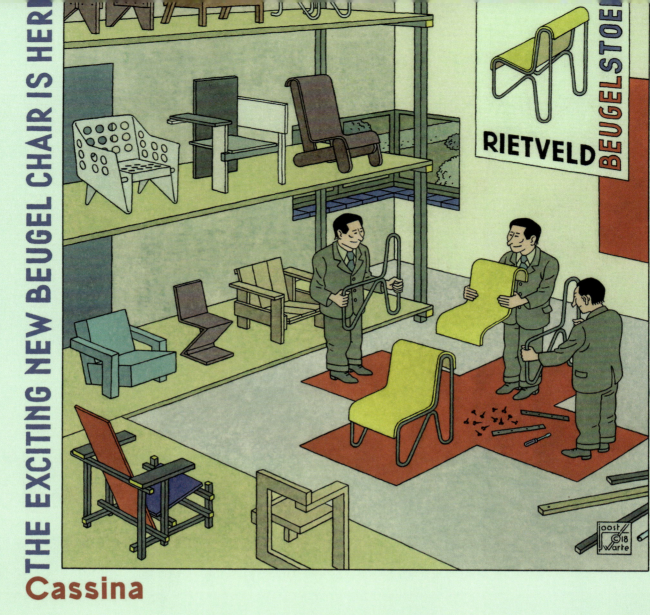

1   Joost Swarte
Rietveld-beugelstoel poster,
2018

2   Red and Blue chair

Gerrit Thomas Rietveld

Gerrit T. Rietveld was born in Utrecht in 1888.

A versatile artist, he began his career in his father's cabinet-making business. He soon opened his own workshop, in which he reinvented furniture in keeping with a wholly personal vocabulary of forms and structures.

In 1918, following his meeting with Theo van Doesburg, he joined the De Stijl movement, bringing together a group of artists who translated certain laws of analysis and deconstruction into ideology. His work quickly became emblematic of the international avant-garde, notably with his Red and Blue armchair. He met many artists such as Bruno Taut, Kurt Schwitters, and El Lissitzky and exhibited his work at the *Aesthetisch uitgevoerde gebruiksvoorwerpen* ("Utilitarian Objects with an Aesthetic Form") at the Museum voor Kunstnijverheid in Haarlem.

In 1921, he received a commission from Truus Schröder-Schräder to design a house in Utrecht. Completed in 1924, Schröder House quickly became the symbol of the Modern Movement in architecture. Rietveld theorized his ideas about the house and its interior, in which he involved the occupant on a daily basis. He wished the occupant to be active in its use and to think about it. The treatment of space is specific, since Rietveld decompartmentalized it to achieve a harmonious spatial effect.

A few years later, in 1928, he became a founding member of the International Congresses of Modern Architecture (CIAM) together with Le Corbusier, Pierre Jeanneret, and André Lurçat, among others. In the 1930s, he received several commissions for private houses, and then put his work as an architect on hold during World War II. In 1944, he became a lecturer at the Amsterdam School of Architecture (until 1955) and then, in 1947, at the Academy of Fine Arts and Technical Sciences in Rotterdam. He traveled to New York and Chicago and then exhibited in Paris with the jeweler Christofle in the exhibition *Dutch Decorative Art* (1947). The following year he exhibited his works at the Salon des Artistes Décorateurs in Paris and at the Triennale di Milano in 1951. Rietveld was one of the great Dutch artists of the interwar period, along with Mondrian, Oud, Van der Leck, and Van Doesburg. His work was presented at major cultural events, such as the exhibition *De Stijl* at the Stedelijk Museum (1951), which traveled to MoMA in New York the following year and the Virginia Museum of Fine Arts in 1958.

Among the hundred-odd buildings he designed throughout his career were the "Row-Houses" and the Juliana Hall in Utrecht, the industrial buildings of Bergeijk, and the Dutch Pavilion at the Venice Biennale in 1954. In 1963 Rietveld was commissioned to build the Van Gogh Museum in Amsterdam (completed in 1973). Rietveld produced furniture steadily all through his prolific career, for a total of more than 350 models. He never ceased to explore the primary qualities of materials. He made his slatted furniture from oak or plane and later turned to curved plywood and aluminum.

After many discussions with the artist's family, represented by his daughter Elisabeth and her husband, Derk Eskes, in 1972 Cassina acquired the rights to reissue Gerrit T. Rietveld's furniture. The architect Daniele Baroni began preliminary reconstruction work on the first two models that went into production: the Zig Zag chair and the Red and Blue armchair. Then, from 1973 onward, Filippo Alison developed iMaestri Collection in parallel. The first prototypes were produced with the assistance of G. A. van de Groenekan, Rietveld's former assistant and loyal collaborator. This made for an interesting comparison between the original construction technique and the technical skills of Cassina's joiners. These pieces would be the subject of several exhibitions, notably in Milan in 1972, at the Hunterian Art Gallery in Glasgow in 1983, and at the MAXXI in Rome in 2011, during the exhibition *Universo Rietveld*. In 1964, he received an honorary doctorate from the Delft University of Technology.

Building Culture

1888	Born in Utrecht	**1900**	Leaves school to join his father Johannes's cabinetry workshop
1917	Opens his own cabinetry workshop in Utrecht — Gerard van de Groenekan becomes his apprentice	**1918**	**Mod. 635 Red and Blue**
1919	**Mod. 636 Elling buffet — Contacts with the magazine *De Stijl***	**1921**	Commission from Truus Schröder-Schräder
1923	**Berlijnse Stoel — Mod. 634 Schröder 1 Mod. 635 Black Red and Blue Zeilmaker version**	**1924**	Schröder House, Prins Hendriklaan 50, Utrecht
1925	Lommen House, Klein Persijnlaan 39, Wassenaar	**1926**	Visits Schröder House with Mart Stam
1927	Meets László Moholy-Nagy — Eerste model armchair in curved plywood	**1928**	Exhibition at the Stedelijk Museum, in collaboration with Truus Schröder-Schräder *ASB* (Architecture, Paintings, Sculpture)
1930	Exhibition of the Union des Artistes Modernes, Pavillon de Marsan, Paris	**1932**	Exhibition of his work at the Museum of Modern Art in Moscow and at the Technische School in Amsterdam — Furniture exhibition

Gerrit Thomas Rietveld

1934 — Mod. 280 Zig Zag / Mod. 281–297 Crate Series

1935 — Mod. 637 Utrecht

1936 — House Mees, Van Ouwenlaan 42, The Hague / Smedes House, Van Weerden Poelmanlaan 1, Den Dolder

1938 — Exhibition at Metz&Co in Amsterdam on the occasion of *Het nieuwe meubel* ("Modern Furniture")

1939 — Wijburg House, Van Ouwenlaan 44, The Hague

1942 — Studies for the aluminum armchair (Aluminiumstoel)

1949 — Smit House, Puntweg 8, Kinderdijk

1951 — Stoop House, Beekhuizenseweg 44, Velp / Slatted furniture for bungalows in holiday homes

Exhibition *De Stijl* at the Stedelijk Museum of Modern Art, Amsterdam

1958 — House Van der Doel, Monnickendammer-rijweg 31c, Ilpendam

1960 — Exhibition *De Stijl* at the Galleria Nazionale d'Arte Moderna, Rome / Exhibition *Meubelen van deze tijd* ("Contemporary Furniture") Metz&Co, Amsterdam

1963 — Steltman-Stoel in oak wood / Van Slobbe House, Zandweg 122, Heerlen

Commission for the Van Gogh Museum in Amsterdam (completed 1973)

1964 — Dies in the Rietveld Schröder House

3   Price list for living room furnishings, 1923

4   Trademark of the Rietveld furniture workshop

Building Culture

Red and Blue

...parte del pezzo, sia pure in diretta relazione spaziale con
...nserva la propria identità; schienale, sedile e aste
...no in tutte e tre le direzioni fondamentali, senza mai
...n un incastro.

Le linee ed i piani sono organizzati in una composizione
verticale-orizzontale dove lo spazio filtra liberamente
senza lasciarsi catturare dalla forma.
Il colore, notevole contributo, dà risalto alla configurazione
spaziale, dematerializzando l'oggetto.

Gerrit Thomas Rietveld

1918
Mod. 635 – 1973

5   Rietveld leaflet, 1974

6   Interior view of the painter Charley Toorop's house Bergen, 1933

7   Detail of the assembly of Red and Blue Rietveld leaflet, 1974

...soprattutto l'insieme sta libero e netto nello spazio... (Rietveld)

Building Culture

This chair consists of six uprights and seven battens with square sections for the frame, two boards for the seat and back, and two solid wood elements for the armrests.

All the parts are assembled with dowels that cross each other at right angles, while the seat and back are nailed to the uprights of the frame.

Rietveld said of it: "I tried to make each element simple, in its most primitive form, depending on the type of use and material." The chair dates from 1918 and was published the following year in the magazine *De Stijl*. G. van de Groenekan, then a young apprentice in Rietveld's workshop, said that the very first version of this iconic chair is the one on which the Master sits, surrounded by his craftsmen, outside his workshop Meubele Makerij.

The chair is very skillfully built since it allows a distribution of the forces on all the structural elements. Subsequently, to suit the needs of its users, the chair was painted Red and Blue, making it a manifesto of the De Stijl movement. The colors reinforced the singularity of this object, a veritable abstract sculpture that goes beyond matter.

Rietveld, who wanted his furniture to be manufactured industrially, stated in 1963: "This chair, made out of two boards and a few slats, was made to show that it was possible to make something beautiful, to create a spatial sculpture using only plain elements of purely industrial manufacture" (Paul Overy, *The Rietveld Schröder house*, Cambridge, MA, 1988, p. 61). It was put into production by Cassina in 1973.

8 Study of the Red and Blue structure
Rietveld leaflet, 1974

Gerrit Thomas Rietveld

Building Culture

Black Red and Blue Zeilmaker version

182

Gerrit Thomas Rietveld

1924

Mod. 635 — 2015

Rietveld used color for the first time to paint his son Jan's crib.

 I asked the apprentice to plane a few slats. In one evening it was ready, and my wife was surprised to find it in the morning. Made of pine wood, it is painted red and yellow and lined with blue fabrics, giving it a festive air.

Gerrit Thomas Rietveld

The first model of this chair was made unpainted and given its iconic colors around 1923. Rietveld also offered monochrome versions to suit the wishes of his customers.

The Black Red and Blue chair was made for Wicher Zeilmaker, a school teacher. It is a variant of the iconic 1918 model, repeating its structure but with a black frame with white terminals and a green seat and backrest.

Building Culture

Elling Buffet

1919

Mod. 636 — 2019

Rietveld built this two-door, four-drawer, two-shelf model, in dark plane wood, for the interior of a house designed by architect J. J. P. Oud in Rotterdam.
It was later made of beech and beech plywood. Cassina has been producing the Elling Buffet since 2019.

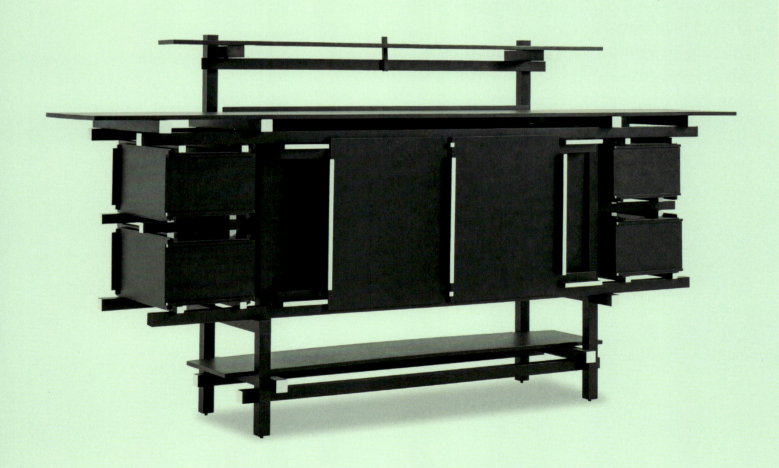

Gerrit Thomas Rietveld

1922

Bolderwagen

1923
Schröder 1
Mod. 634 — 1981

1927

Eerste model

This children's cart is made, like the rest of Rietveld's models, in painted beech and beech plywood. The colors bring out the structure and its other constituent parts.

Rietveld designed this coffee table for Til Brugman's apartment. The renovation of this interior had been overseen by the Hungarian painter and designer Vilmos Huszár, with whom Rietveld had collaborated on a project in Berlin in 1923, for which he designed an asymmetrical table and chair.

The small table perfectly complied with the rules of neo-plasticism: no curves or diagonals, only verticals and horizontals, absence of symmetry, and the search for perfect balance between primary colors (blue, red, yellow) associated with noncolors (gray, black, white). Made of beech by his apprentice Gerard van de Groenekan, the table is asymmetrical and a specific color is applied to each structural element, with each edge picked out in white.

This armchair marked the start of Rietveld's research into the production of a chair made from a single material. With this first model, he managed to free himself from the metal structure to which the seat and the arched wooden back were fixed. Here the seat and backrest are made of a single curved sheet of plywood to which the panels constituting the feet/armrests are attached. In the 1970s Cassina realized a prototype in natural beech plywood in keeping with the 1927 original.

Building Culture

Zig Zag

9 Original drawing of the
Zig Zag chair
Trade document, Metz&Co,
1932–35

Gerrit Thomas Rietveld

1934
Mod. 280 — 1973

Building Culture

With the Birza chair designed in 1927, Rietveld continued his research into industrial production of a monobloc chair. "How can it be that an artifact as simple as a chair has not yet been solved as effectively as a bicycle, or, even better, a spoon?"

Shortly after, he devised his first prototypes of a plywood, fiber, or steel chair. The chosen model, made by Gerard van de Groenekan, consisted of four wooden boards with rectangular sections fastened together with screws and dovetail joints. Cassina faithfully reproduces this constructional detail but eliminates the screws, now structurally unnecessary. Zig Zag has been produced by Cassina since 1973.

A partition that leaves space untouched. It's not a chair, it's a creative folly. I usually call it little Zig Zag.

Gerrit Thomas Rietveld

Gerrit Thomas Rietveld

Building Culture

Utrecht

1935

Mod. 637 — 1988

In 2016, Cassina offered a limited edition called Utrecht C90, which reinterpreted this armchair thanks to a graphic and contemporary fabric designed by the artist Bertjan Pot. The four fabric variants were customized on a computer-controlled Jacquard loom. The BoxBlocks fabric is woven out of eight colored threads combined two by two to create nineteen colors with a perfectly balanced geometric pattern, in which the combination of triangles is never repeated.

Originally designed in 1935 for the Metz&Co department stores for large-scale production, this armchair was Rietveld's first model to embody the notions of comfort and relaxation. The seat and backrest were assembled at right angles to form an L-shaped structure slightly tilted back. The feet and armrests also meet at right angles. The whole is foamed and fully lined.

Gerrit Thomas Rietveld

1934

Crate Series
Mod. 281-287 — 1974

1942

Aluminiumstoel

1963

Steltman-Stoel

This chair is the last project realized by Gerrit T. Rietveld, although it recalls the open structures and asymmetrical shapes of his early days. Initially designed in wood upholstered with leather for the Steltman jewelry shop in The Hague, this model was then made to order in painted oak by Gerard van de Groenekan in the 1960s and 1970s. The principle embodied in the chairs recalls the symbolism of the couple as two independent and opposite forms that together become one. Cassina made prototypes of this model in the 1970s.

Rietveld's first slatted furniture is dated 1934. It is a set of armchairs, table, and bookshelf. Initially, these parts were produced by Rietveld himself and then sold as a kit to be assembled. The following year, Metz&Co launched this series of furnishings with the name "Weekend Meubelen." A few years later, Cassina produced the series with the name "Crate." These crate furnishings were originally unvarnished. The fabric for the cushions of the Crate model, produced by Cassina from 1974 to 1986, was chosen by Rietveld at Metz&Co. It features a De Stijl motif forming colorful geometric patterns, attributed to the Dutch painter B. van der Leck. Production rights now belong to third parties. Cassina retained these rights during the period 1974–86.

Rietveld made this chair with his son Wim (1924–1985), who recalled that it was a difficult job because it was done entirely by hand. The aluminum sheet is hammered and then drilled to make the whole more solid. Rietveld presented his chair at the Salon des Artistes Décorateurs in Paris in 1948, where it was a great success. Cassina undertook the reconstruction of a prototype of this model in 2015.

Building Culture

Marco

Zanuso

194

Marco Zanuso

Architect and designer, Marco Zanuso studied architecture at the Politecnico di Milano from 1935 to 1939, graduating in 1939. After World War II, he opened a practice in Milan and worked as architect, designer, and urban planner.

He quickly proved to be a remarkable designer. He created the Antropus armchair for the Piccolo Teatro di Milano (1949), the iconic Lady armchair (1951), the Triennale sofa (1951), and the Martingala armchair for which he won the Gold Medal at the 10th Triennale di Milano.

He was co-editor in chief, with Ernesto Nathan Rogers, of the magazine *Domus* (1946–48) and editor of *Casabella* (1953–56). At the same time he designed the first Arteluce showroom (1953) as well as the Olivetti complexes in Buenos Aires (1955) and São Paulo (1957).

He joined the CIAM in 1956 and became a member of the Associazione per il Disegno Industriale (ADI) founded by Gio Ponti in 1954. With Alberto Rosselli, he won the prestigious Compasso d'Oro award in 1956, for the sewing machine Mod. 1100/2.

In the same year, Zanuso began an intense collaboration with the German designer Richard Sapper, together producing a significant number of emblematic examples of Italian industrial design. Their constant research into new materials, like thermoplastics, led to the creation of the Antares TV set (1960), the Doney TV set (1962), the K1340 chair (1964), the Grillo telephone (1966), and the FD 1102 radio (1969).

He built the Necchi factory in Pavia (1961–62), Villa Reggiani in Jesi (1970), the Piccolo Teatro in Milan (1974), the IBM buildings in Segrate, Milan (1974–77), and the industrial complex at Santa Palomba, Rome, from 1979 to 1982. He was also a professor at the Politecnico di Milano from 1969 to 1991. During his prolific career, he won three gold medals at the Triennale di Milano and six Compasso d'Oro awards plus the Lifetime Achievement Award.

1 9th Triennale di Milano
Lady armchair, 1951

2 Lady armchairs
Marco Zanuso

Building Culture

1916	Born in Milan	**1939**	Graduates from the Politecnico di Milano
1947	Gold Medal at the 8th Triennale di Milano	**1948**	Office building in Milan
1949	**Mod. 721 Antropus**	**1951**	**Mod. 720 Lady** — Sofa 9th Triennale Senior armchair Bridge chair Crociera armchair
1954	Gold Medal at the 10th Triennale di Milano — Martingala armchair	**1957**	Gold Medal at the 11th Triennale di Milano
1958	Milord armchair	**1960**	Lambda chair (with Richard Sapper) Antares TV set (with Richard Sapper) — Project for a pre-fabricated house (FEAL)
1962	Compasso d'Oro for Doney 14 TV set (with Richard Sapper)	**1964**	**Mod. 722 Woodline**
1965	Ariel TV set (with Richard Sapper) Cambridge bookcase Algol 11 TV set (with Richard Sapper)		K4999 children's chair (with Richard Sapper) — Compasso d'Oro for the K1340 (with Richard Sapper)
			TS 502 radio (with Richard Sapper) — Living room for a single-family home at the exhibition *La casa abitata* in Florence

Marco Zanuso

1966	Algol II TV set (with Richard Sapper)
1967	Compasso d'Oro for the Grillo phone (with Richard Sapper)
	Solo design show
1969	FD 1102 radio (with Richard Sapper) — T 111A bathroom scales Black ST 201
1970	BA 2000 kitchen scales — Villa Reggiani, Jesi
1971	Collegio di Milano inter-university campus
1972	Mobil House in *Italy: The New Domestic Landscape*, MoMA, New York (with Richard Sapper)
1974	Ariante electric fan
1977–1997	Piccolo Teatro Strehler (with Pietro Crescini)
1979	Compasso d'Oro for the Controsoffitto system — Compasso d'Oro for the Ariante fan
1985	Compasso d'Oro Lifetime Achievement Award
1999	Municipal Theater in Bolzano (with Pietro Crescini)
2001	Dies in Milan

Grillo phone Springtime Collection

Living chair and sofa Lombrico modular system

4

3   Marco Zanuso in his studio with the Lady armchair, 1962

4   Portrait of Marco Zanuso

Antropus

Marco Zanuso designed the Antropus armchair in honor of the Italian version of Thornton Wilder's *The Skin of Our Teeth* (Italian title *La Famiglia Antropus*) at the Piccolo Teatro in Milan in 1948–49.

Originally made for Arflex, the armchair is now produced with a metal structure with elastic straps, entirely covered in expanded polyurethane. The seat and backrest are broad for comfort and the side panels, with a sinuous line, act as both structure and armrests. Cassina reissued this model from 2015.

5   Constructional drawing for the Antropus armchair

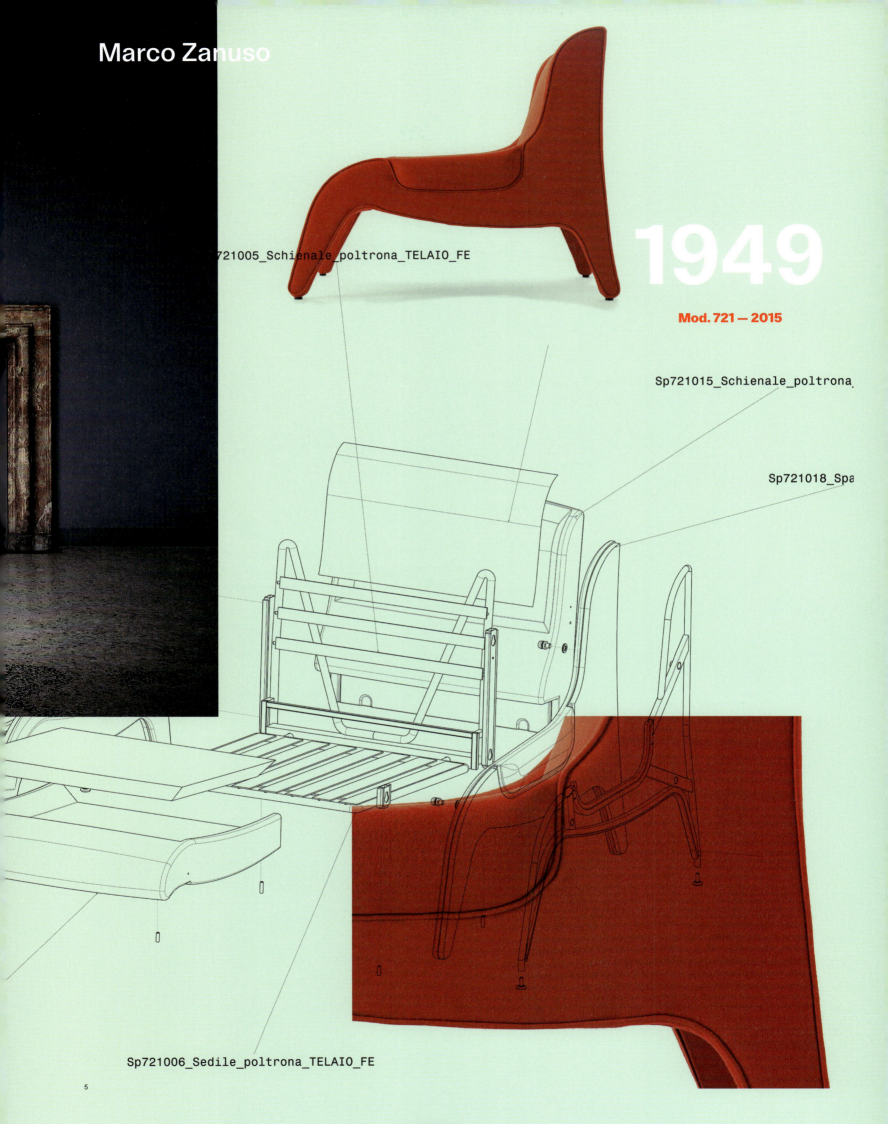

Building Culture

Lady

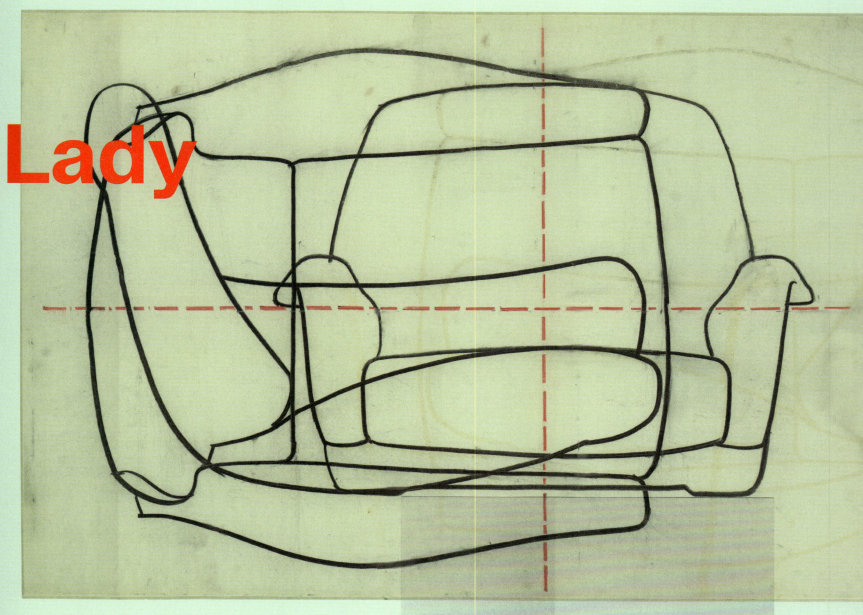

» **Foam rubber makes it possible to revolutionize not just the padding but also its structure and its formal potential. Our prototypes attained an appreciable appearance and new outlines with hitherto unthinkable industrial standards.** »

Marco Zanuso

Marco Zanuso

1951

Mod. 720 — 2015

This is certainly the first armchair whose conception envisioned all the issues involved in its design. Looking ahead, Zanuso realized he had to anticipate all the stages of manufacturing to offer a product that would be both aesthetically and economically attractive. To replace the traditional and expensive work involved in padding with metal springs, he decided to use foam rubber, a new material patented by Pirelli in the 1930s, to make the seat and back of the armchair. The original foam rubber padding was supported by interlacing elastic straps made of Nastro Cord rubber (a material patented in 1948) attached to a wooden frame. The whole rested on metal legs.

The original feature of the armchair was its assembly, because it consisted of elements upholstered separately for faster production.

In 2015, Cassina reissued the Lady armchair, making some changes to the upholstery while retaining the same form as the original versions.

6   Lady armchair
Sketch, section and plan,
1951

7   Cut-out view of the
Lady armchair to show the
inner structure with the
Nastro Cord supporting
straps and foam rubber seat
padding at the 9th Triennale
di Milano, 1951

Building Culture

Woodline

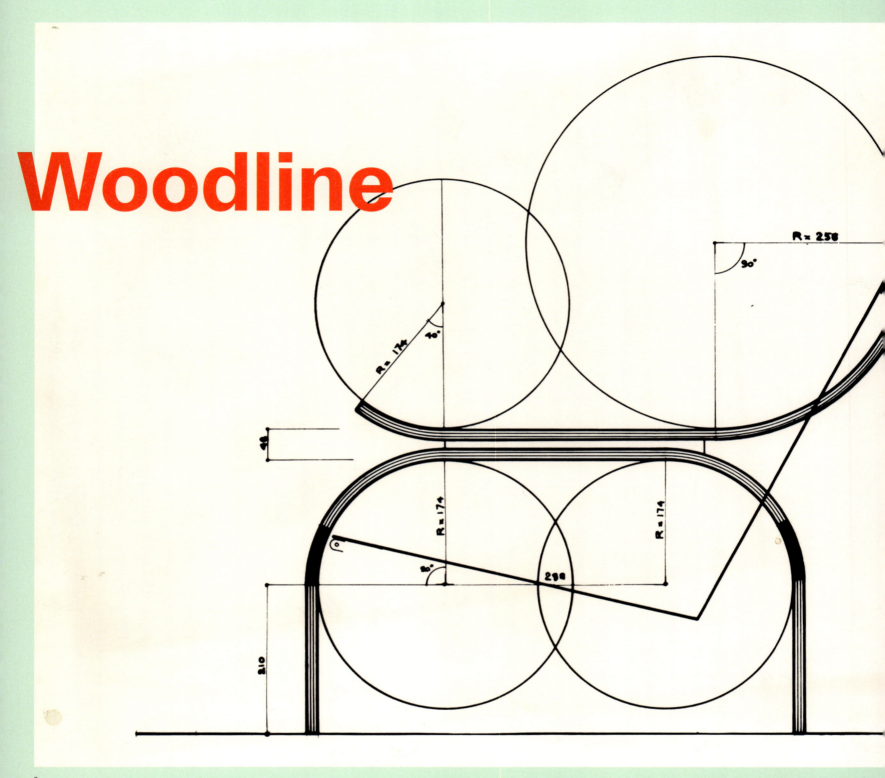

8

 Through the project, I like to give shape to what I call complexity.

Marco Zanuso

8   Drawing of the Woodline armchair, 1964

202

Marco Zanuso

1964
Mod. 722 — 2015

The elegance of the Woodline armchair lies in its curved plywood frame, available in the original version in walnut, rosewood, or black-tinted beech. The armchair's elasticity and suspension were made possible by the slender tempered steel slats forming the seat and back. They are covered with a padded and lined mattress, secured simply with press-studs.

Building Culture

Photos by
DELFINO SISTO LEGNANI

Delfino Sisto Legnani from DSL Studio immortalizes the iMaestri models in museums like Procuratie Vecchie (Venezia), Ca' Scarpa (Treviso), and the Kröller-Müller (Otterlo). Masterpieces of Giacomo Balla, Gerrit T. Rietveld, and Le Corbusier, Pierre Jeanneret, Charlotte Perriand are presented as artworks in these prestigious institutions. Gio Ponti's Superleggera and Leggera chairs are photographed in Edoardo Tresoldi's site-specific installation for the Arte Sella sculpture park in Trentino.

4

Yesterday

4

Today and
Tomorrow

Cassina,
Timeless Elegance

Yesterday Today and Tomorrow

On the Avant-Garde, as a Value of Contemporary Life and a Condition of a Future

CÉLINE SARAÏVA
Curatorial assistant,
Centre Pompidou - Musée national
d'art moderne / Centre de création industrielle
Service design et prospective industrielle

In the constellation of twentieth-century designer furniture, some objects have withstood the test of time. With their longevity, they find themselves in a certain sense ennobled. Their presence in the most prestigious museum collections now endows them with a set of recognized and shared values and contributes durably to their legitimacy. This process of museumification has given them a new status as a work, even a masterpiece. These creations, which are of several kinds, reveal new materials, advances in manufacturing processes, and mutations of forms, while participating in the historiographical interpretation of museums. Without entering into an enumeration of the furnishings that would, of course, be incomplete, here we can take the option of evoking some attributes: wood bent or curved, stamped sheet metal, tubular steel, metal mesh, molded resin, plastics, new methods of fastening, new techniques of padding,

1   View of the Charles Rennie Mackintosh Collection, circa 1980

new finishing methods, and new manufacturing processes. This will have made it clear that their heritage value is most often based on advances, on an experimental dimension of creativity, bound up with the reformist and unacademic outlook of their designers. Creators, always anxious to actualize the present by matching the production of objects with a given period, identify the Zeitgeist, the spirit of the time.

This approach implies always engaging in a process of investigation, of questioning, which is related to the notion of the avant-garde. The words of the American poet David Antin shed a subtle light on this. In his book, *What It Means to Be Avant-Garde*,[1] he tries to imagine the territory of his creation. He says, "I realized I like the fringe because I'm used to it in a certain sense I've always felt I was in the right place and the right place was a place shaded from the bright light at the center of the tablecloth and I liked living there it seemed to be the place where everything meaningful happened." This "fringe" that the writer praises corresponds to a region where the notion of experimentation manifests the opportunity for a real questioning of practices, modes of making by designers, alone capable of restoring the value of contemporary objects and enabling them to withstand the test of time.

Yesterday Today and Tomorrow

But for this virtuous process to be made manifest, around the creators there have to be other protagonists who pick up the signals conveying these new or revolutionary visions in order to shed light on them. It is this position that the brothers Umberto and Cesare Cassina maintained over the years by offering the opportunity to designers, as many as they are varied, to produce and market their creations. Drawing on excellent know-how, prompt investment in research, and fruitful encounters, Cassina has contributed to the emergence of new ideas and design trends, producing innovative furniture. And it is precisely this ability to act as a "scout," or more simply a visionary, that implies a form of "intellectual sophistication," which is already part of a certain form of elegance.

A Phase Favorable to the Avant-Garde

In 1965 Cassina launched the first reissues of furniture creations, designed by Le Corbusier, Pierre Jeanneret, and Charlotte Perriand in 1928 and presented at the Salon d'Automne in Paris in 1929 under the title Équipement intérieur d'une habitation (Interior Equipment of a Dwelling). The Chaise Longue basculante, the Fauteuil tournant, and the Fauteuil Grand Confort and its sofa version were among the first emblematic models of the Modern Movement put into production at Cassina thirty-seven years after their conception. This project owes a lot, as we know, to the exchanges that Cesare Cassina initiated with other Italian manufacturers, and in particular with Dino Gavina, who in 1962 launched a venture unprecedented at that time in Italy: the reissue of the mythical Bauhaus armchair, the model B3 also called the Wassily, designed by Marcel Breuer. Across the Atlantic, in the United States, the same experiment had been initiated, with the same success, by Florence Knoll, who in 1948 had reissued the Barcelona armchair designed by Mies van der Rohe for the German pavilion at the 1929 Barcelona International Exhibition.

That same year, 1965, was marked by the presentation of the exhibition La casa abitata at Palazzo Strozzi in Florence. It proposed to examine the new ways of living in Italy in the 1960s. This Florentine exhibition brought together some of Italy's most outstanding architects and designers, such as Achille and Pier Giacomo Castiglioni, Vittorio Gregotti, and Vico Magistretti—who then presented several pieces of furniture issued by Cassina (the Carimate armchair, Mod. 772 table, Tavolino Mod. T8, Mod. 905 armchair, Mod. 896 armchair), Angelo Mangiarotti, Leonardo Ricci, Leonardo Savioli, Ettore Sottsass, and Marco Zanuso, who displayed their new and creative visions of the contemporary domestic environment in a series of interior designs. It may be recalled here that these devices borrowed the idea of the stand from the first modern trade fairs. The proposals were unprecedented: a dining room prepared for lunch by the Castiglioni brothers; an organic, compact, and nomadic dwelling by Leonardo Ricci; a living cell for a minimal home built out of prefabricated elements by Leonardo Savioli; a bedroom by Ettore Sottsass consisting of an unusual assemblage of colorful furniture and objects made in a wide variety of materials and motifs leading to the "sensory" character of the environment. The creativity of these proposals heralded a paradigm shift in Italian design in the 1960s.

They clearly reflected this exceptional period of creative ferment and ideological debates, described by Andrea Branzi, "(…) where absolute utopia and realism clashed within a cultural system that collaborated extraordinarily effectively with an industrial system itself very dynamic due to the ongoing social changes."[2]

It had become obvious that we were moving from an industrial and unified society, organized around work, to a more fragmented society based on consumption and leisure, in which architecture or the domestic environment were thought of as spaces of discovery and original sensations. Design became a space for communication and debate, a critical space in short, in which it was a question of anti-design, counter-design, or radical design.

It should be remembered here that, in the 1950s, Cassina had already played a pioneering role in Italy in the choice of the prospective dimension of design by working with talented designers and the bearers of new visions, such as Franco Albini, Gio Ponti, or Vico Magistretti, and by relying on the powers of experimentation and manufacturing of its craftsmen. It was the first company to export the image of design made in Italy by becoming involved in the interior design of ocean liners, devised by Gio Ponti. It was also distinguished by winning the Compasso d'Oro in its first edition in 1954 with the Mod. 683 chair designed by Carlo De Carli. In 1957, it was to be equally successful, with the launch of the Superleggera chair, which became an icon of Italian design.

A Collection of Masters Animated by the *New Spirit*

The first reissues of furniture designed by Le Corbusier, Pierre Jeanneret, and Charlotte Perriand were joined in 1973 by those of other great figures of modernity, such as Gerrit Thomas Rietveld or Charles Rennie Mackintosh. The Cassina iMaestri Collection was then officially launched. It would be enriched in the 1980s, 1990s, and 2000s with models by Erik Gunnar

2   Mod. 683 chair designed by Carlo De Carli, awarded the Compasso d'Oro in 1954

3   Sketch of the La casa abitata exhibition, Palazzo Strozzi, Florence, 1965

4   Exhibition view of Salon d'Automne 1929, Paris, with furniture by Le Corbusier, Pierre Jeanneret, and Charlotte Perriand

5   Interior view of Vico Magistretti's booth at La casa abitata exhibition, 1965

Céline Saraïva

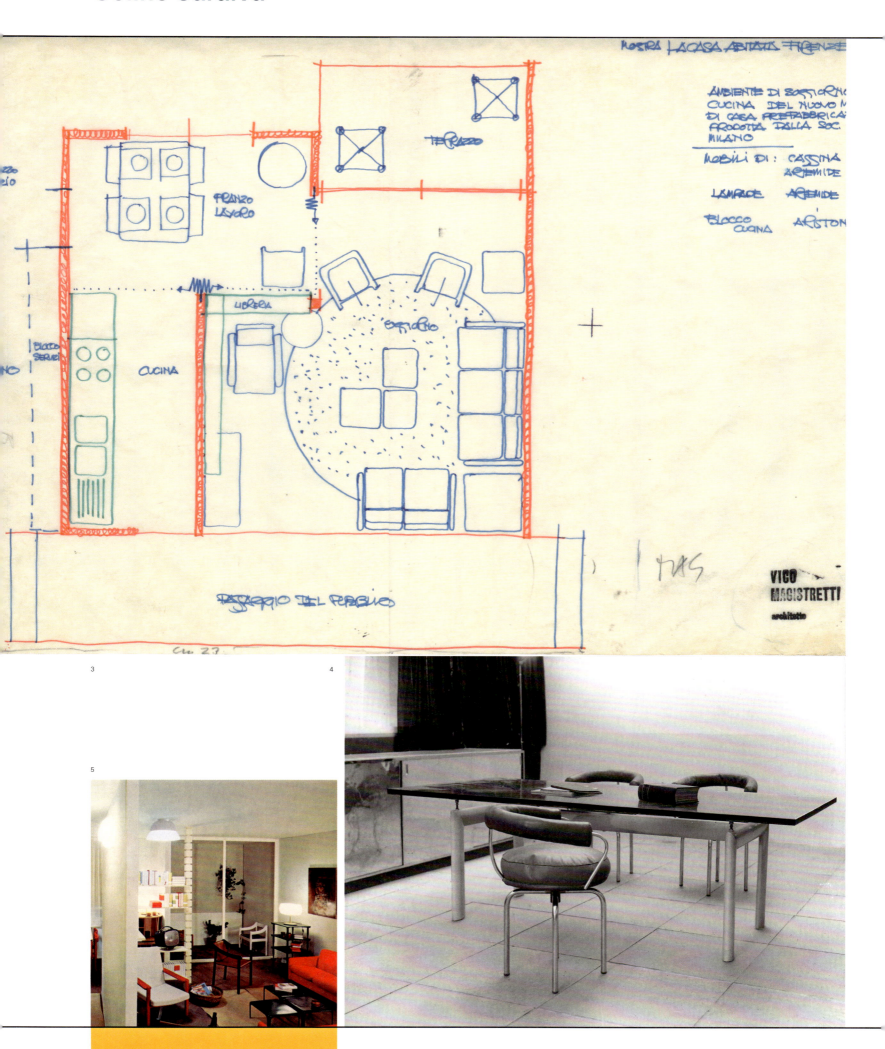

219

Yesterday Today and Tomorrow

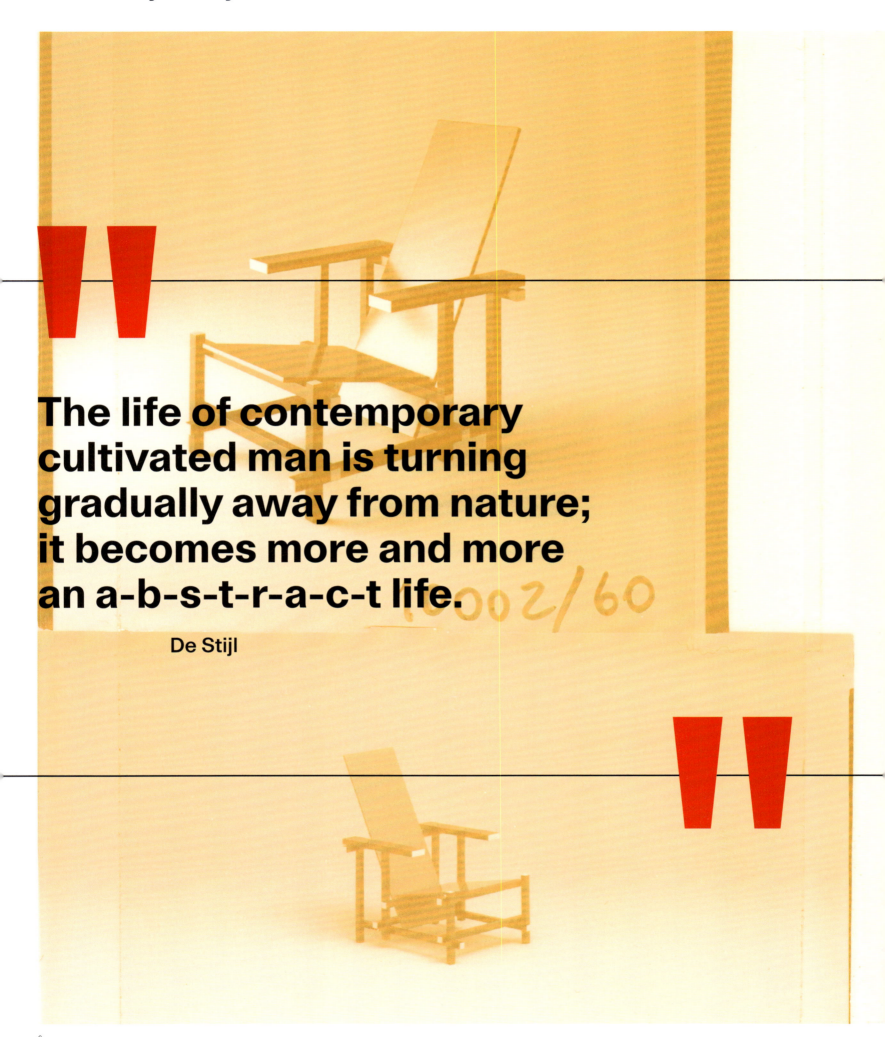

"The life of contemporary cultivated man is turning gradually away from nature; it becomes more and more an a-b-s-t-r-a-c-t life."

De Stijl

Céline Saraïva

Asplund, Frank Lloyd Wright, and Charlotte Perriand, joined by other Masters, Italian this time, such as Franco Albini, Marco Zanuso, Ico Parisi, Giacomo Balla, and more recently, Gio Ponti, Vico Magistretti, and Carlo Scarpa.

Cassina's primary commitment to iconic objects from the Modern Movement at a time when it was no longer a model, may seem contradictory. However, there is no nostalgia in its approach, quite the contrary. By its choice of masters, Cassina goes beyond a need to adopt the ideological values embodied by the modern avant-gardes of the early twentieth century. It is the *New Spirit* formulated by the poet Guillaume Apollinaire and then employed by Le Corbusier. At the time, Art and creation as a whole were meant to reflect the new realities of modern life.

In the early twentieth century, the aim was to put an end to this eclecticism of styles and the overelaborate furniture of the nineteenth century, which sublimated historical references and decoration. This new approach appeared in all industrialized countries: in Germany with Peter Behrens and Walter Gropius, in Austria with Adolf Loos, in Scotland with Mackintosh, then in the Netherlands with the De Stijl movement and the figures of Theo van Doesburg and Gerrit Thomas Rietveld, and in France with Le Corbusier. Even if their approaches varied, they all sought a new aesthetic based on a rational and functional approach to the design of spaces and objects.

The image of the Équipement intérieur d'une habitation, proposed by the trio Le Corbusier, Pierre Jeanneret, and Charlotte Perriand at the Salon d'Automne in Paris in 1929, evokes this approach. We can see how the overelaborate furnishings of the nineteenth century disappeared and objects were freed from the weight of "style." The Chaise Longue basculante, the Fauteuil tournant, and the Fauteuil Grand Confort were the result of this rationalist process focused on the refinement of forms, the use of new materials, such as tubular steel, and new techniques adapted to the Esprit Nouveau, the "new spirit," associated with Functionalist ideology. One might have thought that with this logic of refinement, objects would become poorer. On the contrary, with the free plan formulated by Le Corbusier, modern space has become decompartmentalized and furnishings have acquired a new power of expression that goes beyond their simple function. They act both as authoritative manifestos of modern ideas, bearers of narratives, and as objects with a "poetic function." This "Esprit Nouveau" is a spirit of clarity, geometry, rationality, and perfection, expressed both in the design of these objects and in the aesthetics they convey. It is in this way of being in harmony with the new world that we find a new quality of elegance.

A different form of harmony appeared in this other icon of furniture production: the Red and Blue chair by Gerrit Thomas Rietveld, belonging to the rigorous aesthetic of Neoplasticism, theorized by the Dutch art movement De Stijl. Founded in 1917 by Theo van Doesburg, Piet Mondrian, and Gerrit Thomas Rietveld, among others, the movement aimed to develop an objective "style" appropriate to the modern world, with the idea of a synthesis of the arts. The inaugural manifesto read: "There is an old and a new spirit of the times…"[3] And further on, "The life of contemporary cultivated man is turning gradually away from nature; it becomes more and more an a-b-s-t-r-a-c-t life."[4] This vision of the world is that of a quest for universal harmony. In this context, forms must be produced according to mathematical rules but in keeping with a "cosmic" and completely abstract order. This is expressed by Rietveld's Red and Blue chair, which combines orthogonal lines and flat primary colors in a kind of dynamic and open development of Mondrian's painting into a volume. This form of spatial abstraction with geometric forms, associated with the concept of perfection and a metaphysical order, introduced a new consciousness of beauty that was more universal and in a sense also more timeless.

The encounter between these avant-garde experiences and industrial design was not incongruous. The "reproducibility" of these icons did not detract from their semantic value because they were, for the most part, oriented toward their possible mass production. Professor Filippo Alison, coordinator of the collection, specifies the status of the reissued object: "In our case, the object chosen for the present is an 'archetype,' that is to say a model for a time and a place distant from our own, but on the condition that it embodies formal and decorative predicates likely to signal the significant data of the cultural climate to which it belongs."[5] And Alison concludes, "The work already existed, nothing is reproduced in its entirety, but only in a version more suited to our times, in keeping with the principles that its author himself would have adopted, because the substance of the original object is current."[6] And to ensure the success of this "transposition," Cassina initiated rigorous research into the study of these products, accompanied by the creators or their beneficiaries, while making all its know-how available.

In this way Cassina plays an important part as a transmitter of these historical avant-garde ideas and models of housing most attuned to their time. While some of these products move away from the idea of "functional" furnishings to appear sculptural and more like conceptual objects, they remain catalysts that transform our perception and experience of domestic life. The Cassina iMaestri Collection has brought together these plural languages and embodiments of universally recognized values by revisiting and updating them to adapt them to contemporary needs and tastes.

Since 2008, Cassina has enriched this collection with other emblematic works by the great names of Italian design—Franco Albini, Gio Ponti, Vico Magistretti, Carlo Scarpa, and Marco Zanuso—that the company had produced itself. Thanks to their great purity of expression and their integrity, these creations have also withstood the test of time and become masterpieces of timeless elegance.

6   The Red and Blue chair, photographic proofs, 1973

---

[1] David Antin, *What It Means to Be Avant-Garde*, New York, 1993, p. 6.

[2] Andrea Branzi (ed.), *Il design italiano 1964–1990*, Milan, 1996, p. 30.

[3] In Reyner Banham, *Theory and Design in the First Machine Age*, Cambridge, MA, 1980, p. 151.

[4] Ibid., p. 150.

[5] Filippo Alison, *I Maestri: The Ideology of Reconstruction*, in Giampiero Bosoni (ed.), *Made in Cassina*, Milan, 2008, p. 76.

[6] Ibid., p. 78.

Yesterday Today and Tomorrow

Charles Rennie

Mackintosh

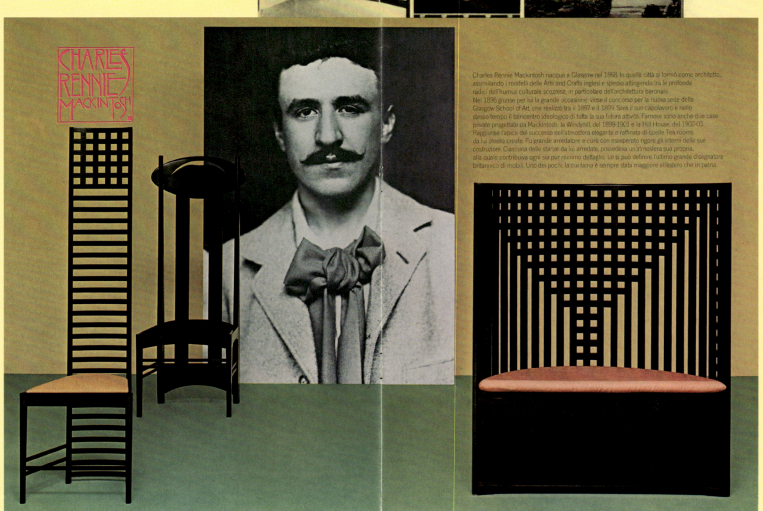

1–2 Excerpts from the Cassina iMaestri catalogue, 1973

Charles Rennie Mackintosh

Charles Rennie Mackintosh was born in Glasgow in 1868. He began his career training as an apprentice at John Hutchinson's agency in Glasgow while attending evening classes at the Glasgow School of Art. With other students (James Herbert MacNair, Frances and Margaret Macdonald), they formed the group "The Four," which made a deep impression on the development of Art Nouveau in Europe, especially following the presentation of their works at the eighth exhibition of the Viennese Secession in 1900. Their style was markedly innovative and absorbed varied influences ranging from Japonisme to the Scottish feudal style. The group's fame spread through Europe from Turin in 1902 to Moscow in 1903.

At the same time, he was working for the firm Honeyman & Keppie, where he was a partner from 1904 until he left in 1913. At the practice, he was in†charge of many projects in Glasgow, such as the design of the offices of *The Herald*, Queen Margaret College Anatomical Department, the Martyrs' Public School, and the famous Glasgow School of Art. He avoided contemporary stylistic movements and his formal vocabulary continued to evolve. In 1896, he met Miss Cranston, an independent businesswoman, the daughter of a tea merchant, who wished to open a number of new tea rooms. From 1897 to 1904, she commissioned him to design and decorate three tea rooms in Glasgow: the Argyle Street Tea Rooms, Ingram Street Tea Rooms, and Willow Tea Rooms, for which he designed custom furniture of geometric shapes. In 1902–03, he built a private villa at Helensburgh, better known as Hill House, where, again, the furniture was taylor made. Thanks to the University of Glasgow, owner of Mackintosh's artistic legacy, and Cassina, all these pieces were reissued in 1973 (Willow 1, Hill House 1, and Argyle). From the beginning of the iMaestri Collection, the company has been involved in defending and promoting Charles Rennie Mackintosh's work through numerous exhibitions: Triennale di Milano (1973), the Museum of Modern Art, MoMA (1975–76), and the Hunterian Art Gallery in Glasgow (1983). Filippo Alison has also written a reference book, *Charles Rennie Mackintosh as a Designer of Chairs*, published by Warehouse Publications.

His artworks are in the collection of the Metropolitan Museum, the Museum of Modern Art – MoMA in New York, and the Victoria & Albert Museum in London.

Yesterday Today and Tomorrow

3   Charles Rennie Mackintosh and Amish R. Davidson Gladsmuir, 1898

4   Back: Margaret Macdonald, Katherine Cameron, Janet Aitken, Agnes Raeburn
Front: Herbert MacNair, Charles Rennie Mackintosh, The Immortals, 1890–93

1868 — Born in Glasgow

1889 — Works for the Honeyman & Keppie firm, Glasgow

1890 — First commission: Redclyffe

1891 — Travels in Italy, France, and Belgium

1893 - 1895 — Offices of *The Herald*, called The Lighthouse, Glasgow

1894 - 1896 — Queen Margaret Medical College

1895 - 1896 — Martyrs' Public School

1897 - 1899 — Glasgow School of Art (1st phase)

1899 — Furnishings of the Argyle Tea Rooms
-
Mod. 302 Argyle
Mod. 310 Argyle set

1899 - 1901 — Villa Windyhill, Kilmacolm
Renovation of 120 Main Street, Glasgow

1900 - 1903 — Renovation and furnishings of Ingram Street Tea Rooms
-
Mod. 305 Ingram Low
Mod. 306 Ingram High

1902 — International Exhibition of Decorative Arts in Turin

Charles Rennie Mackintosh

1902 – 1905
- Mod. 292 Hill House 1
- Mod. 293 Hill House
- Mod. 321 Hill House 2
- Mod. 329 Hous' Hill

1903 – 1904

A partner at Honeyman & Keppie, Glasgow

Willow Tea Rooms
- Mod. 312 Willow 1
- Mod. 326 Willow 2

Interior decoration of Hill House

1904

Scotland Street School

1904 – 1906

1906

Dutch Kitchen for the Argyle Street Tea Rooms

1906 – 1909

Glasgow School of Art (2nd phase)

Oak Room for the Ingram Street Tea Rooms

1907

1911

Cloister Room & Chinese Room for the Ingram Street Tea Rooms

1916 – 1917

Villa Bassett-Lowke Northampton
- Mod. 322 D.S.1
- Mod. 323 D.S.2
- Mod. 324 D.S.3
- Mod. 325 D.S.4
- Mod. 327 D.S.5

Studio house for Harold Squire, Chelsea

1920

1928

Dies in London

227

Yesterday Today and Tomorrow

Argyle set

1897

Mod. 310 — 1982

Scottish entrepreneur Miss Cranston intended to open a series of elegant and refined tea rooms in Glasgow. As a major patron in design, she commissioned Charles R. Mackintosh to design furniture for her new space at 114 Argyle Street. For the different areas decorated by George Walton (Smoking Room, Luncheon Room, and Billiards Room) Mackintosh created furniture specially adapted to the function of each room.

For the central table in the restaurant dining room, Mackintosh designed his first high-backed chair made of solid oak (varnished or stained black) with a horsehair seat. Without any particular function, this high back had a decorative element at the top, made of curved wood pierced by an elliptical pattern.

Argyle
Mod. 302 — 1973

Charles Rennie Mackintosh

1900

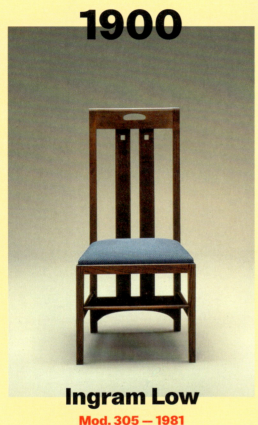

Ingram Low
Mod. 305 — 1981

Ingram High
Mod. 306 — 1981

In 1900 Mackintosh and his wife renovated the White Dining Room of the Ingram Street Tea Rooms. On the upper part of this double-height space they created a striking decorative fresco (158 × 462 cm) of painted plaster and sheets of tin, mother-of-pearl, and glass beads. Below it, vertical silver panels were affixed to the white walls to reflect and diffuse the natural light. This highlighted the solid oak furniture, with its vertical lines recalling the structure of the interior of the building. Cassina has reproduced the model of the chair as well as the high-backed chair of the Ingram Street Tea Rooms.

 Just now, we are working on two large panels for the frieze … Miss Margaret Macdonald is doing one and I am doing the other. We are working them together and that makes the work very pleasant.

Charles Rennie Mackintosh

Yesterday Today and Tomorrow

Hill House

5   Broadsheet poster of The Hill House, Helensburgh

6   Sketch of the Revolving Bookcase for Hous' Hill, Nitshill, Glasgow, 1904
Drawing by Filippo Alison, end of the 1980s

7   Study of a pattern, reproduction of a watercolor painting by C. R. Mackintosh made by Filippo Alison

Hill House 1
Mod. 292 — 1973

Nitshill High - Nitshill Low
Mod. 307 - 308 — 1989

Charles Rennie Mackintosh

1902 - 04

Hous' Hill
Mod. 329 — 1989

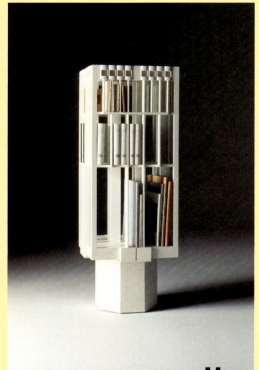

In 1902, Mackintosh received the commission to design the residence of the publisher Walter W. Blackie at Helensburgh on the heights of Glasgow. He worked on the overall project, creating the interiors as well as the custom furniture. Once again, he worked with his wife, Margaret Macdonald, a recognized artist of the Arts & Crafts movement, who produced refined designs for spaces previously disregarded, such as the fireplaces. The decoration is extremely sophisticated and each room was designed for a specific purpose. For the bedroom of the house, Mackintosh designed the Hill House high-back chair made of ebony-stained oak. It was the only black furnishing in a setting finished entirely in shades of cream and white. Installed as a decorative element, it punctuates the space with its slender structure and its high openwork back.

Hill House Set
Mod. 293 — 1985

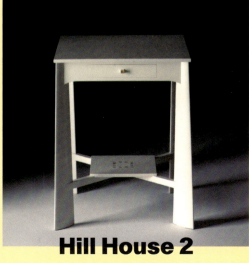

Hill House 2
Mod. 321 — 1989

Yesterday Today and Tomorrow

Willow

8 Drawing for The Dug-Out, Willow Tea Rooms, Glasgow, 1917

9 Cassina carpentry workshop
Meda, Italy

10 Willow Tea Rooms, Glasgow
View from the stairwell between ground and first floor, 1917

Willow 1

Charles Rennie Mackintosh

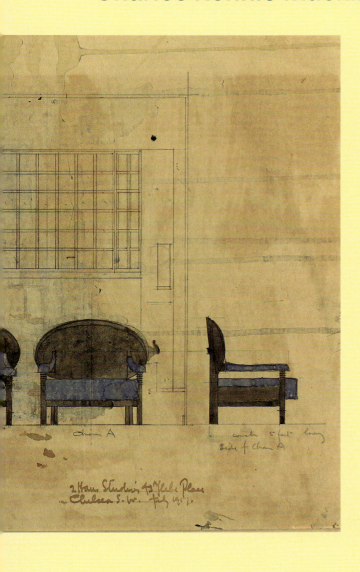

1904

Mod. 312 - 326 — 1973/1974

From 1903 to 1904 Mackintosh worked on the renovation of the Willow Tea Rooms at 215-217 Sauchiehall Street in Glasgow. Miss Cranston gave him a free hand in the whole project, from the facade to the interior design. For the decoration, he once again designed specific furnishings adapted to the spaces and its uses. The Willow easy chair was designed for the ground floor of the Tea Rooms to serve as a seat for the manager. Made of solid ebony-stained oak, its high curved back decorated with a lattice pattern separated the space without obstructing the view. Finally, its large volume emphasized the importance of the person occupying it and her position in relation to the staff.

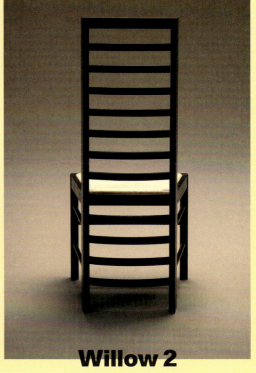

Willow 2

Yesterday Today and Tomorrow

Bassett-Lowke

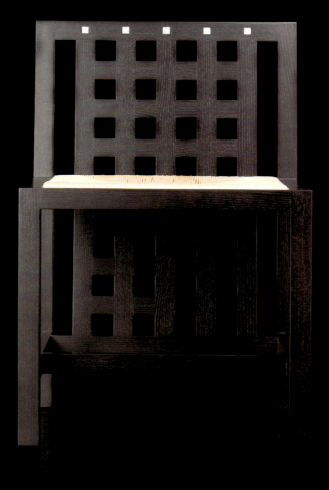

D.S.3
Mod. 324 — 1975

Charles Rennie Mackintosh

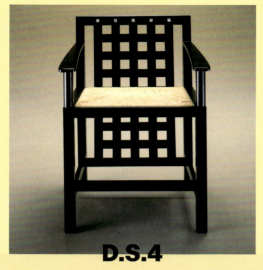

D.S.4
Mod. 325 — 1975

1918

D.S.5
Mod. 327 — 1975

D.S.1
Mod. 322 — 1975

In 1916 Mackintosh decorated Mr W. J. Bassett-Lowke's house at 78 Derngate, Northampton. This furniture has been developed by Cassina on the basis of Mackintosh's watercolors kept at the University of Glasgow.

D.S.2
Mod. 323 — 1975

Yesterday Today and Tomorrow

Le Corbusier

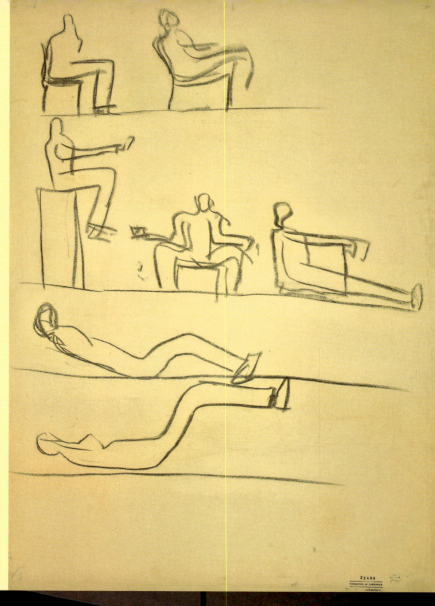

1   Study by Le Corbusier of different sitting positions

2   Interior view of Villa Savoye by Le Corbusier and Pierre Jeanneret
Furniture by Le Corbusier, Pierre Jeanneret, Charlotte Perriand

Le Corbusier

Charles-Édouard Jeanneret was born in 1887 in La Chaux-de-Fonds (Switzerland), the world capital of watchmaking located near Neuchâtel. In 1905 he started working on his first house for the engraver Louis Fallet. After his travels and training with modernist architects such as Peter Behrens and Auguste Perret, in 1912 he built Villa Jeanneret-Perret for his parents, and in 1916 the house of the Swiss watchmaker Anatole Schwob, where he applied his Dom-Ino system made possible by the use of concrete. The following year he moved to Paris and opened his architectural practice.

In 1920, he took the pseudonym Le Corbusier and published articles in the review *L'Esprit Nouveau* on architecture, urbanism, art, and interior design.

In 1922, his cousin Pierre Jeanneret (1896–1967), also an architect, joined him as a partner in his office, which moved two years later to 35 Rue de Sèvres in Paris. Together they undertook the construction of several so-called Purist projects, such as the Maison La Roche-Jeanneret (1923–25), now the headquarters of the Fondation Le Corbusier, the Petite Maison au bord du Lac Léman at Corseaux, and the Maison-Atelier Lipchitz-Mietschaninoff in Boulogne-Billancourt.

For the International Exhibition of Modern Decorative and Industrial Arts in Paris (1925), he built the Pavillon de l'Esprit Nouveau with Pierre Jeanneret, in which he combined architecture and furnishings, including the famous Casiers standard.

In April 1927, he devised "the different ways of sitting which seats had to be adapted to" and, in October, hired Charlotte Perriand to develop the furniture program: "lockers, chairs, and tables," announced in 1925 at the Pavillon de l'Esprit Nouveau.

He published his manifesto, "Five points for a new architecture, a consequence of modern technologies" used since the early 1920s.

• By using pilotis, reinforced concrete pillars, "the house is supported in the air, far above the ground, and the garden passes under the house."

• There is also a garden "on the house, on the roof," made possible by the use of reinforced concrete. The garden roofs should be planted with flowers, shrubs, trees, and grass.

• The open-plan layout inside frees the partitions from their structural function, since the floors now rest on the pilotis.

• The facade becomes an independent envelope.

• The strip windows stretch from end to end of the building, so letting in light and offering views of the landscape.

An icon of this modernist architecture, Villa Savoye (1929) is the archetype of the minimum housing presented at the CIAM congress.

The following year, with Pierre Jeanneret, Le Corbusier built the Pavillon Suisse of the Cité Internationale Universitaire de Paris and published the book *Précisions*. Together with Pierre Jeanneret and Charlotte Perriand, he took part in the first exhibition of the Union des Artistes Modernes (UAM) at the Pavillon de Marsan, Musée des Arts Décoratifs de Paris.

After the Palais du Peuple and the Asile Flottant, Le Corbusier built the Cité de Refuge in Paris (1933) for the Salvation Army. This was a shelter for the homeless with three hundred places, in which he continued his research into social housing. For the Universal Exhibition in Brussels in 1935, Le Corbusier, Pierre Jeanneret, and Charlotte Perriand collaborated with other members of the UAM and the CIAM groups, exhibiting together La Maison du jeune homme, specially designed for "an intellectual athlete."

Yesterday Today and Tomorrow

His last completed work in the UAM was a "cabine sanitaire" (sanitary cubicle) designed with Charlotte Perriand and Pierre Jeanneret. It was exhibited in 1937 at the UAM Pavilion in the International Exhibition of Arts and Technologies in Modern Life in 1937. In the same year, he published *When the Cathedrals Were White*, a book presenting his impressions of travel and analyzing American life and architecture during a year spent in North America.

After World War II, he built Curutchet House (La Plata, Argentina) in 1949 as well as various religious buildings, including the Chapelle Notre-Dame-du-Haut at Ronchamp (1950–55) and the Convent Sainte-Marie de La Tourette (1960). He had regularly visited Roquebrune-Cap-Martin since the late 1930s and stayed at Villa E-1027 built by Eileen Gray and Jean Badovici. In 1949 he decided to build a shed and workshop-house based on the Modulor on a plot of land adjacent to the "L'Étoile de mer," a café owned by his friend Thomas Rebutato.

Built in 1952, this "château" measuring 3.66 × 3.66 m would become his only vacation home. At the same time, he built several large residential buildings in exposed concrete resting on pilotis called Unité d'habitation in Marseille (1952), Nantes-Rezé (1955), Briey (1956), Berlin Charlottenburg (1957), and Firminy (1962).

Among his most emblematic works are: Villa Stein (1926), Villa Savoye in Poissy (1929) with Pierre Jeanneret, the Unité d'habitation in Marseille (1947–52), the Chapelle Notre-Dame-du-Haut in Ronchamp (1950–55), the Cabanon in Roquebrune-Cap-Martin (1952), the city of Chandigarh, the capital of Punjab, built after the independence of India (1950–1962), the convent of Sainte-Marie de La Tourette (1957–60), the ZHLC Exhibition Pavilion (Zurich, Switzerland 1960–67), and the Carpenter Center for the Visual Arts at Harvard University, Cambridge, in the US (1961–63).

Le Corbusier died on August 27, 1965, and was buried in the cemetery of Roquebrune-Cap-Martin with his wife Yvonne. The Le Corbusier Foundation, recognized as a public utility, was founded in 1968.

Le Corbusier's work is regularly the subject of major exhibitions around the world. A transnational series of seventeen works or sites designed by Le Corbusier has been inscribed on the World Heritage List since 2016.

3 Interior of the Maison La Roche, 1923–25

Le Corbusier

4   Le Corbusier in his apartment in Paris sitting on the sofa; the sofa is covered with a hand woven fabric

5   The rooftop terrace of the Unité d'habitation in Marseille with furniture by Le Corbusier, Pierre Jeanneret, Charlotte Perriand

Yesterday Today and Tomorrow

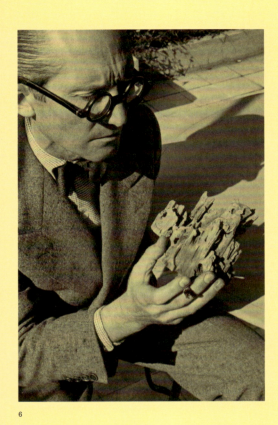

6

1887	Born in La Chaux-de-Fonds (Switzerland)	**1904**	Enters the higher course of decoration directed by Charles L'Eplattenier
1905 - 1911	Villa Fallet, Villa Jaquemet, and Villa Stotzer in La Chaux-de-Fonds and designs their furnishings	**1912**	Villa Jeanneret-Perret in La Chaux-de-Fonds and Villa Favre-Jacot at Le Locle
1920	Founds the review *L'Esprit Nouveau* with Paul Dermée and Amédée Ozenfant	**1922 - 1924**	Villa Besnus, Vaucresson (France), and the Maison Ozenfant studio-home, Paris
1923 - 1924	Publishes *Vers une architecture* and then *L'Art décoratif d'aujourd'hui*	**1923 - 1925**	Maison La Roche–Jeanneret in Paris Designs with Pierre Jeanneret of metal-framed tables for homes
1924 - 1926	After the project of Lège, he builds the Quartiers Modernes Frugès, Pessac (France)	**1925**	**Pavillon de l'Esprit Nouveau with Pierre Jeanneret** — **Designs the Casiers standard**
1927	Theorizes the five points of modern architecture		Devises the "new ways of sitting"
1928	Founds the CIAM (International Congresses of Modern Architecture)	**1929**	**Development and presentation at the Salon d'Automne of furniture produced with Pierre Jeanneret and Charlotte Perriand**

6 Le Corbusier
7 Le Modulor by Le Corbusier

Le Corbusier

1929 — Villa Savoye and the gardener's lodge, Poissy (France)

1930 - 1934 — Immeuble Clarté, Geneva (Switzerland) and Immeuble Molitor on Rue Nungesser-et-Coli, Paris

1934 — 5 Canapé, Appartement Le Corbusier

1943 - 1946 — Theorizes Le Modulor, a scale of proportions based on the human body
- Publication of the *Athens Charter* (1943)

1950 - 1962 — Designs the city of Chandigarh (India)

1951 - 1957 — Villa Shodhan, Villa Sarabhai, the Mill Owners' Association Building, and the Museum, in Ahmedabad (India)

1952 — Cabanon, Roquebrune-Cap-Martin (France), for which he designs murals and furnishings, including the LC14 stool

Inauguration of the Unité d'habitation in Marseille

Unités d'habitation in Briey, Firminy, Berlin and Nantes-Rezé
-
Desk LC16
Stool LC14

1957 — Unités de Camping, Roquebrune-Cap-Martin and design of the coat rack in colored wood, LC17

Maison du Brésil, Cité Internationale Universitaire de Paris, for which he designs the bedroom furniture with Charlotte Perriand

1958 — Designs the LC15 meeting table for his workshop

Dies at Roquebrune-Cap-Martin

1965 — First edition of the metal furniture by Cassina

2006 — Replica of the Cabanon exhibited at the Triennale di Milano

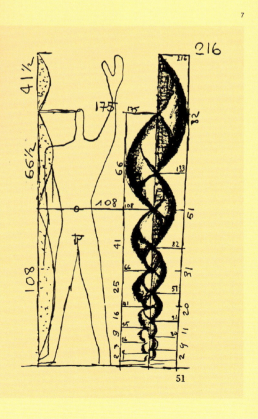

243

Yesterday Today and Tomorrow

Cabanon

8 Interior of the Cabanon by Le Corbusier, 1952

9 Replica of the Cabanon of Le Corbusier in Roquebrune-Cap-Martin Cassina, 2006

Le Corbusier

10 Le Corbusier in the Cabanon

11 Replica of the interior of the Cabanon, MoMA New York, 2013

1952

> **My cabin is nice and my hut installed last summer fifteen meters away is a perfect refuge.**
>
> Le Corbusier

"Today, architecture is concerned with the home, with ordinary, everyday housing for normal, everyday people. It is no longer preoccupied with palaces. This is a sign of the times.

On 30 December 1951, on the corner of a table in a small café on the Côte d'Azur, as a present for my wife on her birthday, I sketched the project for a 'hut' that I built the following year on top of a rock beaten by the waves. This project was done in three-quarters of an hour."

This iconic building is the culmination of Le Corbusier's research into the minimum living cell and the application of his theoretical work on the Modulor. In his *Œuvres complètes*, Le Corbusier describes his Cabanon as, "a room measuring 366 × 366 cm and 226 cm high (...). Prefabricated in Ajaccio (Corsica) and assembled mechanically, the exterior and roof are independent of the problem posed here. The functioning of this building exceeded all expectations."

Le Corbusier specified the list of the furnishings of the Cabanon during a site visit in June 1952. The interior walls were to be made of plywood panels, so marking the difference from the facade of pine logs. The floor, of wooden boards, was to be painted yellow and the ceilings, in sheets of hardboard, would be painted white, green, and ocher. The interior is simple but functional. Three windows only and an integrated ventilation system which was then repeated in Chandigarh. As a seat, Le Corbusier used a solid wooden stool pierced with a hole to serve as a handle on each of its sides. It could be used vertically or horizontally as needed. Its dovetail assembly gives its edges an aesthetic quality. Cassina reissued this model in solid chestnut as LC14.

In 2006, Cassina, in collaboration with the Fondation Le Corbusier and the Triennale di Milano, decided to present a faithful reconstruction of the hut in the gardens of the museum. The exhibition then traveled to the Royal Institute of British Architects (RIBA) in 2009. In 2013, it was presented at the exhibition *Le Corbusier: An Atlas of Modern Landscapes* at the MoMA in New York.

A total work of art, the Cabanon, with its murals on one wall and two wooden shutters, is the epitome of Le Corbusier's architectural and artistic research. It was listed as a Historic Monument in 1996, labeled a Heritage of the Twentieth Century, and registered as a World Heritage Site in 2016.

Yesterday Today and Tomorrow

1952

LC14 Tabouret, Nantes-Rezé 1952 – 57
2010

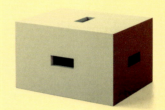

12 Interiors of the Maison Radieuse, Unité d'habitation, Nantes-Rezé

LC16 Table de travail avec rayonnages, Unité d'habitation, Nantes-Rezé 1957
2018

The Maison Radieuse de Rezé near Nantes in France is the second Unité d'habitation built by Le Corbusier after the one in Marseille. This imposing building 52 m high, 108 m long, and 20 m wide has nearly 300 "ascending" or "descending" duplex dwellings that testify to his research into collective housing.

"This Unité d'habitation benefited from the experience gained in Marseille. Similar in its principles, it is different in some of its modes of construction and innovations. Its artificial floor comprised bays of four posts instead of two. This may involve a loss of plasticity or elegance, but it does not entail any loss of quality.

The dimensions, shape, and proportion of the typical loggia that made the Unité on Boulevard Michelet so successful were carefully preserved. But the glass pane was greatly improved, becoming the fourth wall of the room. Nantes-Rezé is the consecration of Marseille, since it stemmed from the spontaneous request by the future occupants, who came together animated by magnificent people of faith and courage." (Le Corbusier). Under the name LC16, Cassina has reissued a small oak desk designed for the children's rooms in the Unité d'habitation. It consists of a writing desk with a single central foot attached to a shelf unit.

Le Corbusier

1956 – 57

LC17 Portemanteau, Unités de Camping, Roquebrune-Cap-Martin 1957
2010

 My furniture is perfect. My two seats are two empty whisky crates scavenged from the sea.

Le Corbusier

LC15 Table de conférence, Atelier Le Corbusier, Paris 1958
2010

Between 1956 and 1957, in exchange for the plot of land on which he built his Cabanon, Le Corbusier designed five camping units arranged facing the sea for Thomas Rebutato (the owner of the restaurant "L'Étoile de mer-Chez Robert" in Roquebrune-Cap-Martin). Their wooden frame rests on reinforced concrete pilotis, and the facade, made of wooden cladding, adopts a very marked polychromy contrasting with Eileen Gray's villa E-1027 built just below.

The five units, or "cells," each measuring 8 sq m, demonstrate Le Corbusier's research into modular and economical leisure accommodation. For the interior, he used some of the features devised for the Cabanon, such as the walls lined with plywood, the sanitary column consisting of a washbasin and cupboards, and the principle of painted hardboard panels for the ceiling.

The coat rack in the entrance is reissued by Cassina as LC17. Its solid oak knobs repeat and interpret the original coloring.

This meeting-room table was designed in 1958 by Le Corbusier for his studio at 35 Rue de Sèvres in Paris. Its originality lies in the combination of geometric forms and opposing materials: a round oak top rests on a cube-shaped structure in black, gray, and green varnished steel. It was edited by Cassina in 2010 in oak or walnut.

Yesterday Today and Tomorrow

Chambre d'étudiant Maison du Brésil

Le Corbusier / Charlotte Perriand

1957
2018

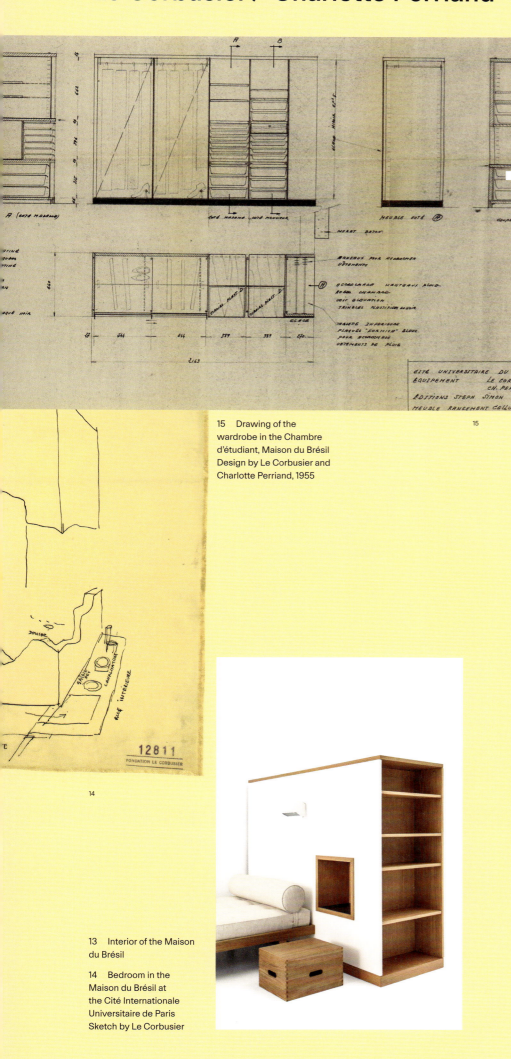

15 Drawing of the wardrobe in the Chambre d'étudiant, Maison du Brésil Design by Le Corbusier and Charlotte Perriand, 1955

13 Interior of the Maison du Brésil

14 Bedroom in the Maison du Brésil at the Cité Internationale Universitaire de Paris Sketch by Le Corbusier

The Maison du Brésil is a five-story, reinforced concrete building located in the Parc de la Cité Internationale Universitaire de Paris. Originally entrusted to the Brazilian architect Lúcio Costa, the Brazilian government's commission was finally built by Le Corbusier, who had already designed the nearby Fondation Suisse. Lúcio Costa advised Charlotte Perriand on the interior design of the student rooms.

The compact space of 18 sq m contained a bed with a wooden frame and a square table, both designed by Charlotte Perriand. The wardrobe dividing bedroom from bathroom, designed by Le Corbusier and Charlotte Perriand, was painted on one side, on the other it had gray PVC doors and colored plastic drawers. The walls housed a piece of furniture consisting of a shelf and a slate blackboard designed by Le Corbusier and Charlotte Perriand.

A faithful reconstruction of the furniture of the Maison du Brésil, as designed by Le Corbusier and Charlotte Perriand in 1959, was presented by Cassina in 2018. The stool LC14 Tabouret Maison du Brésil, Paris 1959, by Le Corbusier, was added to the collection in 2010.

Yesterday Today and Tomorrow

Erik Gunnar

Asplund

1 Stockholm Public Library, 1920–28

2 Stockholm Public Library Axonometry, 1929

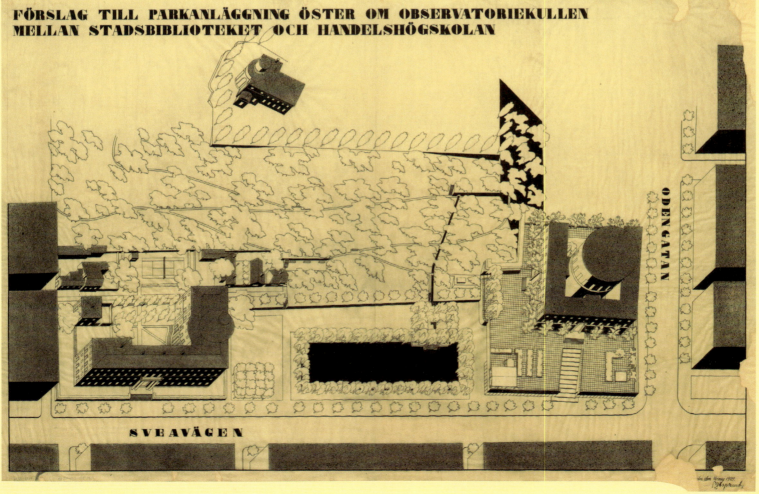

Erik Gunnar Asplund

He was a Swedish architect and designer, active in Sweden in the first half of the twentieth century. His refined oeuvre was influenced by a number of aesthetic currents throughout his prolific career. His early work was in a historical and realist style, in the current of National Romanticism, inspired by the past, simple but original. Then it reflected a neo-classical influence, after his tour of Italy and Greece, as shown by the emblematic achievements of the Karl-Johan School, Villa Snellman, and the Skandia cinemas. Finally, he adopted a more contemporary and functionalist style in the current vein of Modern architecture as in the work of Le Corbusier and Walter Gropius, with the Bredenberg Department Store in Stockholm and the Gothenburg Courthouse, characterized by classic austerity and devoid of ornamentation.

His most important works were the Gothenburg Courthouse (1913–37), the Stockholm Municipal Library (1928), and the Stockholm South Cemetery at Enskede (1915–1940).

In the early 1980s, Cassina began researching furniture by Erik G. Asplund. The choice fell on the model of an armchair made for the Swedish pavilion of the International Exhibition of Decorative Arts in Paris (1925), as well as a chair designed for the Gothenburg Law Courts (1937). Filippo Alison made the first sketches, attempting to get as close as possible to Asplund's original intentions.

These two models of furniture are a perfect example of the challenges inherent in Cassina's reconstruction and reissue program. They also demonstrate the extensive historical and technical research needed to manufacture two furnishings on the basis of different sources.

Yesterday Today and Tomorrow

3 Portrait, undated

4 Original drawing of the Göteborg chair

1885	Born in Stockholm	**1905 - 1909**	Studies at the Royal Polytechnic School in Stockholm
1913	Winner of the competition for the extension to Gothenburg Courthouse		
1913 - 1914	Grand Tour in Italy and Greece		
1915	Wins the competition for Stockholm South Cemetery, with Sigurd Lewerentz		Wins the competition for the Karl-Johan School in Gothenburg
1917	Editor-in-chief of the journal *Architektur*	**1917 - 1918**	Villa Snellman
1921	Solvesborg Courthouse		
1923	Skandia Cinema, Stockholm	**1925**	**Armchair for the International Exhibition of Decorative Arts, Paris - Mod. 500 Senna**

254

Erik Gunnar Asplund

1928 — Stockholm Public Library

1930 — Chief Architect of the Stockholm Exhibition

1931 — Professor at the Stockholm Polytechnic

1934 – 1937 — Chair for the Gothenburg Courthouse - Mod. 501 Göteborg 1 / Mod. 502 Göteborg 2

1935 — Bredenberg Department Store, Stockholm

1937 — Gothenburg Courthouse

1940 — Skövde Crematorium, Enskede Cemetery, Stockholm / Dies in Stockholm

1978 — Exhibition *The Architecture of Gunnar Asplund*, MoMa, New York

1980 — Retrospective exhibition at the Stockholm Museum of Architecture

1989 — Exhibition *Erik Gunnar Asplund, Architecte et designer suédois*, Centre de Création Industrielle, Paris

Yesterday Today and Tomorrow

1925

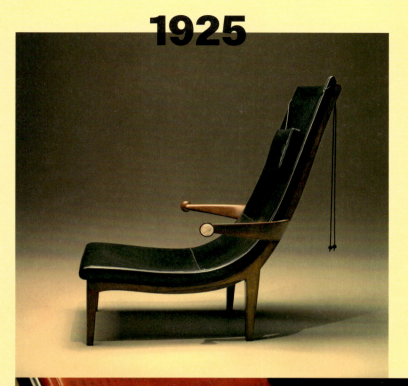

Senna
Mod. 500 — 1983

From April 28 to November 30, 1925, the International Exhibition of Decorative Arts was held in Paris. Between the Place de la Concorde, the Grand Palais, and the Esplanade des Invalides, each country expressed its innovations with the construction of temporary pavilions presenting the most emblematic achievements of modern decorative art. It featured two contrasting architectural currents. The dominant Art Deco style and the modernist current (also known as the international avant-garde). Mallet-Stevens designed the Tourism Pavilion, Josef Hoffmann the Austrian Pavilion, Victor Horta the Belgian Pavilion, Le Corbusier his manifesto Pavillon de l'Esprit Nouveau, and the Constructivist architect Konstantin Melnikov the Russian Pavilion.

Asplund designed the Swedish pavilion in a simple and geometric architecture set off by a facade adorned with columns inspired by the ancient Ionic style. He also worked on the interior, designing a library furnished with a desk, two chairs, a carpet, and an armchair. The armchair was made by the craftsman David Blomberg. It had a mahogany frame and leather upholstery covered with decorative star motifs. The armrests were slightly curved and the tips adorned with classic-style ivory medallions, to which were affixed the faces of a man and a woman. The model produced by Cassina faithfully reproduces the features of the original model now in the Nordiska Museet in Stockholm. The prototyping was overseen by Filippo Alison and Hans Asplund, the architect's son, in the early 1980s.

5   Gothenburg Town Hall
Original drawing by Erik
G. Asplund

Erik Gunnar Asplund

1934 – 37

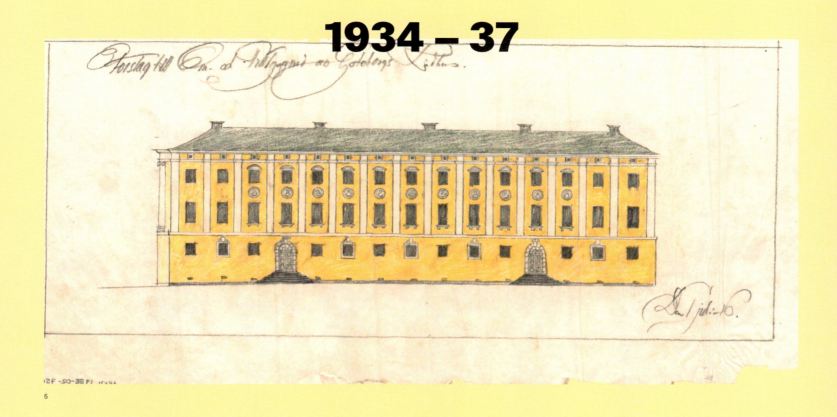

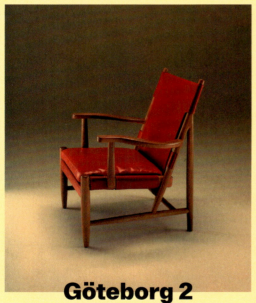

Göteborg 2
Mod. 502 — 1983

To complete the spaces hosting the public, Asplund designed a visitors' chair with classic and harmonious lines. The model was edited by Cassina in 1983 with a natural ash frame and a leather back and seat. The cushion is made of polyurethane foam and polyester padding.

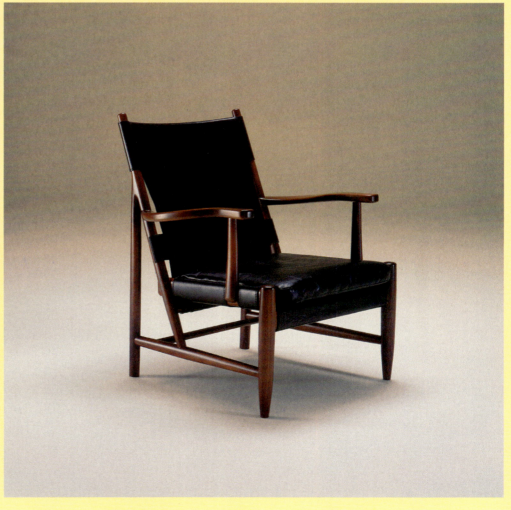

Yesterday Today and Tomorrow

Göteborg 1

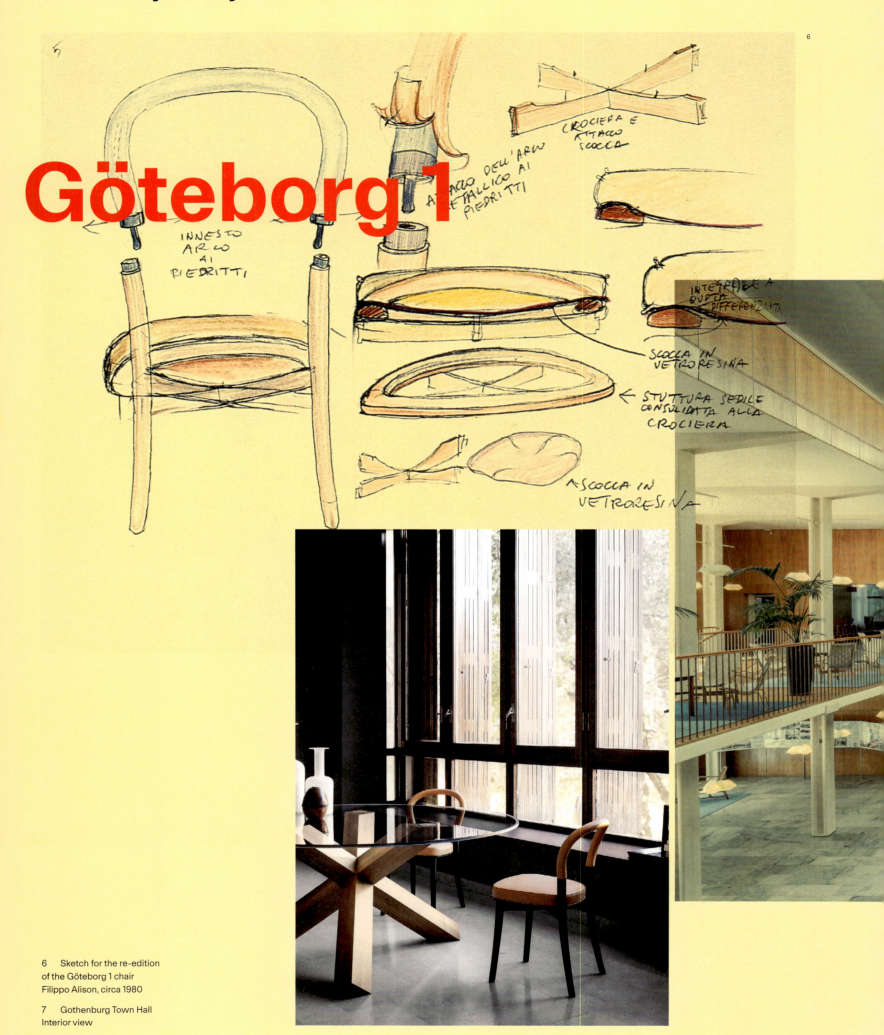

6   Sketch for the re-edition of the Göteborg 1 chair
Filippo Alison, circa 1980

7   Gothenburg Town Hall
Interior view

Erik Gunnar Asplund

1934 - 37

Mod. 501 — 1983

The extension to Gothenburg Town Hall reveals the influence of Le Corbusier's modernist precepts on Asplund's work. He used classical proportions to stress the structure of the building and designed an open plan interior. In the great hall connecting the courtyard of the old building to the extension, Asplund left the structural elements visible and painted the pillars white to stress their function. An impressive glass wall sheds natural light that is reflected on the interior walls, lined with wooden paneling with warm tones. As in all his projects, Asplund designed bespoke furniture for the Gothenburg Town Hall. The 501 model is made of solid ash. Its curved and slightly domed profile pays tribute to the iconic Thonet No. 14 chair, one of the first examples of a chair manufactured on an industrial scale.

Yesterday Today and Tomorrow

Giacomo

Balla

1   Casa Balla, Rome
Interior view

Giacomo Balla

Giacomo Balla was an Italian painter and sculptor born in Turin in 1871. The only son of Giovanni and Lucia Giannotti, he displayed a particular interest in art and attended a three-year course at the Accademia Albertina, where he studied painting, photography, and drawing. Self-taught, he left Turin in 1895 to settle in Rome, where he worked for the rest of his life.

In 1901 in Rome he met Umberto Boccioni and Gino Severini, and painted some of his masterpieces, such as *Streetlight*, now in the MoMA. In 1904, he married Elisa Marcucci, and his first daughter, Luce, was born in the same year. In 1910 he joined the Futurist movement, founded in Italy by Umberto Boccioni and theorized by Marinetti. This avant-garde literary and aesthetic movement is well known for its rejection of the principles of classicism, and its fascination with modernity and speed. "We declare that the splendor of the world has been enriched by a new beauty: the beauty of speed. A racing car with its hood adorned with great pipes like snakes with explosive breath … a roaring car that seems to be racing on the machine-gun, is more beautiful than the Victory of Samothrace." (Filippo Tommaso Marinetti, *Futurist Manifesto*). Futurism was a new conception of the world, embracing all artistic fields.

Balla, who distanced himself from figurative art from 1913 on, began to design sets for films and the theater, decorative objects, tableware, and furnishings. From 1915, his work continued to evolve and brought together his favorite themes, such as light, movement, energy, and speed in a strongly defined creative vocabulary.

In 1929, Balla moved to 39b Via Oslavia, where he conceived the premises as a total work of art. In this experimental laboratory, both home and workshop, Balla, his wife Elisa Marcucci, and their two daughters Luce and Elica, decorated a living space as an artwork in three dimensions. As with his paintings, Balla allows us to evolve in a universe filled with light, deconstructed forms, and colors, in keeping with the dogmas of the Futurist movement.

"In reality, everything is moving, everything is changing quickly. Given the persistence of the image on the retina, moving objects multiply, are deformed, continuing as vibrations precipitated into the space they traverse. Thus a running horse has not four legs but twenty, and their movements are triangular." (*Manifesto of Futurist Painting*, 1910, signed by Giacomo Balla, Umberto Boccioni, Carlo Carrà, Luigi Russolo, and Gino Severini).

Yesterday Today and Tomorrow

2

	Born in Turin		Moves to Rome
1871		**1895**	
	The Street Light – Study of Light - Filippo Tommaso Marinetti's *Futurist Manifesto*		Exhibition at the Salon d'Automne in Paris
1909			
	Joins the Futurist movement - Publishes the *Manifesto of Futurist Painters*	Publishes the *Technical Manifesto of Futurist Painting*	
1910			
	Dynamism of a Dog on a Leash		Works on compositions of collages and paintings
1912		**1913**	
		Exhibition of sculptures at the Galleria Sprovieri entitled *Prima esposizione libera futurista*	Signs the *Manifesto for the Futurist Reconstruction of the Universe*
1914			
	Designs furnishings and tableware		**Paravento Balla**
1916		**1917**	
	The Hands of the Italian People		
1925			

2 Giacomo Balla

264

Giacomo Balla

1929 — Casa Balla, Rome, for which he also designs all the furnishings and carpets

1935 — Made a member of the Accademia di San Luca in Rome

1937 — Quits Futurism in a letter published in the Italian newspaper *Perseo*

1948 — Rejoins Futurism

1949 — Exhibits at MoMA, New York

1955 — Takes part in the 1st Documenta in Kassel

1958 — Dies in Rome

1972 — Retrospective at the Galleria Nazionale d'Arte Moderna, Rome, and the Musée d'Art Moderne de la Ville de Paris

1976 — Exhibition *Giacomo Balla*, Museo Civico di Castelvecchio, Verona

2007 — Furniture exhibited at *Camera con Vista, Arte e Interni in Italia, 1900–2000*, Palazzo Reale, Milan

2008 — Exhibition *Balla. La modernità futurista*, Palazzo Reale, Milan

His best-known works are:

Streetlight, 1909
oil on canvas
Museum of Modern Art, MoMA, New York

Dynamism of a Dog on a Leash, 1912
oil on canvas
Albright-Knox Art Gallery, Buffalo, New York

Girl Running on a Balcony, 1912
oil on canvas
Museo del Novecento, Milan

Plastic Construction of Noise and Speed, 1915
steel and aluminum sculpture
Hirshhorn Museum and Sculpture Garden, Smithsonian Institution, Washington, DC

Boccioni's Fist, 1916–17
painted brass sculpture
Hirshhorn Museum and Sculpture Garden, Smithsonian Institution, Washington, DC

Iridescent Interpenetration - Eucalyptus, 1914
oil on canvas
Former Yves Saint Laurent and Pierre Bergé Collection

Yesterday Today and Tomorrow

Paravento Balla

Giacomo Balla

1917

Mod. 330 — 2020

The original design for the screen he called the *Paravento Balla* dates from 1917. It was first published in 1968 by Maurizio Fagiolo dell'Arco in his book *Balla: Ricostruzione Futurista dell'Universo*. Drawn in pencil and gouache on paper, it is stamped with the *Pugno di Boccioni* ("Boccioni's Fist"), which Balla sometimes used to sign his works instead of his classic signature *Futurballa*. The drawing also contains detailed information on the use of colors and their combinations. "The dark green must be much more beautiful and brighter, the light green (…) a vivid lemon yellow and orange. It could be made in other color combinations.."

This screen consists of three plywood panels of different heights and widths, joined by hinges in satin brass, in keeping with the instructions left on Balla's original drawing. They enable the panels to be positioned as desired and so create a setting to suit its user. The pattern, screen-printed on both sides, allowed the artist to free himself from the usual dimensions of painting and push its limits in two dimensions. Balla filled the space with a varied and contrasting palette of orange, green, and yellow. Here he took the principle of deconstruction to an extreme, representing speed and movement in their most perfect abstraction.

We find these distinctive qualities, dear to the Futurists, on a very beautiful copy of a screen preserved at the Kröller-Müller Museum: *Screen with Speedline* (1916–17). On it he created an extreme deconstruction of the movement and speed of a car in a perfectly abstract composition with a dynamic form. On another screen, the artist's personal copy, entitled *Speedline, Vortex*, we find broad flat colors applied to both sides of the articulated wooden panels. In 1937, he wrote a letter to the Italian newspaper *Perseo* in which he stated that he was moving away from the Futurist movement, which he eventually rejoined in 1948. In 1955, he took part in the first Documenta at Kassel in Germany. Giacomo Balla died in 1958 in Rome.

The dark green must be much more beautiful and brighter, the light green (…) a vivid lemon yellow and orange. It could be made in other color combinations.

Giacomo Balla

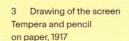

3   Drawing of the screen
Tempera and pencil
on paper, 1917

Yesterday Today and Tomorrow

Photos by
SARAH VAN RIJ &
DAVID VAN DER LEEUW

Sarah van Rij & David van der Leeuw compose veritable dreamlike paintings, in which they invite viewers to enter and create their own scenarios. In a timeless atmosphere, the piece by the Master blends into the colorful composition that surrounds it, so perfectly emphasizing the notion of elegance. Their goal was mainly transforming the pieces almost into surrealistic objects to enhance the artistry of these furnishings.

Anticipating Change

Cassina,
Facing Social
Changes

Anticipating Change

Past into Future

JANE WITHERS
Curator and design consultant

When Gio Ponti unveiled the 699 chair, better known as Superleggera ("beyond light"), in 1957 the skeletal frame brought modernity to an artisanal furniture tradition. Inspired by the nineteenth-century wooden chairs with woven Indian cane seats traditionally made in the village of Chiavari, in Liguria, Ponti merged aesthetic and functional requirements by paring away any unnecessary material to reveal the chair's essential structure—the legs have a triangular section with a maximum diameter of 18 mm. The result was a chair so light that it could be lifted by a child using just one finger—the theme of Cassina's early photographic campaign. A refinement of Gio Ponti's earlier Leggera chair, the name Superleggera references automobile construction technology designed to reduce the weight of racing cars and patented by Carrozzeria Touring in 1936, and used by Ferrari, Alfa Romeo, and Maserati, among others.

Cassina recently returned to Formula One workshops to find the technology to produce an outdoor version of the Leggera. Inspired by a sketch for a metal chair discovered in Ponti's sketchbooks, the product development challenge was to design an outdoor model that maintains the chair's slender

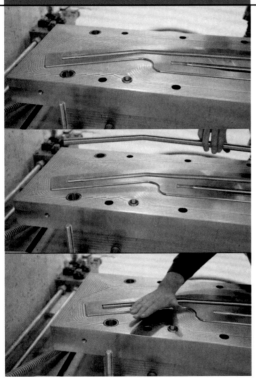

1   The hydroforming technique: phase of the insertion into the mold of the leg tube of a Leggera Outdoor chair

profile and lightness but also addresses durability. The tubular stainless-steel components are manufactured using a hydroforming technique developed to make parts for racing cars, in which hydro pressure is used to expand the tubes into the mold, forming elements with exceptionally thin 8 mm walls. The company has also produced a limited-edition version in collaboration with streetwear brand One Block Down that is left in its raw state, visible welding marks revealing the manufacturing process and giving each chair its own distinct flame patterning. Turn it upside down and you see the screws that allow it to be disassembled and the components repaired, replaced, or recycled. Arguably cultivating a new aesthetic that celebrates the imperfect and highlights process is part of the disruptive actions that are needed as we rethink materials and manufacturing in the transition to more sustainable design. The exhibition *Echoes* staged for the Salone del Mobile 2023, to mark fifty years of the Cassina iMaestri Collection, offers a glimpse into the remarkable archive collection that will form the basis of Cassina's design museum in the years to come. As well as giving us a direct connection to the minds of twentieth-century design pioneers and their use of furniture as a test bed for formal and technological experimentation, it also reveals some of the challenges involved in keeping these classics alive. It is a delicate balance between capturing the intentions of the original designers and meeting twenty-first-century expectations of performance, materials, and technology.

Anticipating Change

Living Archive

It might seem perverse to look to designs from more than half a century or more ago, but if we are to transition to circularity, understanding what makes things last is fundamental. Perhaps the first surprise is that the life stories of these design "classics" are far from static. When Cassina launched iMaestri in the 1970s, the idea was to make these iconic designs by some of the great architects of Modernism available to new audiences via industrial production. This meant not only rethinking how they were made but also initiating what has turned out to be a long philosophical inquiry into our understanding of "reproduction" and "authenticity." Rather like a contemporary staging of *A Streetcar Named Desire*, or a twenty-first-century remake of *The Third Man*, reproducing an important early-twentieth-century design requires analyzing the original design intent and how to communicate this to contemporary audiences as well as addressing contemporary challenges such as sustainability. Each generation brings its own interpretation to the "classics" that reflects not just the manufacturing technologies of the day but also shifting cultural and societal values.

In their day, these Maestri were, of course, radicals who pushed technological, cultural, and social boundaries. Reimagining not just the form and function of furniture but how it was made and what it is made of. "[These are] designers who have worked in their own time with great naturalness and spontaneity, without ever being afraid to experiment, to force the limits of dwelling and to open windows on the future," observes Patricia Urquiola in a recent interview.[1] "Their architecture and design objects can be seen as catalysts for the development and progression of different evolutionary paths. (…) They made objects that resist the filter of time, influencing generations of designers." Arguably, though, we shouldn't just focus on what they did back then but also speculate on what they might do today. In a recent interview with the *Financial Times*, Charlotte Perriand's daughter Pernette Perriand-Barsac says: "I traveled cheek-to-cheek with my mother over many years, so I know exactly what was in her mind." "For Charlotte it was possible to work with every material. She was known for tubular metal but called Madam wood," says Perriand-Barsac in references to the designer's famously chunky wooden pieces for Les Arcs. "By the end of her life she started working with carbon, but this was very expensive. My wish is to one day find a good project so we can use carbon with Cassina. Charlotte would be thrilled…"[2]

In the 1960s, Cassina was one of the first companies to reissue modern classics. The company acquired rights to designs by Le Corbusier, Pierre Jeanneret, Charlotte Perriand in 1964, including the Chaise longue model that it relaunched the following year. The 1960s and 1970s were turbulent decades, and design reflected the political and social mood of upheaval, generating a rash of invention in new forms and materials. In 1972, MoMA's *Italy: The New Domestic Landscape* captured the revolutionary spirit of the time in a now-legendary exhibition that presented Italy as a dominant force in contemporary design and brought a critical lens to the current tasks of design. Exhibits, including Bellini's Kar-a-sutra as well as Joe Colombo's Total Furnishing Unit, explored the possibilities for a radically new furniture and domestic landscape. In 1973 Cassina launched the AeO chair, by Paolo Deganello, a member of Archizoom—a gawky reinterpretation of an armchair using experimental materials and designed for self-assembly. Surprisingly, in that same year Cassina also launched the iMaestri Collection, with reissued pieces by Gerrit Thomas Rietveld and Charles Rennie Mackintosh. I find it fascinating that a firm at the forefront of new industrial processes, material research, and molding polyurethane into forms envisioned by radical designers like Archizoom Associati were also committed to looking to the past, to recreating the work of equally radical but now historic designers. The skills of Meda's craftsmen were tested on remaking remarkable early-twentieth-century pieces like Rietveld's Red and Blue chair and Mackintosh's throne-like chairs for the Willow Tea Rooms and Hill House. But arguably it is this hybrid character, the combination of meticulous craftsmanship and

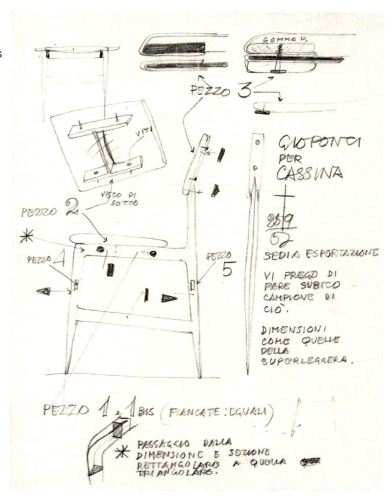

2

cutting-edge technological skills, respect for design's history, and pursuit of the contemporary that still defines Cassina. According to Patricia Urquiola: "The fact that the company has had an articulated and structured vision toward iMaestri, opening up a dialogue with the contemporaries, for over fifty years, is an example of increasing durability, one of the main elements of sustainability."

Rietveld's Zig Zag is a good example of the re-editioning process. The ambitious cantilever construction—one of the earliest examples of a cantilevered chair made from a single material, wood—was one of the first pieces "reinterpreted" by Cassina for the iMaestri Collection in 1973. When Rietveld first produced it in 1934 the rhythmic shape, formal reduction, and implausible structure captured the spirit of De Stijl's bold abstraction. But of course, this daring simplicity hides structural

2 Sketch of a chair for export, Gio Ponti, 1957

3 Details of the dovetail joints of the Zig Zag chair designed by Gerrit Thomas Rietveld. Original version with visible screws and version reissued by Cassina

Jane Withers

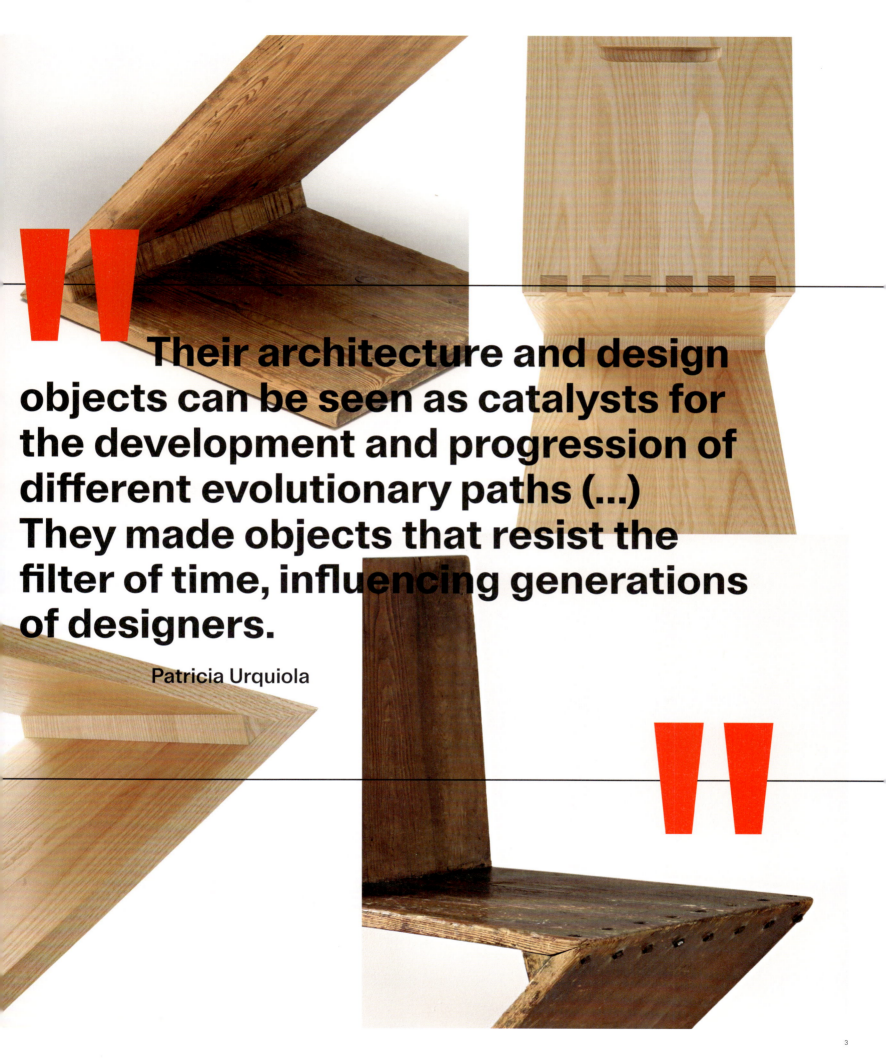

"Their architecture and design objects can be seen as catalysts for the development and progression of different evolutionary paths (...) They made objects that resist the filter of time, influencing generations of designers."

Patricia Urquiola

Anticipating Change

complexity. The original 1934 design has mitered joints reinforced with brass bolts along the front of the seat and the back of the foot, with a dovetail joint construction of the seat back. There are no bolts or screws on the elegant Cassina chair.

Cassina Lab

To address social and environmental responsibility, Cassina launched Cassina Lab in 2020, a collaboration with POLI.design, a unit at the Milan Polytechnic that serves as a bridge between academic research and industry, to promote well-being and circular design. Based at Cassina's plant in Meda, the research unit has been tasked with guiding the transition toward a sustainable product model. Early research projects that are now feeding into production models have focused on life-cycle analysis and extending the circularity of the company's working activities, looking into the use of recycled and low-impact materials and practices, such as disassembly, to extend a product's use and life cycle up to the recovery and recycling of materials and the finished product.

If Italian companies were at the forefront of plastic technology from the 1950s, now that we are aware of the environmental cost of plastic, companies like Cassina are identifying new materials to replace them in furniture. Soriana is a good example—when it was designed in 1969, Afra and Tobia Scarpa experimented with the sculptural possibilities offered by the forming of polyurethane foam to create free forms for seating that transformed our ideas of upholstered furniture. In the updated version, developed in collaboration with Tobia Scarpa as part of the Cassina Lab project, the original polyurethane padding has been replaced with a biodegradable internal one. This padding is made from an organic-based foam composed of biopolymers derived from natural sources and a recycled blown fiber produced from Polyethylene terephthalate (PET), recovered from nonprofit enterprise Plastic Bank®. Polyurethane-foam elements with a percentage of polyols derived from biological sources and recycled PET padding have also been used to develop new versions of the Le Corbusier, Pierre Jeanneret, Charlotte Perriand Collection. At the moment, though, these are offered as options. The challenge is for companies to educate customers to adopt a more conscious approach to consumerism and question the way things are made and the systems of which they are part. Clearly, if this commitment to circular design is to have impact at scale, accurate data and adoption of a transparent methodology for measuring circular performance indicators and certification by a third party are essential.

Longevity

If extending the lifespan of products is a solution in the transition to the circular economy, we need to ask what "design for longevity" actually means. What do we mean by "last a lifetime"; how do we define an "optimal lifespan"? The reality of this currently fashionable longevity mindset was engagingly demonstrated by a graduation project at the RCA a couple of years ago. Andu Masebo exhibited a slight wooden chair that was designed to be as resource efficient as possible with the "lowest possible rate of carbon consumption." Alongside the chair Masebo presented a "contract of material union"[3] binding the purchaser to keep the piece for several decades, a period of time calculated according to the timber's carbon sequestration during growth. If the owner were to sell the chair, they would be obliged to pass on the contractual responsibility to the new owner. Masebo intended this as a provocation, confronting us with the reality of designing for an optimal lifespan and highlighting the responsibilities of both maker and owner to the objects with which we live. "To live in material union is to respect an object beyond simply its monetary value or personal usefulness to us at any given moment in time. It is to fully consider the impact of the materials with which the object was made, the processes and transportation that brought it to be, and the impact of these choices on both human and animal populations as well as the natural life cycles that provided us with the materials in the first place (…) If we were forced to fully consider even one of these variables at the point of purchasing an object, might it change our patterns of consumption and reduce the amount of waste we produce?"[4]

Observing the Cassina iMaestri Collection through the telescope of history, are there lessons we can learn from the long lives of progressive designs from fifty, seventy, or even one hundred years ago? How is it they have managed to surf trends and outlast fashions while other furniture designs have disappeared into the archives? As well as the physical aspect of objects crafted to endure, can we learn from the psychological dimension by exploring how and why they continue to capture our imaginations? A lot less

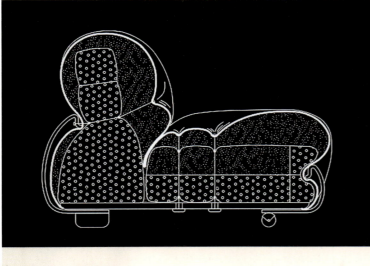

4   Design of Soriana armchair, 2021. The Cassina Lab version replaces the padding with a series of bags filled with BioFoam® microspheres to which is added a layer of blown fiber made from recycled PET

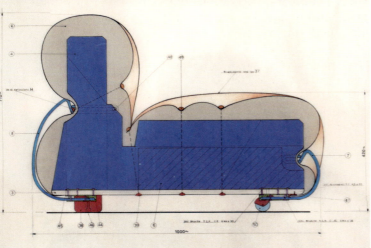

5   Design of Soriana armchair, 1970. The padding was made from polyurethane foam and Dacron

Jane Withers

work has gone into understanding emotional attachment and what makes us hold onto things than physical design for longevity. This was the subject explored in *R for Repair* at the V&A (I was cocurator of the project with designer Hans Tan). The exhibit set out to illuminate the art of repair and, in particular, the notion that creative repair can add character and value to cherished but damaged possessions. Members of the public were invited to submit broken objects along with the story of why they are attached to them. These were then handed over to designers to be not just repaired but creatively renewed. This informal exploration of attachment revealed how stories grow around an object and transform their meaning, and suggests how a creative repair culture might help cultivate personalization and individuality. As the world grapples with the consequences of hyper-consumerism and drowning in waste, there is a growing landscape of initiatives designed to encourage a richer repair culture.

Despite the talk of a repair economy, this has been slow to develop for many obvious reasons, and currently the repair space is led by disruptive players. A straw poll of design colleagues offered a handful of enterprising repair services, like an electrical repair shop in Paris that has pivoted to specialize in mending Tizio lamps. The owner has amassed a store of spare parts that he can draw on to repair and also modify the classic design from the 1970s. In London a few years ago, rather than ship a Wegner chair back to Copenhagen to have a Danish cord seat replaced, I found a local repairer, but when they left on a sabbatical I had to wait a year for its return.

Clearly this underground network needs support if it is to grow into a functioning repair economy. The Right to Repair movement is a coalition of organizations campaigning for system change around repair. Led by sustainability activists, the campaign supports a mix of designing products for repair and supporting repairers. An EU right to repair proposal[5] published in March 2023 takes a step in this direction with an "obligation for Member States to create national online platforms to register repairers, refurbishers, and purchasers of defective goods for refurbishment—with the possibility to extend its scope to include business-to-business relationships as well as community-led repair initiatives." As well as supporting citizens looking for repair options, this is also a step toward legitimizing the role of independent repairers who, at the moment, are often hampered by the difficulty of getting access to parts and information. If current practices emphasize the role owners play in extending a product's lifespan, circularity brings responsibilities for the manufacturer beyond designing a viable route to repair. These responsibilities also include initiating takeback systems needed to support repair and end-of-life services; for brands with global distribution, the logistics of takeback are challenging and require systemic change.

This is another argument for localism. Growing consumer interest in regional production is being driven by several factors: anxiety around global supply chains and some of the human and environmental atrocities that have been uncovered, concern for the environment, as well as the desire to support local communities, businesses, and traditions and the search for more distinctive and higher quality products.

In Italy, specialized manufacturing districts evolved after World War II, and developed through the 1950s and 1960s when economic prosperity increased the demand for home products. Today's Italian furniture industry is the result of these local networks of small to medium businesses specializing in specific sectors. Here the local manufacturing and economy are inseparable from sociocultural relationships, and they are part of a strong tradition historically rooted in each region and one that continuously evolves. Ninety percent of Cassina's suppliers are in northern and central Italy, specifically in Marche, Veneto, and Lombardy, where the company's three production sites are based in Meda.

But localism also raises questions for the future in terms of keeping artisanal skills alive and training new generations in historic crafts. Arguably couture fashion has led in securing the supply chain of craft by supporting artisanal companies. One of the most frequently cited examples is Chanel, which is well known for its policy of actively preserving highly specialized artisan skills. The company has purchased a number of struggling, highly specialized French ateliers that have catered historically to haute couture houses and bespoke clients, including the famous embroidery firm Lesage, as well as specialist button-makers, floral fabric artisans, feather-makers, and boot-makers. However, Chanel only accounts for part of their business and the workshops are operated independently, also supplying to competing houses.

However, for design, the challenge is as much related to developing skills around new materials and technologies as traditional crafts. This year Cassina launched Moncloud, a new sofa by Patricia Urquiola that is the result of intensive research and development by Cassina Lab: Moncloud's curvaceous shape is not obtained through molding polyurethane, as would have been usual practice in the past; instead the structure is a metal framed seat dressed in ample cushioning made from recycled PET fiber.

Perhaps counterintuitively, the most significant benefits of placing twentieth-century iMaestri at the heart and mind of the twenty-first-century company is the belief in the power of research it brings and encouraging a mindset that values new ideas and experimentation.

6 Moncloud sofa by Patricia Urquiola composed of a metal framed seat dressed in ample quilted cushioning made from recycled PET fiber, 2023

[1] Patricia Urquiola in an interview with the author, May 2023.
[2] Jackie Daly, "The Passion and Politics of My Mother, Charlotte Perriand," *Financial Times*, April 26, 2023. Pernette Perriand-Barsac on growing up with a design legend and evolving her legacy.
[3] Andu Masebo, Material Union, 2022, https://andumasebo.com/In-Material-Union.
[4] Rain Noe, "Fantastic Product Design Student Work: Andu Masebo's 'In Material Union' Chairs," *Core 77*, February 24, 2022, https://www.core77.com/posts/112592/Fantastic-Product-Design-Student-Work-Andu-Masebos-In-Material-Union-Chairs.
[5] Not Yet Accessible, Affordable nor Mainstream: Campaigners Tighten the Screw on New EU Right to Repair Proposal, by Cristina Ganapini, Repair.eu, 22 March, 2023, https://repair.eu/news/not-yet-accessible-affordable-nor-mainstream-campaigners-tighten-the-screw-on-new-eu-right-to-repair-proposal/.

Anticipating Change

Charlotte Perriand

Anticipating Change

1 Exhibition view of UAM
Musée des Arts Décoratifs
Paris, 1985

2 Perspective view drawing
of Chambre de la Maison
de la Tunisie
Charlotte Perriand, 1952

Charlotte Perriand

Charlotte Perriand was born in Paris in 1903. After studying at the Union Centrale des Arts Décoratifs, she was an immediate success when she presented her *Bar sous le toit* at the Salon d'Automne in 1927. Engaged by Le Corbusier as a partner in charge of the furniture program, she developed metal furnishings with them. After fitting up several interiors (Villa La Roche, Villa Church, Villa Savoye, project for Villa Martinez), she worked on the Pavillon Suisse of the Cité Internationale Universitaire de Paris and the Cité de refuge for the Salvation Army.

As a member of the UAM and the CIAM, she presented La Maison du jeune homme at the 1935 Brussels International Exhibition, with René Herbst and Louis Sognot, in collaboration with Le Corbusier and Pierre Jeanneret.

A socially committed artist, she denounced the appalling living conditions in the capital in a photomontage entitled *La Grande Misère de Paris*, which she presented at the Salon des Arts Ménagers in 1936. She also designed a giant photomontage in the waiting room of the Ministry of Agriculture to promote the agricultural reforms of the Popular Front (the creation of the Wheat Board and various public bodies).

In 1937, Charlotte Perriand designed, in collaboration with the engineer André Tournon, the Refuge bivouac. It was shown at the Pavillon de l'Union des Artistes Modernes. She created her first free-form table in 1938 and took part the following year in the interior design of a hotel at Méribel-les-Allues. She went to Japan in 1940, invited by the Ministry of Commerce and Industry as an advisor for Japanese industrial art, on the initiative of Junzo Sakakura. In Tokyo and Osaka, she organized the exhibition *Sélection, tradition, création* at the Takashimaya department stores. She left Japan in 1942 and lived in Indochina until 1946.

On her return to France, she created many pieces of furniture for the interior design of various buildings at Méribel-les-Allues and then designed the prototype kitchen for Le Corbusier's Unité d'habitation in Marseille. Under the aegis of the UAM, she took part in the creation of the Formes Utiles movement, which marked the birth of design in France, and created part of the set design for the *Formes Utiles, objets de notre temps* exhibition at the Musée des Arts Décoratifs in Paris. In 1950, she created the interior design and layout of the Maison de l'étudiant de Médecine in Paris (Michel Weill, Guy Lagneau, Jean Dimitrijevic, architects). In 1952, she completed the interior design and furnishings of the Maison de la Tunisie, then the Maison du Mexique at the Cité Internationale Universitaire de Paris, for which she designed a new bookcase system consisting of metal vertical elements. In the same year, with Jean Borot, she presented a shower-bath and wall-hung WC unit at the Salon des arts ménagers.

Anticipating Change

In 1953 she moved to Japan, working on the exhibition *Proposition d'une Synthèse des Arts, Paris 1955. Le Corbusier, Fernand Léger, Charlotte Perriand*. For this event, she designed new furnishings soon issued by the Takashimaya department store. In France, she took part with Jean Prouvé in the creation of the Galerie Steph Simon in Saint-Germain-des-Prés, which issued her furnishings from 1956 to 1970, including the high and low versions of the Mexique table, the Table à gorge, stools, bookcases, storage systems, drawers, sideboards, offices, etc.

She designed the Air France offices in London (Peter Braddock, operational architect) in 1957 and then the following year, she designed the interior of the Air France offices in Tokyo (Junzo Sakakura, operational architect). In Paris, she designed a table and a bed for the student rooms of the Maison du Brésil (Lúcio Costa, Le Corbusier, architects), and, with Le Corbusier, a wardrobe-storage unit and a wall chalkboard.

3

From 1962 to 1968, she traveled in Latin America, where she met the architects Lúcio Costa and Oscar Niemeyer. She moved in Brazilian artistic and intellectual circles and met Roberto Burle Marx, Jorge Amado, and Luis Carlos Barreto. In Rio de Janeiro, she designed the interiors and furnishings of the Air France offices as well as Jacques Martin's official apartment, for which she designed the Rio coffee table, a collector's piece called the Rio bookcase, a large bench, and a large free-form dining table in jacaranda wood.

In 1966, she created the interior design and furniture of the residence of the Japanese ambassador in Paris (Junzo Sakakura, architect, J. H. Riedberger, operational architect; Jean Prouvé collaborated on the project as an engineer).

Finally, from 1967 to 1988, she led the team responsible for the creation of the iconic Les Arcs winter sports resort in collaboration with the Atelier d'Architecture en Montagne, including Gaston Regairaz, Guy Rey-Millet, Pierre Faucheux, Robert Rebutato, Alain Tavès, and Bernard Taillefer. She also designed the interiors and furnishings of all the buildings.

In 1983, she was made a Chevalier of the Légion d'Honneur. She died in Paris in 1999.

3 Exhibition view of *Synthèse des Arts* Tokyo, 1955

4 Color range of fabrics selected by Charlotte Perriand, 1979

5–6 Exhibition view of *Le Monde Nouveau de Charlotte Perriand* Fondation Louis Vuitton, Paris, 2019

Charlotte Perriand

Her work has been the subject of numerous exhibitions, including *Charlotte Perriand* at Centre Pompidou, Paris (2005), *Charlotte Perriand 1903–1999: de la photographie au design* at the Petit Palais, Paris (2011), *Charlotte Perriand et le Japon* at the Museum of Modern Art, Kamakura, Hiroshima City Museum of Contemporary Art, and Meguro Museum of Art, Tokyo (2011).

In 2012, the Refuge Tonneau was presented at the Salone del Mobile in Milan with interiors faithfully reproduced by Cassina. True to its policy of reconstruction, Cassina reproduced the prototypes of her Japanese period exhibited during *Charlotte Perriand et le Japon* at the Musée d'Art Moderne de Saint-Étienne (2013), as well as several models for *Le Monde Nouveau de Charlotte Perriand* at the Fondation Louis Vuitton in Paris in 2019.

On the occasion of the exhibition *Charlotte Perriand: The Modern Life* at the Design Museum in London (2021), Cassina produced a prototype of the Banquette Air France. The Refuge Tonneau was also exhibited at the Wilmotte Foundation during the Venice Architecture Biennale.

Anticipating Change

7 Charlotte Perriand, 1928

8 Charlotte Perriand and Filippo Alison Cassina, Meda, circa 1985

1903 — Born in Paris

1921 – 1925 — Studies at the École des Arts Décoratifs

1926 — Takes part in the Salon des Artistes Décorateurs (SAD) with her Coin salon - First furniture in metal, wood, and glass

1927 — Sets up her workshop in Place Saint-Sulpice and designs Le Bar sous le toit

7 Fauteuil tournant
8 Tabouret tournant
9 Tabouret

Le Bar sous le toit at the Salon d'Automne - Joins Le Corbusier and Pierre Jeanneret's office

1928 — Dining room suite consisting of an extendable table, chairs, and swivel stools at the Salon des Artistes Décorateurs (SAD)

1929 — Resigns from SAD and founds the Union des Artistes Modernes (UAM)

1933 — Member of the Congrès Internationaux d'Architecture Moderne (CIAM)

1935 — La Maison du jeune homme at the Universal Exhibition in Brussels with René Herbst and Louis Sognot

1937 — Master builder for the Pavillon des Temps Nouveaux (Le Corbusier and Pierre Jeanneret, architects)

Presentation of a sanitary cubicle prototype with Le Corbusier and Pierre Jeanneret

Presentation of the Refuge bivouac with engineer André Tournon at the Pavillon de l'UAM. Ends collaboration with Le Corbusier's office

1938 — **First free-form table for her own use at her workshop in Montparnasse - Mod. 539 Bureau Boomerang**

1940 — **Leaves France for Japan Mod. 522 Tokyo Chaise Longue Mod. 532 Tokyo Dormeuse D04 Vérité and Graffiti**

1941 — Exhibition Sélection, tradition, création, Takashimaya department stores, Tokyo and Osaka

Charlotte Perriand

1943 - 1946
Leaves Japan for Indochina Pavilion of Handicrafts, Hanoi, 1943
-
Mod. 528 Indochine

1947
Mod. 533 Doron Hotel

1952 - 1956
Mod. 526–536 Nuage and Nuage à plots
Mod. 527–531 Mexique Mexique Stool
Mod. 530 Guéridon J.M.

1953 - 1954
Mod. 523–524 Tabouret Méribel–Berger
Mod. 512 Ombra
Mod. 517 Ombra Tokyo
Mod. 514 Refolo

1955
Exhibition *Proposition d'une synthèse des arts. Paris 1955.* Le Corbusier, Fernand Léger, Charlotte Perriand, Takashimaya department store, Tokyo

1956 - 1970
Editions Steph Simon:
Mod. 513 Riflesso
Mod. 525 Table en forme libre

1957
Refurbishment of Air France offices in London

1958
Interiors of the Air France offices in Tokyo
-
Interior design of the Maison du Brésil

1960 - 1962
Chalet at Méribel-les-Allues in the Alps (her own property)

1962 - 1969
Interior design of the residence of the Japanese ambassador in Paris
Mod. 515 Plana
Mod. 529 Rio
Mod. 537 Paravent Ambassade

1967 - 1988
Urban design and architecture of most of the Arc 1600 and Arc 1800 ski resorts, Savoy

1972
Mod. 511 Ventaglio

1985
Mod. 520 Accordo
-
Charlotte Perriand: Un Art de Vivre, Musée des Arts Décoratifs, Paris

1999
Dies in Paris

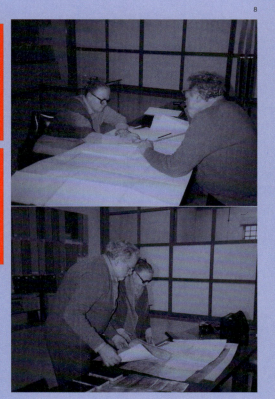

Anticipating Change

Refuge Tonneau

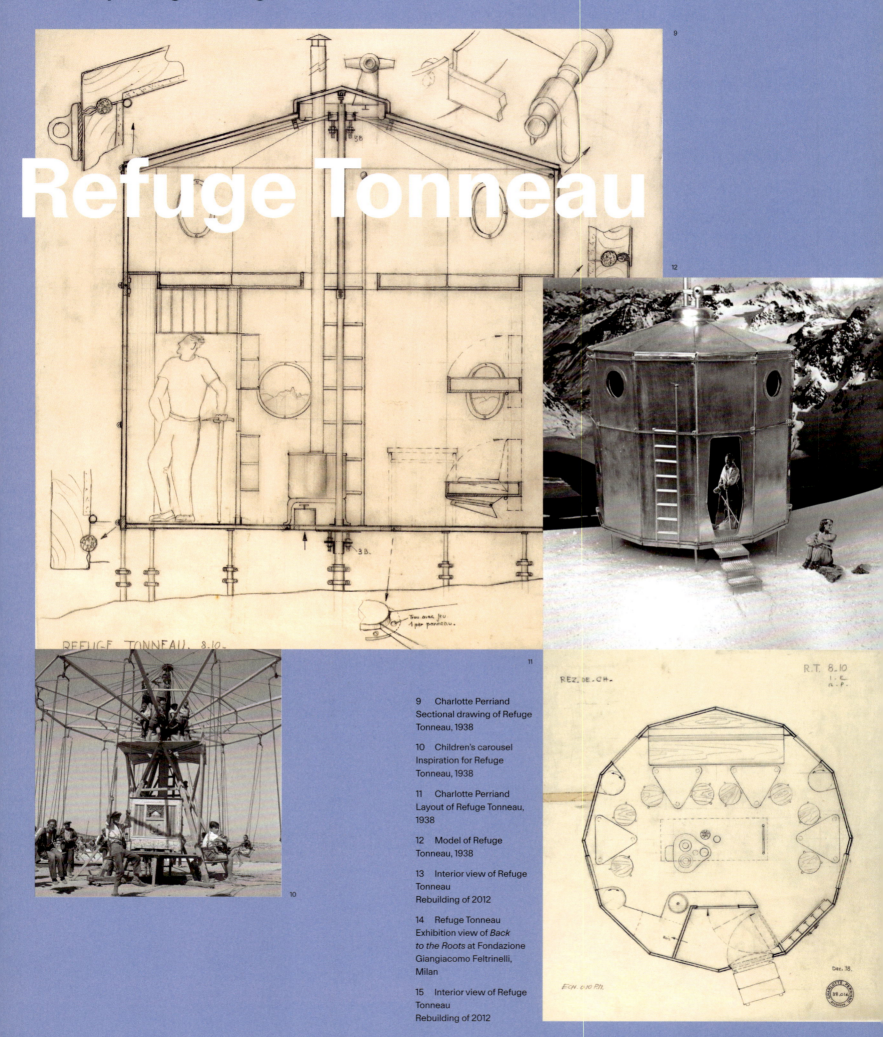

9 Charlotte Perriand
Sectional drawing of Refuge Tonneau, 1938

10 Children's carousel
Inspiration for Refuge Tonneau, 1938

11 Charlotte Perriand
Layout of Refuge Tonneau, 1938

12 Model of Refuge Tonneau, 1938

13 Interior view of Refuge Tonneau
Rebuilding of 2012

14 Refuge Tonneau
Exhibition view of *Back to the Roots* at Fondazione Giangiacomo Feltrinelli, Milan

15 Interior view of Refuge Tonneau
Rebuilding of 2012

Charlotte Perriand

1938

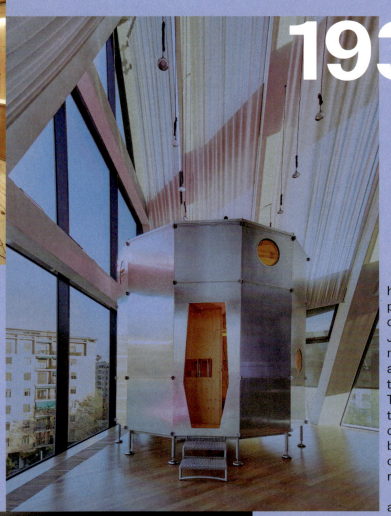

The futuristic lines of this mountain hut were inspired by a fairground ride photographed by Charlotte Perriand when on holiday in Croatia. Together with Pierre Jeanneret, she designed a lightweight metal structure with prefabricated aluminum components in order to be easy to transport and built in only three days. The refuge stands on stilts, allowing it to be installed on all terrains, even steep ones. Finally, its shape prevents it from being too sensitive to the wind, and its coating, made of aluminum, helps through radiation to clear the snow around it.

The interior is laid out around a central metal shaft and its compact furnishings comprise eight beds set on two levels.

In 2012, Cassina presented a faithful reconstruction of the Refuge Tonneau at the Salone del Mobile in Milan. It was then presented at the retrospective *Le Monde Nouveau de Charlotte Perriand* at the Fondation Louis Vuitton in Paris in 2019 and in Venice, at the Fondation Wilmotte in 2021.

Anticipating Change

16   Desk for Jean-Richard Bloch
Paris, 1938

17   Sketch of the Chaise Longue, bamboo version
Charlotte Perriand, 1940

18   Sketch of the Dormeuse daybed
Charlotte Perriand, 1940

19   Charlotte Perriand looking at the prototype of the Chaise Longue version in wood
Frankfurt, 1986

1938

Bureau Boomerang
Mod. 539 — 2022

1937

Table à Plateau Interchangeable
Mod. 535 — 2019

In 1938, Charlotte Perriand was commissioned by the French writer, journalist, and poet Jean-Richard Bloch to design the pieces of furniture of his office on the premises of the daily newspaper *Ce Soir*. To accommodate a number of staff members, she created a large boomerang-shaped desk with a solid wood top supported by three feet with organic lines of different forms.

She reinterpreted this model in 1943, during her stay in Indochina, where a similar desk was made for the director of the Cité Universitaire in Hanoi and then for the office of Jacques Martin, director of Air France in Rio de Janeiro, Brazil. Cassina began editing this desk in 2022.

The structure of the base of the table with an interchangeable top consists of three legs with a circular section in ash wood, connected by three crosspieces on which rests the table top. Designed for Charlotte Perriand's Parisian workshop in the Montparnasse district of Paris, this coffee table was originally made entirely of wood. Cassina now offers it with an extra-clear tempered glass or marble top.

« **No other material has more infinite possibilities than bamboo.** »

Charlotte Perriand

Charlotte Perriand

1940

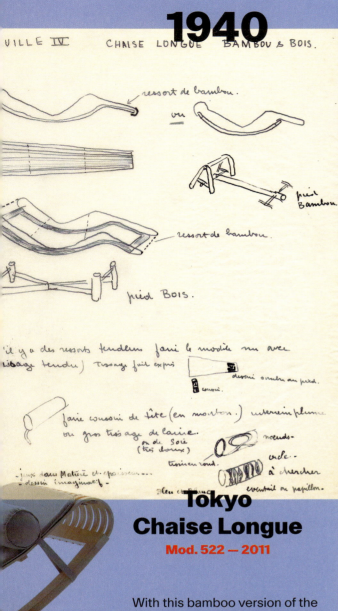

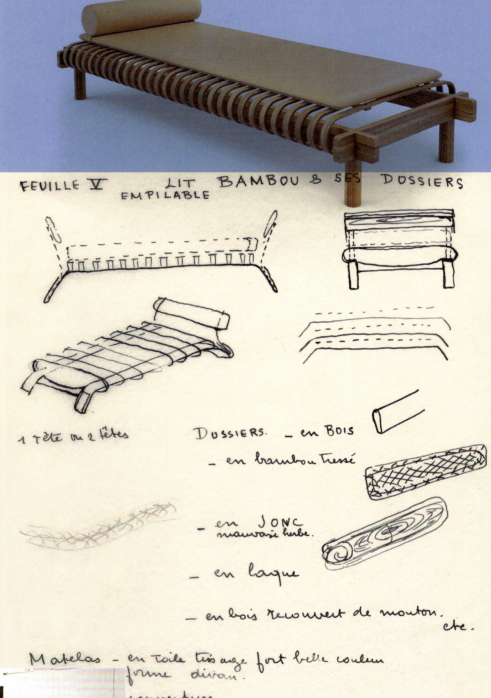

Tokyo Chaise Longue
Mod. 522 — 2011

With this bamboo version of the 1928 Chaise longue, Charlotte Perriand replaced the elasticity of tubular steel with bamboo or wooden slats. This one-off piece, preserved at the Musée des Arts Décoratifs in Paris, has been edited by Cassina since 2011.

Tokyo Dormeuse
Mod. 532 — 2021

Presented beside the Chaise longue basculante, this wooden and bamboo daybed has been reissued by Cassina in a solid teak version.

Anticipating Change

20 Exhibition view of *Sélection, tradition, création* Tokyo, 1941

21 Charlotte Perriand with Junzo Sakakura and Japanese craftsmen, 1940

22 Exhibition view of *Sélection, tradition, création* Tokyo, 1941

23 Interior view of Doron Hotel Méribel, 1947

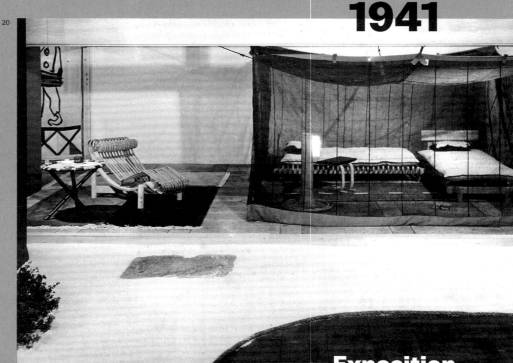

1941

Exposition « Sélection, tradition, création »

The exhibition *Sélection, tradition, création* opened at the Takashimaya department store in Tokyo in March 1941. Charlotte Perriand presented Japanese objects she had chosen that nurtured a dialogue with her own works made of bamboo and wood, the only materials available during the Pacific War. The exhibition space was enclosed by fixed or sliding partitions and Noren bamboo blinds, reflecting her continuing research into spatial design.

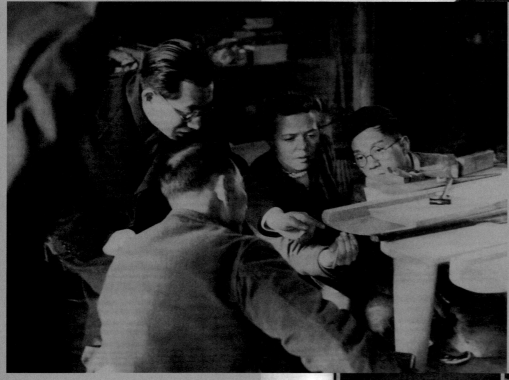

Charlotte Perriand

1943

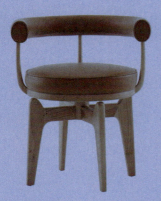

1947

Doron Hotel
Mod. 533 — 2020

In 1946, Charlotte Perriand was again invited to Méribel-les-Allues by the English developer Peter Lindsay, who entrusted her with the interior design and furnishings of several buildings. For the Hotel Le Doron, she created an armchair with a solid wood frame. The seat and back are lined with leather.

Indochine
Mod. 528 — 2014

Designed by Charlotte Perriand during her stay in Indochina (now Cambodia, Laos, Vietnam), this armchair is the wooden adaptation of the famous Fauteuil tournant. The model initially had three legs and then four.

Anticipating Change

Nuage

The Nuage à plots, Tunisie-type, and the Nuage à joues, Mexique-type, bookcases were issued from 1956 onward by the Steph Simon gallery, then by Cassina under the name Nuage (from 2012) and Nuage à Plots (from 2021). Modular storage units of the Mexique type can be installed crosswise as a screen to partition the space or set against a wall. The addition of colored aluminum sliding doors allows for many personalized compositions.

24 Copy of the SPADEM patent registration for the Mexique bookshelf, 1954
Design by Charlotte Perriand

25 Air France offices, London, 1957
Interior design by Charlotte Perriand (Thomas and Peter Braddock, project architects)

26 Casiers bookcase, 1952
Design by Charlotte Perriand

27 Sketch for the bookcase screen
Air France offices, London, 1957
Design by Charlotte Perriand

298

Charlotte Perriand

1952 – 56

Mod. 526 — 2021

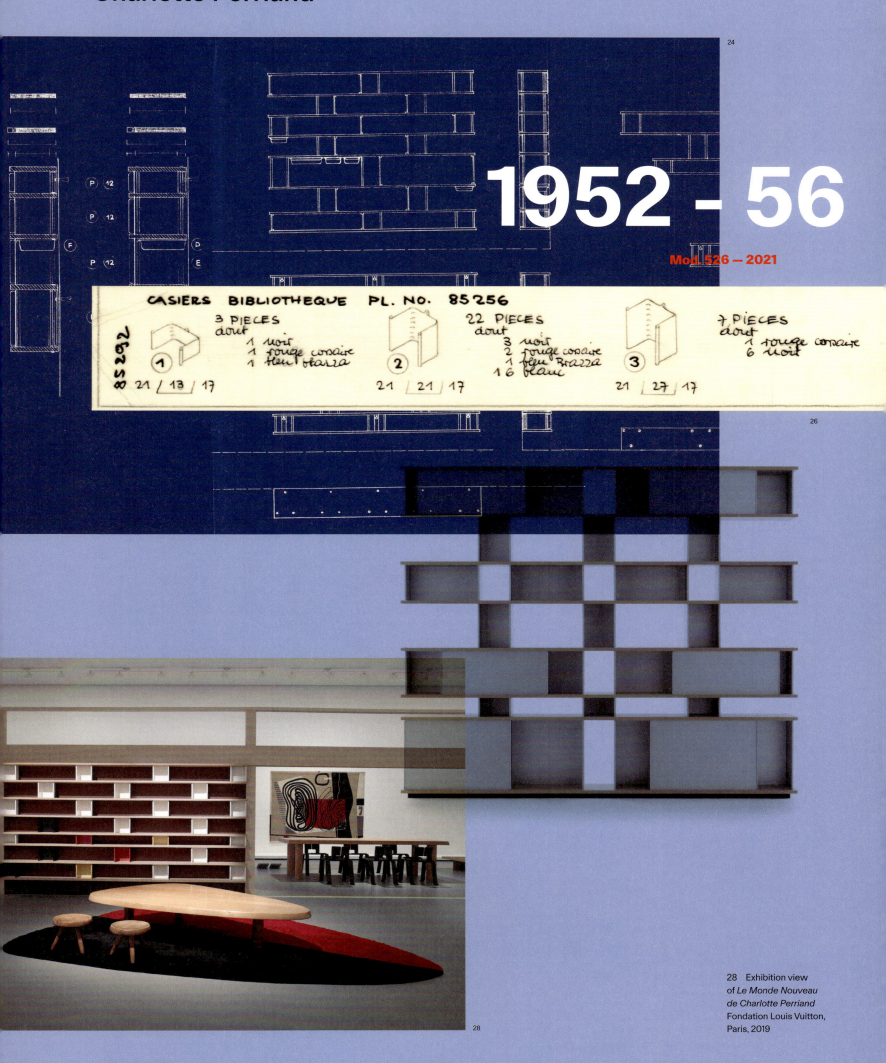

28 Exhibition view of *Le Monde Nouveau de Charlotte Perriand* Fondation Louis Vuitton, Paris, 2019

Anticipating Change

1953 – 54

Guéridon J.M.
Mod. 530 — 2016

Ombra Tokyo
Mod. 517 — 2009

Charlotte Perriand moved to Tokyo in 1953 where she designed the Air France stackable table (1953) for Jacques Martin's apartment. The following year she created the Ombra stackable chair, made of a unique bent plywood sheet, as well as a double chaise longue and a stackable low armchair.

1952

Petit Bureau en Forme Libre
Mod. 538 — 2021

Refolo
Mod. 514 — 2004

Charlotte Perriand imagined the small free-form desk in 1937 while designing her studio apartment in the Montparnasse district. This model is now produced in solid walnut or mahogany by Cassina.

Charlotte Perriand

1952 – 56

Mexique
Mod. 527 — 2014
Mexique Stool
Mod. 531 — 2019

The Maison du Mexique building was designed by architect Jorge L. Medellin and built by his brother, engineer Roberto E. Medellin. It's a modern building of ninety-two rooms with interior designs by Charlotte Perriand and Jean Prouvé. Perriand designed a triangular table in solid wood with rounded corners and slightly beveled edges. The metal legs were produced by Ateliers Jean Prouvé and the wooden tops by André Chetaille. For the Maison du Mexique, she created a custom-made bookcase, which is— with the one she made for the nearby Maison de la Tunisie—the first example of her modular storage system composed of wooden shelves and metal plots.

29 Editions Steph Simon Trade document for low tables, 1956

30 Technical drawing of Mexique table, 1952

Anticipating Change

1955

« Proposition d'une synthèse des arts »

At the same time, she was actively working on an exhibition entitled *Proposition d'une synthèse des arts. Paris 1955. Le Corbusier, Fernand Léger, Charlotte Perriand*. After many setbacks, the event opened in the Tokyo Takashimaya department store in March 1955. In the exhibition catalogue, Perriand explained why: "To express the collaboration between artists and industrial producers; to reaffirm the relationship of unity between architecture, painting, and sculpture." She went on to explain that "all these elements: architecture, furniture, everyday objects, tapestries, polychrome sculpture, wall canvases, which complement one another, will have to strive for unity."

The exhibition space was divided into several rooms with amenities responding to different uses: reception, dining room, bedroom, and office. These spaces were fully furnished by Charlotte Perriand with new pieces, such as the Ombra stackable chairs and armchairs in curved plywood and the Tokyo bench in slats of hinoki wood. She segmented the exhibition spaces by using bookcases with lacquered sheet metal plots that enabled her to present the artworks by her friend Fernand Léger. The space was also enlivened by large tapestries and paintings by Le Corbusier.

1958

Tabouret Méribel–Berger
Mod. 523 - 524 — 2011

Riflesso
Mod. 513 — 2004

For the Steph Simon gallery, Charlotte Perriand designed a collection of what she called free-form furniture in solid wood consisting of a three-drawer chest, a desk, tables (high and low), and a low chest. They were made by her cabinetmaker André Chetaille and then reproduced by Cassina in a contemporary edition.

Charlotte Perriand

31   Charlotte Perriand at her exhibition *Proposition d'une synthèse des arts*
Tokyo, 1955

32   Exhibition view of *Proposition d'une synthèse des arts*
Tokyo, 1955

33   Sketch for Charlotte Perriand's Rio table in cane, 1962

1962

Rio
Mod. 529 — 2015

1959

Table en Forme Libre
Mod. 525 — 2011

For the apartment of Jacques Martin, she custom made pieces of furniture using traditional Brazilian materials and techniques. She created a very imposing bookcase and a huge bench in Jacaranda wood and rattan. The round coffee table was faithfully reproduced by Cassina in 2015. Named Rio, the table is also available with a marble top.

Anticipating Change

1969

Plana
Mod. 515 — 2004

Paravent Ambassade
Mod. 537 — 2021

Starting in 1966, Charlotte Perriand designed the interiors and furniture of the residence of the Japanese ambassador in Paris, built by the architect Junzo Sakakura. Among her many creations for the residence, she adapted the design of the large bench and coffee table made for the apartment in Rio de Janeiro and designed a screen made from the wooden offcuts from her stools made by André Chetaille.

Charlotte Perriand

1972

1985

34 Japanese ambassador's residence in Paris (Junzo Sakakura, architect, J. H. Riedberger, project architect) View of the Reception room Paris, 1969

35 Sketch of the Ventaglio table, 1972 Design by Charlotte Perriand

Ventaglio
Mod. 511 — 2004

Charlotte Perriand created the table that opens like a fan for the ground floor of her chalet at Méribel. Designed to seat up to ten people, a prototype was made in fir wood in 1972. It has been produced since 2004 by Cassina, which offered it in black-tinted oak or natural oak.

Accordo
Mod. 520 — 2009

In 1985, Charlotte Perriand was the subject of a retrospective exhibition at the Musée des Arts Décoratifs in Paris, whose design and scenography she oversaw. On this occasion, she designed a carpet and a glued laminated coffee table. This model was produced in 2009 by Cassina under the name Accordo.

Anticipating Change

Photos by
TOMMASO SARTORI

Tommaso Sartori wished to photograph these pieces as sculptures, presented alone on raw and mineral materials such as the lava basalt of the Etna volcano and the concrete of *Grande Cretto* by Alberto Burri.
Art and organic materials here contrast in two different universes to create striking and powerful images.

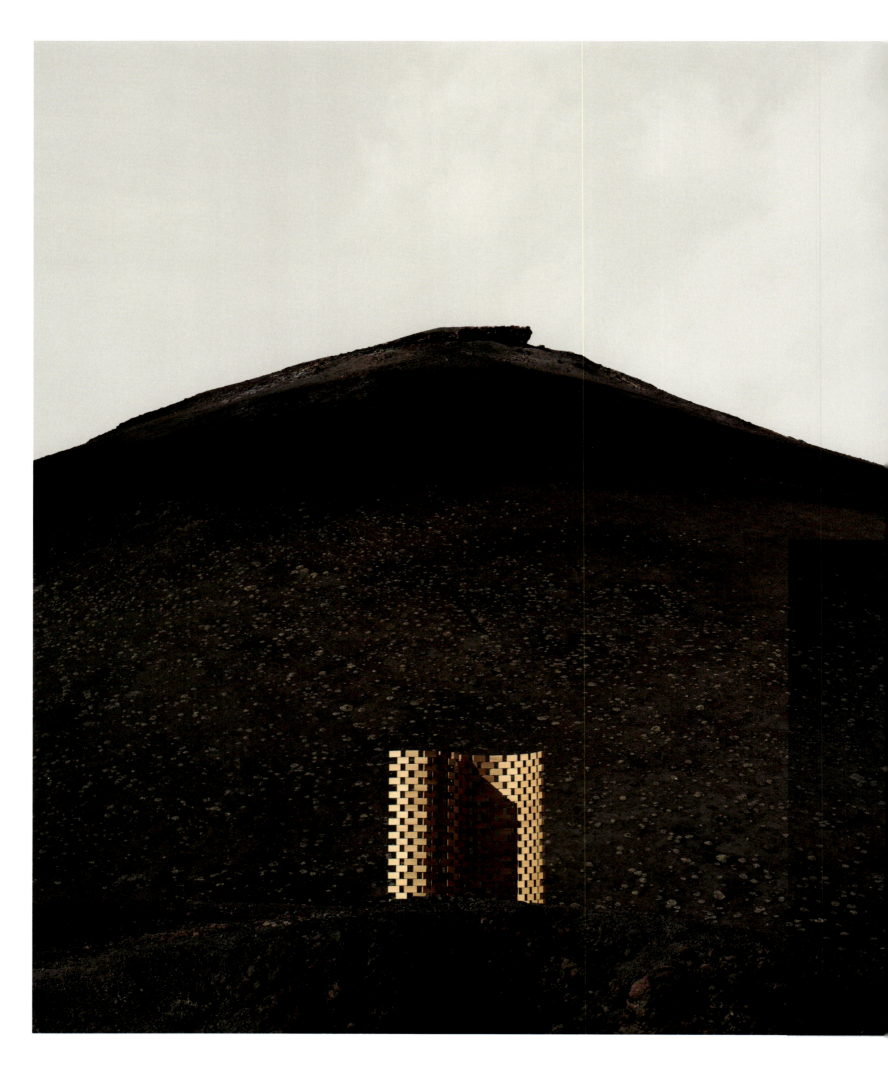

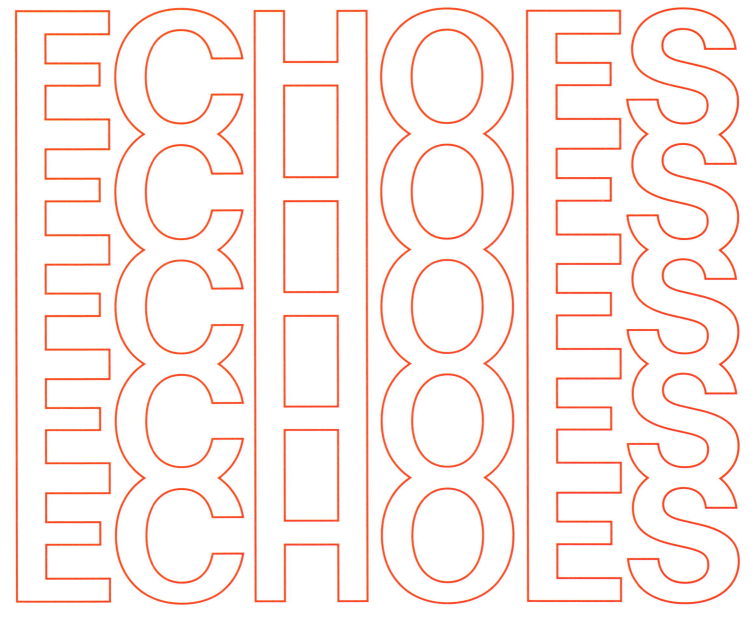

1927 **1952** **1953** **1954** **1955**

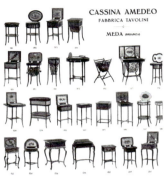

Birth of the company
Amedeo Cassina

646 Leggera,
Gio Ponti

Figli di Amedeo Cassina, forniture
navali e alberghiere catalogue

807 Distex,
Gio Ponti

851 Mariposa,
Gio Ponti

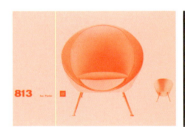

813
Ico Parisi

683
Carlo De Carli
Compasso d'Oro

691
Ico Parisi

687
Gio Ponti

1957 1958 1963 1964 1965

839
Ico Parisi

865
Ico Parisi

121
Afra & Tobia Scarpa

845
Gio Ponti

Mod. 892, Mod. 115 Carimate,
Vico Magistretti

905
Vico Magistretti

928
Vico Magistretti

699 Superleggera,
Gio Ponti

325

1965   1967   1968

925
Afra & Tobia Scarpa

Marema,
Gianfranco Frattini

Beginning of the
Le Corbusier© Pierre Jeanneret©
Charlotte Perriand© Collection

4 Chaise longue à réglage continu,
Le Corbusier
Pierre Jeanneret
Charlotte Perriand

122
Vico Magistretti

Carlotta,
Afra & Tobia Scarpa

Ciprea,
Afra & Tobia Scarpa

1971   1972

Moloch (Bracciodiferro)
Gaetano Pesce

Golgotha (Bracciodiferro)
Gaetano Pesce

Soriana,
Afra & Tobia Scarpa
Compasso d'Oro

First advertising campaign of the
Le Corbusier© Pierre Jeanneret©
Charlotte Perriand© Collection
—
Opening of the showroom
in Via Durini, Milan

Le Corbusier© Pierre Jeanneret©
Charlotte Perriand© Collection
Poster

1972

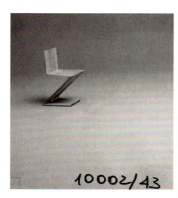

Zig Zag,
Gerrit Thomas Rietveld

Showroom Cassina
Via Durini, Milan
—
Presentation of the
Gerrit Thomas Rietveld Collection

Kar-a-sutra,
Mario Bellini
prototype car, presented at the
exhibition *Italy: The New Domestic
Landscape*, MoMA, New York

Red and Blue
Gerrit Thomas Rietveld

1973

Birth of
iMaestri Collection

Showroom Cassina
Via Durini, Milan
—
Presentation of the
Charles Rennie Mackintosh
Collection

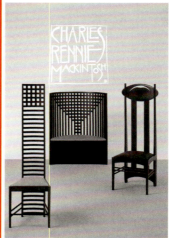

1974

AeO,
Archizoom
Paolo Deganello

Maralunga,
Vico Magistretti

Presentation of iMaestri
Collection, Showroom
in Via Durini, Milan

Terra (Bracciodiferro)
Alessandro Mendini

1975   1976   1977

iMaestri Collection
Poster

La Rotonda,
Mario Bellini

Cab,
Mario Bellini

Cassina
and Vico Magistretti Poster

1978　1980　1982　1983

20 Casiers Standard,
Le Corbusier
Pierre Jeanneret
Charlotte Perriand

Tramonto a New York,
Gaetano Pesce

Torso,
Paolo Deganello

Tangram,
Massimo Morozzi

Senna,
Erik Gunnar Asplund

7 Fauteuil tournant,
by Charlotte Perriand included
in the Le Corbusier©
Pierre Jeanneret©
Charlotte Perriand© Collection

Sansone,
Gaetano Pesce

Genoa,
Vico Magistretti

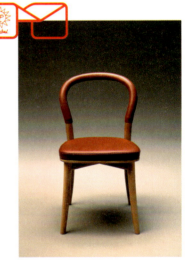

Göteborg 1,
Beginning of the
Erik Gunnar Asplund Collection

Wink,
Toshiyuki Kita

1985 　　1986 　　　　　1987 　　1988

Showroom Cassina
Via Durini, Milan
—
Presentation of the
Frank Lloyd Wright Collection

Exhibition catalogue *Ricerca e Design. La ricostruzione nella Collezione Cassina iMaestri*, Palazzo delle Albere, Trento

I Feltri,
Gaetano Pesce

Utrecht,
Gerrit Thomas Rietveld

Brochure for the 20th Anniversary of the Le Corbusier© Pierre Jeanneret© Charlotte Perriand© Collection

Taliesin 1,
Frank Lloyd Wright

Midway 2,
Frank Lloyd Wright

Cannaregio,
Gaetano Pesce

Cardigan,
Vico Magistretti

1989   1991   1992   1993   1996

Robie 3,
Frank Lloyd Wright

Artù,
Isao Hosoe

Diwan,
Danube,
Sottsass Associati

Revers,
Andrea Branzi

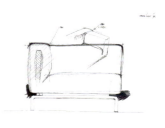

Met,
Piero Lissoni

Portovenere,
Vico Magistretti

Compasso d'Oro to Cassina for its innovative role and for contributing to the overall enhancement of the project culture

Hilly,
Achille Castiglioni

1997 1998 2004 2006 2007

Presentation of the new iMaestri Collection brochures, showroom in Via Durini, Milan

L.W.S. Lazy Working Sofa, Philippe Starck

Ventaglio,
Ombra,
Beginning of the
Charlotte Perriand Collection

Reconstruction of the interior of the Cabanon by Le Corbusier

Boboli,
Rodolfo Dordoni

Privé,
Philippe Starck

2008   2009   2010   2011

Luisa,
Beginning of the
Franco Albini Collection

80th anniversary of the company,
book and exhibition
Made in Cassina

Hola,
Hannes Wettstein

Cicognino,
Franco Albini

Plurima,
Charlotte Perriand

Tre Pezzi,
Franco Albini

Tabouret LC14,
Presentation of new models
for the LC Collection,
Showroom in Via Durini, Milan

Veliero,
Franco Albini

1 Fauteuil
dossier basculant Outdoor,
Le Corbusier
Pierre Jeanneret
Charlotte Perriand

2012

Nuage,
Charlotte Perriand

Reconstruction of the interior
of the Refuge Tonneau,
Charlotte Perriand
and Pierre Jeanneret

2013

Collaboration
with Karl Lagerfeld

les grands trans-Parents,
Man Ray

2014

Bramante,
Kazuhide Takahama

Indochine,
Charlotte Perriand

8,
Piero Lissoni

2015

Beginning of the
Marco Zanuso Collection

Woodline,
Marco Zanuso

336

2016 2017 2019

Lady,
Marco Zanuso

Beam,
Patricia Urquiola, Cassina's Art Director from 2015

Hommage à
Pierre Jeanneret Collection

Reconstruction of the Salon d'Automne by Le Corbusier, Pierre Jeanneret, Charlotte Perriand. Exhibition *Le Monde Nouveau de Charlotte Perriand*, Fondation Louis Vuitton, Paris

50th anniversary of the
Le Corbusier® Pierre Jeanneret® Charlotte Perriand® Collection

90th anniversary exhibition at the Fondazione Giangiacomo Feltrinelli in Milan, Italy,
book *This Will Be The Place*

Presentation
of the new corporate philosophy:
The Cassina Perspective

Leggera reissue,
Gio Ponti

Elling Buffet,
Gerrit Thomas Rietveld

2019 2020   2021

Extension of the
Cotone family,
Ronan & Erwan Bouroullec

Table à plateau interchangeable,
Charlotte Perriand

Sengu Sofa,
Patricia Urquiola

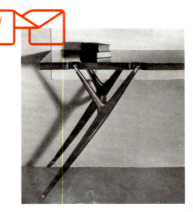

PA' 1947,
Beginning of the
Ico Parisi Collection

Paravent Ambassade,
Charlotte Perriand

Paravento Balla,
Beginning of the
Giacomo Balla Collection

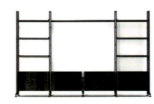

Infinito,
Franco Albini

875,
Ico Parisi

Beginning of the
Cassina Pro Collection

Cassina LAB

Birth of Cassina LAB

Soriana reissue,
Afra & Tobia Scarpa

2022

Radio in Cristallo,
Franco Albini

Bureau Boomerang,
Charlotte Perriand
for Cassina Pro

Dudet,
Patricia Urquiola

Leggera outdoor,
Gio Ponti

2023

Flutz,
Michael Anastassiades

Esosoft,
Antonio Citterio

Four new authors join
the iMaestri Collection:
Vico Magistretti,
Carlo Scarpa,
Gio Ponti, and
Charles & Ray Eames

50th anniversary of iMaestri Collection

Table Monta,
Limited edition
Charlotte Perriand

Beginning of Cassina Lighting
Eitie,
Tobia Scarpa

ECHOES Exhibition, Milan Design Week 2023

PATRICIA URQUIOLA
Art Director Cassina

AGOSTINO OSIO
for Alto Piano

(...) **In labyrinths of coral caves
The echo of a distant time
Comes willowing across the sand
And everything is green and submarine** (...)

Pink Floyd, "Echoes"

***Echoes, 50 Years of iMaestri* is an opportunity to reflect on the innovative element of the Cassina method. Timeliness, its value, the continuity of its path, the opening of a dialogue to define the guidelines for the future. Highlighting the importance of research, experimentation, authorship, originality. And how this process can lead to values that go beyond contemporaneity, an example of sustainability of thought, of ideas.**

This is how Federica Sala and I devised an exhibition for the anniversary-event, during the Salone del Mobile 2023, that bears the same title as the book, one going beyond its time frame as an "open work," recalling Umberto Eco. A tool that allows different interpretations, an individual path, an open container, to open a conversation.

In the historic vault at Palazzo Broggi, the former headquarters of the Credito Italiano, the ideal protection for the pieces on display, we descend into the heart of the company: drawings, archival documents, videos, sketches, museum furnishings, prototypes, as well as original reconstructions. A space-time path of research, not definition. Characterized by the constant presence of a red Cassina light, which with the changes of light and sounds, envelops everything in a liquid atmosphere ... And everything is red and submarine.

Palazzo Broggi, Milan, April 2023

342

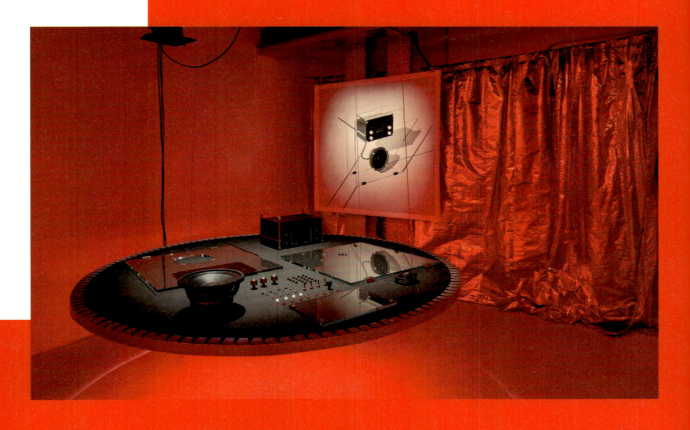

Palazzo Broggi, Milan, April 2023

344

Palazzo Broggi, Milan, April 2023

346

Bibliography

General References

Pier Carlo Santini,
Gli anni del design italiano.
Ritratto di Cesare Cassina
Electa, Milan, 1981

Giampiero Bosoni,
Made in Cassina
Skira, Milan, 2008

Irene de Guttry, Maria Paola Maino,
Il mobile italiano degli anni '40 e '50
Editori Laterza, Rome, Bari, 1992

Maura Santoro,
Filippo Alison. Un viaggio tra le forme
Skira, Milan, 2013

Giuliana Gramigna,
Repertorio generale tipologico dell'arredo domestico italiano, 1950–2000
Umberto Allemandi, Turin, 2021

R. Craig Miller,
Modern Design in the Metropolitan Museum of Art 1890–1990
Metropolitan Museum of Art, New York, 1990

Emilio Ambasz,
Italy: The New Domestic Landscape. Achievements and Problems of Italian Design, exh. cat. (New York, MoMA, The Museum of Modern Art), MoMA, New York in collaboration with Centro Di, Florence, 1972

Marie-Ange Brayer,
Futurissimo. L'utopie du design italien 1930–2000
Centre Pompidou, Paris, 2021

Deyan Sudjic, Maria Cristina Didero, Catharine Rossi,
SuperDesign: Italian Radical Design, 1965–76
Monacelli Press, New York, 2017

Raymon Guidot,
Histoire du Design, 1940–2000
Hazan, Paris, 2000

Albrecht Bangert,
Italienisches Möbeldesign
Verlag Modernes Design, Munich, 1985

Virgilio Vercelloni,
La storia del paesaggio urbano di Milano
Officina d'Arte Grafica, Florence, 1989

Franco Albini

Federico Bucci, Giampiero Bosoni,
Il design e gli interni di Franco Albini
Electa, Milan, 2009

Franca Helg,
Franco Albini, 1930–1970
Rizzoli, New York, 1981

Luigi Spinelli,
I luoghi di Franco Albini. Itinerari di architettura
Electa, Milan, 2006

Michele Ugolini, Amedeo Zilioli,
Franco Albini. Uffici INA a Parma
Alinea Editrice, Florence, 1991

Antonio Piva, Vittorio Prina,
Franco Albini 1905–1977
Electa, Milan, 1998

Stephen Leet,
Franco Albini, Architecture and Design, 1934–1977
Princeton Architectural Press, New York, 1990

Erik Gunnar Asplund

José Manuel López-Peláez,
Erik Gunnar Asplund
Stylos, Barcelona, 1990

Peter Blundell-Jones,
Gunnar Asplund
Phaidon Press Ltd., London, 2005

Luca Ortelli,
La pertinence de Gunnar Asplund: du cimetière boisé à l'exposition de Stockholm
Metispress, Paris, 2019

Erik Gunnar Asplund: architecte et designer suédois, exh. cat. (Paris, Centre de Création Industrielle, Centre Georges Pompidou, February 15 – April 17, 1989)
Regirex-France, Paris, 1989

Gustav Holmdahl, Sven Ivar Lind, Kjell Ödeen,
Gunnar Asplund architect 1885–1940: plans, sketches and photographs
Svenska Arkitekters Riksförbund, Byggförlaget, Järfälla, 1981

Giacomo Balla

Ada Masoero,
Nel giardino di Balla: Futurismo, 1912–1918
Mazzotta, Milan, 2004

Filippo Tommaso Marinetti,
Le Manifeste Futuriste
Le Figaro, Paris, 1909

Didier Ottinger,
Le futurisme à Paris
Centre Pompidou, Paris / 5 Continents, Paris–Milan, 2008–09

Maria Drudi Gambillo, Teresa Fiori,
Archivi del Futurismo, vol. II
De Luca, Rome, 1962

Maurizio Fagiolo dell'Arco,
Balla. Ricostruzione futurista dell'universo
Bulzoni, Rome, 1968

Maurizio Fagiolo dell'Arco,
Futur Balla
Italian University Press, Rome, 1985

Virgilio Vercelloni,
L'avventura del Design: Gavina
Jaca Book, Milan, 1987

Le Corbusier

Willy Boesiger, Oscar Stonorov,
Le Corbusier - Œuvre complète Volume 1: 1910–1929
Birkhäuser Verlag GmbH, Basel, 1995

Willy Boesiger,
Le Corbusier - Œuvre complète Volume 2: 1929–1934
Birkhäuser Verlag GmbH, Basel, 1995

Max Bill,
Le Corbusier - Œuvre complète Volume 3: 1934–1938
Birkhäuser Verlag GmbH, Basel, 1995

Willy Boesiger,
Le Corbusier - Œuvre complète Volume 4: 1938–1946
Birkhäuser Verlag GmbH, Basel, 1995

Willy Boesiger,
Le Corbusier - Œuvre complète Volume 5: 1946–1952
Birkhäuser Verlag GmbH, Basel, 1995

Arthur Rüegg,
Le Corbusier : Meubles et intérieurs, 1905–1965
Fondation Le Corbusier – Scheidegger & Spiess, Zurich, 2012

Le Corbusier,
Mon œuvre
Hatje Cantz Verlag GmbH, Stuttgart, 1960

Le Corbusier,
"Modulor II (la parole est aux usagers)"
L'architecture d'Aujourd'hui, 1955–59, Boulogne, 1955

Charles & Ray Eames

Eames Demetrios,
An Eames Primer: Revised Edition
Rizzoli, New York, 2013

Eames Demetrios,
Eames: Beautiful Details
AMMO Books LLC, Los Angeles, 1999

Gloria Koening,
Charles & Ray Eames: 1907–1978, 1912–1988: pionniers du modernisme de l'après-guerre
Taschen, Cologne, 2005

Brigitte Fitoussi,
Eames
Assouline, Paris, 1999

Qu'est-ce que le design?: Joe C. Colombo, Charles Eames, Fritz Eichler, Verner Panton, Roger Tallon, exh. cat. (Paris, Palais du Louvre, Pavillon de Marsan, October 24 – December 31, 1969)
Centre de Création industrielle, Paris, 1969

Arthur Drexler,
Charles Eames. Furniture from the design collection, The Museum of Modern Art, New York
Museum of Modern Art, New York, 1973

Charles Rennie Mackintosh

James Macaulay,
Charles Rennie Mackintosh
Norton, New York and London, 2010

Roger Billcliffe,
Charles Rennie Mackintosh: The Complete Furniture, Furniture Drawings and Interior Designs
Lutterworth, Guildford, Surrey, 1980

Guido Laganà,
Charles Rennie Mackintosh: 1868–1928
Electa, Milan, 1990

Peter Fiell,
Charles Rennie Mackintosh: 1868–1928
Taschen, Cologne, 2004

Louise Campbell,
"A Model patron: Bassett-Lowke, Mackintosh and Behrens"
The Journal of the Decorative Arts Society, no. 10, 1985

Vico Magistretti

Gabriele Neri,
Vico Magistretti. Architetto milanese
Electa, Milan, 2021

Vanni Pasca,
Vico Magistretti.
L'eleganza della ragione
Idea Books, Milan, 1991

Vanni Pasca,
Vico Magistretti, Designer
Rizzoli, New York, 1991

Fulvio Irace, Vanni Pasca,
Vico Magistretti. Architetto e designer
Electa, Milan, 1999

Anniina Koivu,
Vico Magistretti, Storie di Oggetti
Triest Verlag, Zurich, 2020

Beppe Finessi,
Vico Magistretti
Corraini, Mantua, 2003

Marco Biagi,
Vico Magistretti. Architetture Milanesi
Fondazione Vico Magistretti, Milan, 2010

Ico Parisi

Roberta Lietti,
Ico Parisi Catalogo ragionato 1936–1960
Silvana Editoriale, Cinisello Balsamo, 2017

Roberto Aloi,
Mobili Tipo: Presentazione dell'Arch. Agnoldomenico Pica,
Hoepli, Milan, 1956

"Mobili italiani per l'America"
Domus, no. 292, March 1954

Domus, no. 339, February 1958

Domus, no. 342, May 1958

Domus, no. 314, January 1956

Ico Parisi,
Operazione Arcevia. Comunità essenziale
Cesare Nani, Como, 1976

Flaminio Gualdoni,
Ico Parisi la casa
Electa, Milan, 1999

Charlotte Perriand

Jacques Barsac,
*Charlotte Perriand. L'œuvre complète
Tome 1: 1903–1940*
Norma, Paris, 2015

Jacques Barsac,
*Charlotte Perriand. L'œuvre complète
Tome 2: 1940–1955*
Norma, Paris, 2015

Jacques Barsac,
*Charlotte Perriand. L'œuvre complète
Tome 3: 1955–1968*
Norma, Paris, 2017

Jacques Barsac,
*Charlotte Perriand. L'œuvre complète
Tome 4: 1968–1999*
Norma, Paris, 2019

Jacques Barsac,
Charlotte Perriand. Un art d'habiter
Norma, Paris, 2005

Marie-Laure Jousset,
Charlotte Perriand, exh. cat. (Paris, Centre Pompidou, December 7, 2005 – March 27, 2006)
Centre Pompidou, Paris, 2005

Arthur Rüegg,
Charlotte Perriand. Livre de bord 1928–1933
Infolio éditions, Gollion, 2004

Gio Ponti

Gio Ponti, "Senza aggettivi"
Domus, no. 268, March 1952

Lisa Licitra Ponti, Germano Celant,
Gio Ponti: The Complete Work 1923–1978
Thames & Hudson, London and New York, 1990

Ugo La Pietra, *Gio Ponti*
Rizzoli, Milan, 1996

Giulio Castelli, Paola Antonelli, Francesca Picchi,
La Fabbrica del design. Conversazioni con i protagonisti del design italiano
Skira, Milan, 2007

Graziella Roccela, *Gio Ponti*
Taschen, Cologne, 2017

Sophie Bouilhet-Dumas, Dominique Forest, Salvatore Licitra, *Gio Ponti Archi-designer*
UCAD, Paris, 2018

Salvatore Licitra, Stefano Casciani, Lisa Licitra Ponti, Brian Kish, Fabio Marino, *Gio Ponti*, Karl Kolbitz (ed.)
Taschen, Cologne, 2021

Gerrit Thomas Rietveld

Marijke Küper, Ida van Zijl,
Gerrit Th. Rietveld 1888–1964, The Complete Work
Central Museum, Utrecht, 1992

Ida van Zijl, *Gerrit Rietveld*
Phaidon Press Limited, London, 2016

Peter Vöge, *The Complete Rietveld Furniture*
010 publishers, Rotterdam, 1993

Paul Overy, Lenneke Büller, Frank den Oudsten, Bertus Mulder, *The Rietveld Schröder House*
Thoth Publishers, Bussum, 1992

Bertus Mulder, Ida van Zijl,
The Rietveld Schröder House
Princeton Architectural Press, New York, 1999

Carlo Scarpa

Carlo Scarpa, Francesco Dal Co, Giuseppe Mazzariol,
Carlo Scarpa: The Complete Works
Electa / Rizzoli, New York, 1985

Sandro Bagnoli, Alba Di Lieto,
Carlo Scarpa: Il design per Dino Gavina
Silvana Editoriale, Cinisello Balsamo, 2014

Virgilio Vercelloni,
L'avventura del Design: Gavina
Jaca Book, Milan, 1987

Robert McCarter,
Carlo Scarpa
Phaidon, London, 2013

Guido Beltrami,
Carlo Scarpa: Architecture and Design
Rizzoli, New York, 2007

Sergio Los,
Carlo Scarpa
Taschen, Cologne, 2002

Marco Zanuso

François Burkhardt, *Design Marco Zanuso*
Motta Editore, Milan, 1990

Gillo Dorfles, *Marco Zanuso designer*
Editalia, Rome, 1971

Paolo Fossati, *Il design in Italia, 1945–1972*
Einaudi, Turin, 1972

Antonio Piva, *Marco Zanuso: Architettura, Design e la costruzione del benessere*
Gangemi Editore, Rome, 2007

Vittorio Gregotti, "Marco Zanuso, un architetto della seconda generazione"
Casabella-Continuità, no. 216, September 1957

Photographic Credits

Photographers

© Carlotto: pp. 17, 217, 329 (11, 13)

© Grafica Salvatore Gregorietti: pp. 29, 34

© Matteo Monti: p. 30

© Jean Collas: pp. 32 (10), 153, 219 (↓)

© David Bordes: p. 34 (14)

© G. Thiriet: p. 36 (16)

© Paola Pansini: p. 37 (↑)

© Valentina Sommariva: pp. 39 (↑), 100, 103 (↓), 116, 118, 130, 132, 134–135, 181, 184, 186, 187, 294, 336 (5)

© De Pasquale + Maffini: pp. 39 (↓), 40, 42, 105, 120, 121, 168–169, 171, 182, 190, 201, 267, 279, 289, 293, 297, 301, 303, 305, 335 (7), 336 (12), 338 (1, 4)

© Olivier Martin Gambier: pp. 44 (27), 244

© Albin Salaün: p. 44 (28)

© C. Vanderberghe: p. 45 (29)

© Mattia Balsamini: pp. 59, 60–61, 62–63, 64–65, 66–67, 68–69

© Masera: pp. 80, 326 (6)

© Stefano de Monte: pp. 33 (↑↓), 73, 76, 80, 84 (↑), 85, 89, 123, 126, 128, 134 (↓), 135 (↑),136 (↑), 137, 138, 139, 190 (↓), 194, 199, 201 (↑), 203, 232 (↓), 249, 294–295, 303 (↑), 305 (→), 336

© Giorgio Casali: p. 82

© Francesco Dolfo: pp. 91, 336 (17)

© Bruno Falchi & Liderno Salvador: pp. 94, 230, 327 (3, 4)

© Orjan Bjorkdahl: p. 96

© Aldo Ballo: pp. 99, 101 (↓), 103, 106, 109 (↑), 109, 231, 325 (6, 7, 10), 326 (1, 2, 7), 328 (6), 329 (9), 330 (3, 4), 331 (11), 332 (5)

© Leo Torri: pp. 104, 331

© Mario Carrieri: pp. 107, 108, 191, 196–197, 229 (↓), 231, 233, 234–235, 240, 256, 257, 258, 264, 331 (5, 8)

© Confalonieri e Negri: pp. 112 (↓), 324 (6, 7, 10), 325 (3, 5)

© Richard Blin: p. 126

© Giuliano Carraro: p. 136

© Maurice Scheltens & Liesbeth Abbenes: pp. 141, 142–143, 144–145, 146–147, 148–149

© Mario Mulas: pp. 156, 159, 164

© Oriani Origone: pp. 166–167, 170

© Eva Besnyö: pp. 178–179 (5)

© Nicola Zocchi: pp. 188, 324 (9), 325 (1), 327 (7), 329 (12)

© Farabola: pp. 194 (1), 200

© Giuseppe Brancato: pp. 43, 179, 183, 189 (↑), 198, 228, 235, 334 (6)

© Delfino Sisto Legnani: pp. 205, 206–207, 208–209, 210–211, 212–213

© Mimmo Capurso: p. 218

© Gruppoquattro Romano Brenna: p. 220

© Walter Prina: p. 228 (↑)

© Paul Kozlowski: p. 238

© Radiodiffusion et Télévision françaises: p. 241 (↑)

© André Steiner: pp. 242, 245

© Willy Boesiger: p. 244 (10)

© Photo industrielle A. Hamonic: p. 246 (12)

© Lucien Hervé: p. 248 (13)

© Rosenberg C.G.: p. 252

© Oscar Enqvist: p. 254

© Giovanni Frigerio: pp. 257, 333 (14, 15, 16)

© Lasse Olsson: p. 259

© Stefan Giftthaler: p. 262

© Sarah van Rij & David van der Leeuw: pp. 269, 271, 273, 275

© Ernst Moritz: p. 281

© Pierre Jeanneret: p. 290

© Charlotte Perriand: p. 292 (10, 11, 12)

© Omar Sartor: pp. 293 (14), 336 (13)

© Karquel: p. 297 (22)

© Paola Pansini: pp. 297 (↓), 299

© Marc Domage: p. 299 (26)

© Pernette Perriand Barsac: p. 304 (34)

© Tommaso Sartori: pp. 306–307, 308–309, 310–311, 312–313, 314–315, 316–317, 318–319, 321

© Fondazione Palazzo Albizzini – Collezione Burri, Città di Castello: pp. 311, 313, 314–315, 316–317

© Pratelli: p. 325 (8)

© Benedetti & Pisani: p. 326 (9)

© Gruppoquattro Romano Brenna: p. 328 (1, 4)

© Valerio Castelli: p. 328 (2)

© Carlo Dani: p. 328 (3, 5)

© Luciano Marco Boschini: p. 330 (1)

© Luca Merli: p. 331 (7)

© Basilico: pp. 329 (8), 331 (9, 10)

© Carlo Orsi: p. 329 (10)

© Maurizio Galimberti: p. 332 (11)

© Bella & Ruggeri: p. 332 (9)

© Efrem Raimondi: p. 333 (17)

© Mattew Donaldson: p. 334 (2)

© Santi Caleca: p. 334 (7)

© Karl Lagerfeld: p. 336 (3)

© Paola Pansini: p. 339 (11, 15)

© Luca Merli: p. 339 (16)

© Andrea Bartolucci: p. 339 (23)

© Agostino Osio for Alto Piano: pp. 341, 342–343, 344–345, 346–347, 348–349

Unidentified photographers

pp. 23, 28, 30–31, 83, 84, 86–87 (6, 7), 89, 90–91, 96–97, 112 (1), 114–115, 121, 128, 132, 155, 219, 226–227, 288, 291, 302

Archives

© Archivio Storico Cassina: pp. 17, 19, 20, 23, 29, 34–35, 36–37 (16, 18), 39 (21), 40–41 (22, 23, 24), 42–43, 48–49, 50–51, 52–53, 54–55, 56–57, 74, 75, 76, 80, 83, 84–85 (4, 5), 86–87 (6, 7), 88–89 (8, 9), 90–91, 94 (1), 97, 99, 101, 103, 104, 106–107, 108–109, 112 (2), 119, 132, 155, 156, 159, 164, 174 (2), 178–179, 180, 184–185, 187, 191, 196, 197, 217, 219, 220, 224, 226–227, 228–229, 230–231, 232–233, 234–235, 240, 241 (5), 245 (11), 248–249, 256–257, 258, 280, 282, 286, 288–289, 291, 293, 295 (18), 299 (27), 300

© Fondation Le Corbusier
pp. 26 (1, 2), 28 (3), 30 (5, 6), 31 (6, 7, 8), 36 (15), 41 (24), 44 (26, 27), 154, 238, 240–241, 242–243, 244–245, 246–247, 248–249

© Archives Charlotte Perriand
pp. 26 (1, 2), 32–33 (9, 10, 11), 34 (12), 36–37, 38 (19, 20), 45 (28), 249, 286 (2), 288–289 (3, 4), 292–293 (9, 10, 11, 12), 294–295 (16, 17, 18), 296–297 (20, 21, 22), 298–299 (24, 25, 26, 27), 300 (28), 301 (29, 30), 302–303 (31, 32, 33), 304–305 (34, 35)

© MAMbo: p. 30

© Fondation Louis Vuitton / David Bordes: p. 34 (14)

© Eames Office, LLC, 2023: pp. 48, 49, 50, 51, 52, 53, 54, 55, 56, 57

© Università Iuav di Venezia, Archivio Progetti, Fondo Giorgio Casali: p. 82

© Phillips Auctioneers LLC: pp. 86–87, 90 (↑), 91 (↓), 122 (↑), 281

© Archivio Studio Magistretti – Fondazione Vico Magistretti: pp. 94, 96, 98, 102 (7), 104–105 (8, 9), 106–107 (10, 11), 108–109 (12, 13, 14), 219

© Archivio del Design Ico Parisi: pp. 112 (1), 114–115, 116–117, 118 (7), 120–121, 122

© Fondazione Franco Albini: pp. 75, 126, 128, 130–131, 132–133, 134–135, 136–137, 138–139

© Archivio Carlo Scarpa Museo di Castelvecchio di Verona, Archivio S. Bagnoli: pp. 162, 168–169, 171

© Archivio Carlo Scarpa Museo di Castelvecchio di Verona, Fondo Cassina: p. 162

© Gerrit Rietveld / Rietveld Foundation / Centraal Museum Utrecht % Pictoright Amsterdam 2023: pp. 176 (3), 186 (9)

© Centraal Museum Utrecht: p. 281, ph. Ernst Moritz

© Maria Austria Instituut, Amsterdam: pp. 178–179 (5)

© AdM Fondo Marco Zanuso: pp. 194, 200, 202

© Archivio Famiglia Zanuso: p. 197

© Archivio ADI Design Museum: p. 218, ph. Mimmo Capurso

© The Glasgow School of Art: pp. 230 (5), 232 (9)

© The Hunterian, University of Glasgow: p. 233 (10)

© Getty Research Institute: p. 248 (13)

© Bridgeman Images: p. 266

© SIAE: p. 266

© Fondation Louis Vuitton / Marc Domage: p. 299

Every effort has been made in good faith to trace the copyright holders and obtain permission to reproduce the works that appear in this book. The Publisher may be contacted by entitled parties for any iconographic sources that have not been identified.

Acknowledgments

CEO Cassina
Luca Fuso

Art Direction Cassina
Patricia Urquiola

Edited by
Ivan Mietton

Graphic Art Direction
Nicola Aguzzi, Undo-Redo

Editorial Coordination
Federica Sala

Historical Research
Ivan Mietton

Iconographic Research
Ivan Mietton
Barbara Lehmann

Texts
Ivan Mietton
Emanuele Coccia
Beatriz Colomina & Mark Antony Wigley
Domitilla Dardi
Barbara Lehmann
Céline Saraïva
Jane Withers

Photographers
Mattia Balsamini
Agostino Osio for Alto Piano
Sarah van Rij & David van der Leeuw
Delfino Sisto Legnani, DSL Studio
Tommaso Sartori
Scheltens & Abbenes

Set Design Chapter 1 & 4
Greta Cevenini

Production
NOP—NOP

Locations
The Home of the Human Safety Net,
Procuratie Vecchie, Piazza San Marco, Venezia

Rietveld Pavilion,
Kröller-Müller Museum, Otterlo

Ca' Scarpa,
Fondazione Benetton Studi Ricerche, Treviso

Edoardo Tresoldi, *Simbiosi*
Arte Sella, Val di Sella, Trento

Parco dell'Etna, Catania

A. Burri, *Grande Cretto di Gibellina*
Gibellina, Trapani

ADI Design Museum:
Alessandra Fontaneto

Fondazione Franco Albini:
Paola Albini, Marco Albini, Elena Albricci,
Arianna Mongardi

Arte Sella

Maria Austria Instituut

Alessandro Balla, Patrizia Balla, Vittorio Balla

Fondazione Benetton Studi Ricerche

Silvana Beretta

Andrea Bocchiola

Christian Boisson

Fondazione Burri

Santi Caleca

Laura Caronni

Ca' Scarpa

Adele Cassina

Centraal Museum Utrecht:
Natalie Dubois, Frederik Markusse

Fondation Le Corbusier:
Brigitte Bouvier, Benedicte Gandini,
Isabelle Godineau, Arnaud Dercelles

Serena Crespi

Céline Degoulet

Stefano De Monte

Eames Office:
Demetrios Eames, Eckart Maise, Kelsey Williams

Ente Parco dell'Etna

Ulrich Fiedler

Justine Forest

Maurizio Galimberti

Getty Research Institute:
Virginia Mokslaveskas

Tiziana Giacovani

Comune di Gibellina

The Glasgow School of Art, Archives and Collections

Beatrice Gobbi

The Hunterian, University of Glasgow:
Graham Nisbet

Kröller-Müller Museum

Fondazione Vico Magistretti:
Margherita Pellino

Archivio del Moderno:
Elena Triunveri, Micaela Caletti, Paola Giudici

Sara Nosrati

Agostino Osio for Alto Piano

Lasse Olsson

Oriani Origoni

Carlo Orsi

Archivio del design di Ico Parisi:
Roberta Lietti

Archivio Gianfranco Pardi

Archives Charlotte Perriand:
Pernette Perriand, Jacques Barsac

Phillips Auctioneers LLC:
Elie Massaoutis, Antonia King, Sophia Garbagnati

Pictoright: Sander van der Weil

Gio Ponti Archives:
Salvatore Licitra, Paolo Rosselli

Rietveld Foundation:
Martine Eskes, Mieke Rietveld, Wim Rietveld,
Paula Rietveld

Chiara Rodriquez

Laurent Rotgé

Maura Santoro

Studio Scarpa:
Tobia Scarpa, Ilaria Cavallari

Archivio Carlo Scarpa, Museo di Castelvecchio:
Ketty Bertolaso

Vittoria Speziali

Talent and Partner

Archivio Emilio Tadini e Casa Museo:
Melina Scalise

The Home of the Human Safety Net

Edoardo Tresoldi

Università Iuav di Venezia, Archivio Progetti:
Teresita Scalco

Joost Swarte

We Folk

The Willow Tea Rooms Trust

Rosa Zambelli

Federica Zanuso, Lorenza Zanuso, Susanna Zanuso,
Ietvart Zarmanian

cassina.com
Instagram @cassinaofficial
Facebook @Cassina
LinkedIn @Cassina
Pinterest @cassinaspa
YouTube @cassinachannel

Translation from Italian into English
and from French into English
Richard Sadleir

© Fondazione Palazzo Albizzini – Collezione Burri,
Città di Castello, by SIAE 2023
© GIACOMO BALLA, by SIAE 2023
© Charlotte Perriand, by SIAE 2023
© FLC, by SIAE 2023
© Pierre Jeanneret, by SIAE 2023
© Gerrit Rietveld/Rietveld foundation c/o Pictoright
Amsterdam, by SIAE 2023

pp. 311, 313–317
Alberto Burri, *Grande Cretto*, 1984–89. Gibellina

© 2023 Mondadori Libri S.p.A.
Distributed in English throughout the World
by Rizzoli International Publications Inc.
300 Park Avenue South
New York, NY 10010, USA

ISBN: 978-88-918385-8-2

2023 2024 2025 2026 / 10 9 8 7 6 5 4 3 2 1

First edition: February 2024

All rights reserved. No part of this publication
may be reproduced, stored in a retrieval
system, or transmitted in any form or by any
means, electronic, mechanical, photocopying,
recording, or otherwise, without prior consent
of the publishers.

This volume was printed at O.G.M. S.p.A., Padua
Printed in Italy

Visit us online:
Facebook.com/RizzoliNewYork
Twitter: @Rizzoli_Books
Instagram.com/RizzoliBooks
Pinterest.com/RizzoliBooks
Youtube.com/user/RizzoliNY
Issuu.com/Rizzoli